Anya Schiffrin is the director of the media and communications program at Columbia University's School of International and Public Affairs. She spent ten years working overseas as a journalist in Europe and Asia. She is the editor of *Bad News: How America's Business Press Missed the Story of the Century* and a co-editor, with Eamon Kircher-Allen, of *From Cairo to Wall Street: Voices from the Global Spring* (both published by The New Press). She is married and lives in New York City.

GLOBAL MUCKRAKING

100 Years of
Investigative Journalism from
Around the World

Edited by

Anya Schiffrin

THE NEW PRESS

NEW YORK
LONDON

Published in the United States by The New Press, New York, 2014
Distributed by Perseus Distribution

LIBRARY OF CONGRESS CATALOGING-IN-PUBLICATION DATA
Global muckraking : 100 years of investigative journalism from around the world / edited by
Anya Schiffrin.
     pages   cm
   Includes bibliographical references.
   ISBN 978-1-59558-973-6 (paperback)—ISBN 978-1-59558-993-4 (e-book)
1. Investigative reporting.   I. Schiffrin, Anya, 1962–   editor of compilation.
   PN4781.G57   2014
   070.4'3—dc23   2014015614

The New Press publishes books that promote and enrich public discussion and understanding
of the issues vital to our democracy and to a more equitable world. These books are made
possible by the enthusiasm of our readers; the support of a committed group of donors, large
and small; the collaboration of our many partners in the independent media and the not-for-
profit sector; booksellers, who often hand-sell New Press books; librarians; and above all by
our authors.

www.thenewpress.com

Book design and composition by dix!
This book was set in Janson Text LT Std

Printed in the United States of America

10   9   8   7   6   5   4   3   2   1

CONTENTS

Anticolonialism

Corruption

Oil and Mining

The Environment and Natural Disasters

Food Shortages and Famine

Military and Police

Rural Life

Women

INTRODUCTION
ANYA SCHIFFRIN

As newspapers in many countries today are in crisis—hit by declines in circulation and lack of advertising—it is refreshing to be reminded of some of the moments in history when reporting really mattered. This book is a collection of pieces that launched campaigns, exposed military atrocities, and called for justice for the downtrodden and the colonized. Reading these articles, one is amazed at how contemporary many seem and how much in common the journalist of our time has with the journalist of fifty or one hundred years ago.

Most journalists working today have little idea of the breadth of exposure reporting[1] that has been published around the world, not just now but in the past. In the United States, we think of the muckrakers of the Progressive era and their crusades for food safety, or against big oil and banking. South Africans may know *Drum* magazine, which was published in the 1950s and '60s and gave voice to a number of black writers who wrote about life under apartheid. In much of Latin America, India, and Africa there is a familiar legacy of anticolonial writing as well as a type of journalism known as "development communications" that was born in the postcolonial era.

But although journalists may know the history of reporting in their own countries, they don't necessarily know anyone else's. One of the purposes of *Global Muckraking* is to bring together pieces that have been published around the world since the nineteenth century. Leading scholars, journalists, and activists provide the historical context in which they were published and explain the impact they had. By placing these pieces next to each other and highlighting their similarities, I hope this book will educate, inspire, and delight.

Even more, exploring the historical roots of contemporary journalism shows that battles that make the headlines today—against corruption, human rights abuses, and corporate exploitation—are subjects that journalists have been exposing for more than a century. The fact that journalists have been calling attention to some of the same problems for more than a hundred years might make one despondent, but it shouldn't: their writing had significant impact even when it was not as fully effective as could be hoped. In many cases, if not most, the worst abuses were halted. Journalism succeeded in mobilizing public pressure or at least in engaging the elites who had decision-making powers so that they could take (or not take) necessary measures. That the battles are still going on should simply remind us that new abuses, new forms of corruption, are always emerging, providing new opportunities and new responsibilities for the media.

A Surprising Modernity

Not only have the same subjects been covered for many years, but the tactics used to wield influence and to persuade are also still in use. Some examples include fair trade campaigns and consumer boycotts, public relations efforts, and corporate and government pressure on journalists to toe the line. Any journalist working today will relate to much of what took place in the last century.

Moreover, it turns out that many of the questions we grapple with today about business models for media—the role and impact of investigative reporting, the line between journalism and advocacy, the financing of investigative reporting—are questions that have come up in the past. For this reason, it's instructive to take a look back.

A Historical Moment

This book begins with a moment in history when there was a wave of committed and campaigning journalism. Social unease with the excesses of colonialism and industrialization, missionary zeal, the rise of the labor movement, and a general climate of intellectual ferment and political activism as well as the increasing ease of communication all contributed. In the United States the muckrakers benefited from a rise in paid circulation, which they thought would liberate them from the pressures of advertising. Overseas, some of the large media houses we know today were getting started or establishing themselves. Audiences were growing thanks in part to the railway and telegraph, which made it easier to gather and distribute news. Newspapers and pamphlets brought together communities of people both physically and ideologically. Once connected, these audiences began to have shared views partly because being able to read the same documents helped create and shape public opinion across regions and even continents. Ideas like slavery being evil or colonialism being wrong could and did spread, partly because of the printed word. Some of the pieces of journalism in this book reflect this broadened awareness that crossed national boundaries.

But many of the stories told here are local in scope, and it was years before they caught the attention of a global audience. Geographic distance, the lapse of time, language barriers, government censorship, a natural interest in the news of one's own country, and the lack of commercial appeal are all reasons some of the stories didn't spread at the time and why so much of this global reporting is no longer remembered. Another reason is the simple fact that journalism is about what happened today or yesterday. It is about news, not history, even if journalism is often described as the first draft of history.

King Leopold's Ghost

We start with a piece by the writer Adam Hochschild, who introduces the work of E.D. Morel, the journalist who campaigned long and hard against the brutal conditions in the Belgian Congo. Morel was so outraged by the situation in the Congo that in the early part of the twentieth century he started a newspaper, the *West African Mail*. Although the paper ran advertising from companies that did business in the Congo, Morel exposed the forced labor and torture endemic to the rubber business that enriched Belgian king Leopold and others involved in the growing international market for vulcanized tires. Hochschild's book, *King Leopold's Ghost*, published in 1998, was a bestseller that brought home to a wide audience the violence of colonialism in the Congo and the role of the campaigners who exposed and fought against it. In *King Leopold's Ghost*, Hochschild explains how journalists and missionaries raised awareness about the terrible conditions. Exposing these atrocities became a critical part of campaigning against them, and Hochschild argues that, although rooted in the antislavery movement of the eighteenth and nineteenth centuries, the campaign for reform in the Congo was in fact a modern human rights campaign.

King Leopold's Ghost introduced millions of readers to three men who sounded the alarm about the Congo and wrote about the terrible conditions there, often drawing on reports from missionaries who had gone up the river and seen for themselves what was taking place: the African American soldier and writer George Washington Williams, E.D. Morel, and British consul Roger Casement. Williams and Morel illustrate the global nature of global muckraking. Neither was from the Congo but they wrote about it. Nor were they from Belgium, but they still sought to influence its government.

Hochschild describes the propaganda war that raged over two decades as missionaries and former abolitionists campaigned intensively for an improvement in conditions and for the king to give up his claim to the land.[2] King Leopold responded to the criticism with public relations tactics that are all too familiar today. The king hired lobbyists, charmed journalists with invitations to his palace, and even funded a magazine telling his version of events. *The Truth About the Congo*, as it was called, was handed out to passengers taking the comfortable night train to Brussels.

Hochschild makes clear that the task of investigative reporting has often not been an easy one. George Washington Williams, who was instrumental in exposing the abuses in the Congo, founded his own newspaper to get his message out, interviewed King Leopold, wrote the searing *Letter to King Leopold*, and was accused of libel. A story not unfamiliar to today's journalists.

After reading *King Leopold's Ghost*, I wondered what other hard-hitting journalism was exposing similar conditions in developing countries. Were journalists also covering Latin America and Asia in the same way? Where could I find their work? What happened next to Morel and Casement? Following the trail of Casement and Morel led me to other important episodes of global exposure journalism in very different parts of the world. There was, in fact, a treasure trove of writing from around the world, as the articles collected here make clear.

From Congo Crusaders to Amazon Advocates

Casement's subsequent story is described in *The Devil and Mr. Casement*, written by historian Jordan Goodman, who also has a piece in this book. At the turn of the last century, conditions for rubber workers in the Peruvian Amazon were brutal. Benjamin Saldaña Rocca had bravely covered the subject in his newspaper *La Sanción*, in Iquitos, Peru's main Amazonian city. But word didn't spread internationally until a young engineer, Walter Hardenburg, brought copies of *La Sanción* to London and shared them with the Anti-Slavery and Aborigines Protection Society,[3] a campaigning organization founded in the 1830s to protect the rights of indigenous people. Saldaña Rocca had been writing about the Peruvian Amazon Company, which was listed in London, and the resulting pressure spurred the foreign office to send Roger Casement to investigate. Casement's report was published in 1912 and estimated that thirty thousand indigenous people had died during the twelve years that the Peruvian Amazon Company had been operating. The result of the reporting and the campaign was further investigations by the U.S., Peruvian, and UK governments and arrest warrants for some company officials. Goodman notes that in the end the campaigning didn't have much impact, arguing that it was World War I and the growth of rubber in Malaya that weakened the rubber trade in Peru.

But the story of the journalism and the campaign illustrates the point made by communications scholar Clifford Bob in his book *The Marketing of Rebellion: Insurgents, Media and International Activism*. Bob argues that in the crowded world of good causes, knowing how to get attention is key, and local causes are often not taken up internationally unless they can find support from overseas campaigning organizations that can serve as the intermediaries between the local NGOs and the international community.

Corporate Conscience

Next on my reading list—chasing the trail of global muckraking, a trail in which Casement and Morel once again make an appearance—came two books about the journalists who exposed the conditions on the cocoa plantations in West Africa more than one hundred years ago. Lowell Satre's book *Chocolate on Trial: Slavery, Politics and the Ethics of Business* and *Chocolate Islands: Cocoa Slavery and Colonial Africa*, written by Catherine Higgs, describe how the renowned Cadbury family grappled with the question of working conditions on the African cocoa plantations of its suppliers. Just as companies today worry about their supply chains, so did the Quaker, abolitionist families that ran Britain's top chocolate companies. They weren't sure whether to boycott their suppliers and needed to know whether the laborers on the plantations were there of their own free will or if they were slaves.[4]

It took about eight years for the Cadburys to decide to boycott their suppliers in São Tomé and Príncipe. Along the way there were dueling press coverage, fact-finding reports, and lawsuits brought by the Cadburys against newspapers that accused them of dawdling instead of boycotting. Roger Casement appears in this story as he goes to Angola in 1902[5] to check out conditions there, and campaigning journalist E.D. Morel sides with the Cadburys. This would be surprising, except that William Cadbury funded Morel's newspaper and his Congo Reform Association.[6] By 1909 the British chocolatiers were persuaded that it was time to boycott African cocoa beans. The U.S. manufacturers weren't, and their demand for cocoa drove up world prices, showing once again that boycotts work only if everyone sticks to them.

Reading these books made me want to read nineteenth-century newspapers, so off I went to the library. Some of the newspapers were hard to find and had deteriorated. Looking through newspaper collections in Calcutta and Delhi (probably the best in India), I found torn pages and missing copies. Other times, the paper crumbled in my hands. The digitization of newspapers has not happened quickly enough to save these back issues. Even when technology has intervened, digitized versions are hard to read and search and lack the context that comes with being able to hold and smell the hard copy of an entire newspaper or year of newspapers.

Where the holdings are in good shape—at the British Library, Library of Congress, or Columbia University, for example—the collections are being moved off-site, making browsing through them almost impossible. Orders need to be placed days in advance, and there are limits to how many newspapers will be brought out at one time. Having to wait can make it difficult to follow a thread or quickly move to the next article in a series.

Hidden Gems

Since the newspapers can be so hard to find, the collection of writings in this book is even more important. Historians and scholars who have spent years tracking down and studying reporting from around the world have saved us the trouble by painstakingly going through their files or back to research libraries to find their favorite examples, resulting in some gems that, until now, remained lost in time.

Newspapers as we know them now didn't really exist until the turn of the twentieth century. Looking at eighteenth- and nineteenth-century newspapers from India and West Africa, I was struck by how much they resemble today's blogs. They are often random and personal, containing information that can be inconsistent, unpredictable, and attributable to a variety of sources, not all of them reliable.

The range of what was considered news also varied greatly. One unusual story I read while in the Library of Congress that was deemed worthy of print was a two-part series about a man kicked off a boat near Malta. The coverage included a debate in the letters column about whether he was taken off because he had a contagious disease, or whether he was kicked out by the rapacious captain who wanted to re-rent the cabin to a large family who would pay more for their passage. On a wintery morning in Calcutta, I stumbled upon a long article about a parliamentary debate on the sanitary conditions for "coolies" working in Assam, alongside a letter from London about how everyone was reading George Eliot's *Middlemarch* this season.

And yet despite the noise and the randomness of news choices, there was plenty of serious writing being done in the nineteenth century. Of course, it was not in the same style as today's newspaper articles. But it was there. Sometimes it was turgid coverage of parliamentary discussions. At other times, there was more passion and more editorializing and more campaigning. Often, the style was quietly amusing and witty. It was a different kind of writing than we usually see today but its impact could be profound. There were global campaigns that used information and journalism, as well as pamphlets, public meetings, and government investigations, to raise awareness, and they accomplished their advocacy aims.

Across countries and decades, many journalists went to great lengths and took personal risks to expose injustice and wrongdoing. In some cases they became activists and crusaders, campaigning to bring the perpetrators to account. In other cases, the atrocities spawned the journalism. Benjamin Saldaña Rocca in Peru and E.D. Morel in the Congo were so outraged by the abuses they saw that they became journalists and founded newspapers in order to expose the injustices they had witnessed in the gathering of rubber. The newspapers and pamphlets (like today's blogs) that resulted were often not financially sustainable and it sometimes took years for the writing to have an impact. But they carried on. This book is full of examples.

Even when justice wasn't served, these intrepid reporters at least tried to bear witness and were sometimes vindicated by history. One example is Gareth Jones, whose exposure of the famine in Ukraine under Stalin may not have saved lives at the time, but it set the record straight for the future. Another is Patricia Verdugo, who wrote a chilling account of one of the death squads operating in Pinochet's Chile. Her journalism—with its emphasis on evidence and establishing the chronology of events—ended up becoming valuable testimony about what happened in that dark period of the country's history and was used later by investigators seeking to establish the facts of what had happened.

National Bias

National bias colored journalism then as it does now. One of the points that Adam Hochschild makes in *King Leopold's Ghost* is that this bias also colored the debate about conditions in the Congo. Journalists lined up on different sides, depending on which country they were from, with the Belgian and German reporters defending the conditions in King Leopold's colony. The same is true of the debates about conditions in the cocoa plantations of São Tomé and Príncipe. It was the British press (particularly Henry Nevinson) that kept alive the discussion of slavery in Portuguese West Africa.[7] More contemporary examples of this bias toward national interest include the U.S. media coverage of the Iraq War or the different national responses to the documents revealed by WikiLeaks. These are just two examples of the many different ways that national media frame global news events for their domestic audiences.

The Line Between Advocacy and Journalism

Just like today's journalists, the journalists of one hundred years ago relied on information from documents, firsthand experience, and from being on the scene, interviewing witnesses and, in some cases, advocates and campaigners. Often the news trickled down from academics or lawyers who later faded into the background as the media ran with the story. In other cases, the journalists more explicitly crossed the line into advocacy—again, as many do today.

Many publishers dream of a world in which media houses would be financially strong, independent, and able to carry out investigations without help. In reality, investigative journalism is often underwritten by foundations and philanthropists. So too in the past. As many of the essays in the book discuss, advocacy organizations and NGOs gave information to reporters and worked closely with them as they developed their stories. In this sense the missionaries who printed pamphlets and ran campaigns and worked with journalists are perhaps the forerunners of today's human rights campaigners.

The exposé in this book of Nestlé's infant food formula marketing practices demonstrates these close ties. Pieces on the subject, written by the same person, were published both by the media and by an influential NGO. Author Mike Muller was a card-carrying member of Britain's National Union of Journalists when he wrote the first big report on the Nestlé's baby milk scandal (published by War on Want) as well as a 1974 article for *New Scientist* that was critical of the baby food industry. As his piece in this book makes clear, Muller thinks of himself as an activist and that the journalism was critical to the campaign. There had been complaints for decades about the use of infant food formula, including a speech made in 1939 in Singapore by a renowned scientist who specialized in infant diseases,[8] but it was not until the 1970s that the consumer boycott spread and new codes of conduct were introduced.

Labor stories too were often based on reporting done by advocacy organizations that helped journalists with data and contacts that reporters followed up on. The pieces you'll read here about the sweatshops run by subcontractors to clothing and shoe manufacturers Nike and Kathie Lee Gifford are examples of this kind of reporting.

Another kind of story was the testimonial by the policeman or soldier who had blood on his hands and wanted to confess. Ernesto Semán introduces a piece by the famous Argentine journalist Horacio Verbitsky, who interviewed Adolfo Scilingo, the naval officer who pushed Argentine dissidents out of helicopters during that country's military dictatorship. Similarly, Anton Harber introduces a piece from the *Weekly Mail* in South Africa, a small alternative paper that ran a confession by Albert Nofemela, who admitted to having been part of a police hit squad aimed at antiapartheid activists.

Beyond the Fold

Some of the forms of journalism that existed in the nineteenth century will seem unfamiliar today. But others will seem similar: the importance of pamphlets has long since receded but blogs have replaced them. Just as happens today, stories were turned into books and ended up having a longer shelf life and more impact than they would have had as an ephemeral newspaper article. *Red Rubber*, E.D. Morel's book that exposed the brutal conditions in King Leopold's Congo, is just one example. But there are others, such as *Os Sertões*, the rambling and intense chronicle of Brazil's military expansion into the hinterland that was written by Euclides da Cunha.

The Power of Print

It's a pleasure to read the pieces in this book and important to understand the historical context in which they appeared. There are also larger questions as to why ideas spread at certain times. A vast amount of scholarship exists on this subject generally, but my focus is the journalism. Why does something become news? Trafficking of people, hunger, foot binding, exploitative labor conditions, military and police atrocities have gone on for centuries. So what suddenly makes them a story, to be read about and sometimes acted upon? What conditions impel journalists to explore a topic, and why does it resonate, or not?

Stories Didn't Always Spread

Language, political control, and technological barriers were bigger blocks to the spread of news in the past than they are today. Newspapers often covered what was of interest in their region or country while—even after the invention of the telegraph—news from remote places overseas took weeks or months to arrive. The rise of the Internet, social media, and citizen journalism has changed all that. News does indeed travel faster now, even if it is often ignored when it arrives.

When Do Campaigns Happen?

Although many stories often didn't spread, didn't go global, or were just shrugged off by their readers, they sometimes did catch fire. In their book *Activists Beyond Borders*, Margaret E. Keck and Kathryn Sikkink compare successful campaigns, such as those by the missionaries against foot binding in China, with campaigns around the same time that didn't do much, such as the missionary-led campaign against female genital mutilation in Kenya. Journalism, on its own, could not bring about change. There needed to be local support and local elites ready to transform their societies. (Understanding why that might be so would take us well beyond this book.) Today we refer to the importance of "media ecologies" and "information ecosystems," expressions that imply many things need to happen in order for one advocacy campaign or series of articles to have an effect. In today's world, the barriers to entry for news creation and dissemination are low, but audience fragmentation makes it hard to get a sustained and regular following.

This may mean that sociologist Clifford Bob's ideas about the marketing of causes are even more relevant. Successful activists in developing countries understand that mounting a global campaign requires forming connections with Western organizations that will support them and promote their cause. Having a spokesman who is media savvy, has lived in the West, and speaks English helps, says Bob, who cites Aung San Suu Kyi, Ken Saro-Wiwa, and the Dalai Lama as examples. In his introduction to a piece by Nigeria's Ken Saro-Wiwa, Bob explains the way Saro-Wiwa, who was originally preoccupied with the independence of the Ogoni people in the Niger Delta, broadened his campaign so that it appealed to global environmental activists.

Economist Alexander Dyck has written about how sensitive companies are to reputational effects.[9] The example of Benjamin Skinner's reporting about the terrible conditions on the fishing boats in chapter 9 is a case in point. These boats were chartered to New Zealand, the owners and officers were largely Korean, and the sailors were Indonesian. But New Zealand turned out to be responsive to the name and shame effect, and so were the large American companies that bought the fish.

The impact of the story and research was tremendous, and New Zealand's law was rewritten within months. That story was based on the research of a PhD candidate at the University of Auckland Business School who got the story out through a journalist who was then able to get space for it in *Bloomberg Businessweek*, demonstrating yet again the importance of amplification and the fact that traditional media outlets with strong brand names may have the influence that many of the disparate websites of the twenty-first century, with their fragmented readership and weak finances, often don't.

All in the Timing

Timing is also critical. As Columbia University's Graduate School of Journalism professor Sheila Coronel notes, the flowering of exposure reporting is often accompanied by periods of political transition. There are different kinds of transitions that can produce investigative journalism. Countries in transition to democracy generally see a large increase in the number of media outlets (think Spain after Franco, France after World War II, Indonesia after Suharto, Burma in 2013, Ghana after Jerry Rawlings left office in 2001). Periods of political tension and rivalry between factions in power can lead to leaks that make news.

The presence of larger social movements also may enhance the likelihood of journalistic campaigns being successful. This is illustrated here in the chapter by historian Jayeeta Sharma, who describes the connections between the activists who worked on the "coolie problem" and Brahmo Samaj, which she characterizes as an important modernizing sect that sought to reform Hindu social practices across India.

The anticolonial journalism in this book is another example: many anticolonialist fighters knew how to use the power of the press. But the writings of the anticolonialist journalists were particularly effective because they came at a period when there were vast upheavals in the French and British colonies and widespread political movements calling for independence following World War II.

Of course, for these larger social movements to exist, there has to be a climate in which they are permitted. As historian Philippe Peycam describes in his introduction to a piece by Vietnamese anticolonial writer Nguyễn An Ninh, the French allowed the Vietnamese to open newspapers because the French wanted support from an educated, urban middle class. This turned out to be a mistake for the French colonialists as the new, educated urban elites used their newspapers to call for freedom from the French.

This book is full of those spaces in which journalism crept in and then soared. Even under oppressive regimes such as those in Pinochet's Chile, China, and Vietnam, some journalists were able to push the limits and publish. Sometimes it was economic or environmental stories, as these have often been allowed when other kinds of exposure reporting was not. When there was an opening in society, or a responsive government, or a company that was worried about its reputation, the journalism could catch on and have an effect. Sometimes it took a reporter abroad to write the first big piece, after which it would amplify and reverberate back to the country where the event took place but, because of government or other kinds of censorship, could not be reported on.

Financial Problems

Another point in common with today is that after the first wave of excitement during political transitions, most media outlets don't survive financially. In fact, many of the hard-hitting newspapers of the last decade, such as *Taraf* in Turkey or *Next* in Nigeria, ran into economic problems.

One thing that has not changed over the last hundred-plus years is that there is not much of a market for investigative reporting. Periods like the Progressive era in the United States, from 1900 to 1905, when there was lots of revenue to fund the muckraking magazines, is the exception, not the rule. Generally, advertising is hard to come by, subscriptions rarely provide enough revenue, and even the most deep-pocketed proprietor soon tires of the pressure and extensive lawsuits that accompany seriously independent and critical reporting. The drive to maximize profits can also hurt good journalism, as sensationalism sells. Without an audience for serious reporting, the media are forced to dumb down their coverage in order to make money.[10]

This problem has become particularly salient today in the era of the Internet. For decades newspaper advertising helped fund investigative reporting—an unlikely marriage that seemed to work. The Internet has thrived on blogging and opinion and on citizen reporting—typically not based on expensive investigative reporting—and aggregating, taking stories produced elsewhere. While it may have enhanced the dissemination of knowledge that has already been produced, it has yet to develop a business model that would support extensive investigative reporting on new subjects. As advertising has shifted to Internet sites like Google and Facebook and away from the media, there is hope that these companies will use their revenues to finance the kind of reporting featured in this book.[11] It's not clear how much the West Coast tech companies will contribute in the future, but they have already influenced philanthropy in the media sector by helping spur the fashion for metrics and hard data that demonstrate the impact of journalism.[12]

Measuring Impact

The foundations that increasingly fund exposure journalism are, like other media development donors, under pressure to demonstrate impact and to find ways to quantitatively measure outcomes. Donors want results and try constantly to figure out how to gauge the impact of the money they give. They hope that ever more sophisticated technology and data will be able to provide information as to what concrete results are achieved by in-depth reporting. Journalists, squeezed by these demands, scramble to find ways to prove their worth.

This book takes a longer view and, as such, is hopeful but not fully conclusive. I've outlined here some of the circumstances in which exposure reporting and campaigning works. It's also known under what circumstances media usually won't be able to perform the watchdog function very effectively: repression that is as tight as Stalin's Russia, controls that are rigorous and well enforced, and proprietors aligned with business interests who squash investigative journalism and use their outlets to support their friends in government or their own business interests.

In taking the longer view, this book provides an important note of caution to those who seek large and immediate impact. It's clear that journalism is only part of a bigger picture. But when the circumstances are right, journalism does make a difference. For example, stories read by policy makers can spur them to action. Journalism can also help influence societal changes that ensure that "circumstances are right," that there is an openness to critiques identifying societal abuses of the kind this collection of articles exemplifies. Some of these societal changes occur slowly. But stories—written over and over again, over a span of years, sometimes decades—can sometimes have a cumulative effect. In part this is because by framing an event in a certain way the media can change how society looks at it. The case of Nike is an example: over years the way the media portrayed the problem of labor conditions in the factories changed.[13] As the media coverage became more sophisticated, so did our understanding of the problems and how to address them. I believe the world is better today as a result of the investigative reporting of the kind contained in much of this book. And this is so even if it's also clear that the same kinds of problems reappear, sometimes over and over again, and are written about over a span of decades.

Selection of Articles

Researching this book, I found that the same kinds of stories kept reappearing across countries and across time: slavery and trafficking; the brutality of labor conditions; human rights violations committed by the military; rural poverty and the difficult conditions of rural areas, often faced by women; corruption; and environmental and natural disasters that exposed the weakness of government. This book seeks to reflect these themes, but it should be clear that this book is in no way comprehensive. There are many stories and many journalists that I did not include. Still, it is remarkable that such a large fraction of global muckraking is reflected in the kinds of stories represented here.

In making choices, I usually went for the readable, the significant, or the compelling. I eschewed stories that didn't travel, no matter how important they were, or which were reported over such a long period in such small increments that they didn't make sense for the outside reader. I favored reporting by journalists in the global south and I focused on the subjects that they covered (including mining and oil, life in the countryside, and anticolonialism). Because of space reasons, we had to cut and condense many of the pieces. The research for this book was a group effort and was supplemented by asking dozens of investigative journalists and historians from around the world to nominate their candidates for the best examples of global muckraking.

It turned out that corruption stories were particularly difficult. Many of these kinds of stories were submitted for inclusion but, too often, they are interesting only to the insider, as the characters are often unknown internationally. Detailed descriptions of shell companies, licensing allocation, and balance sheets—while important to exposing misdeed and corruption—are not terribly meaningful to the reader who has not followed the story from the beginning. Though the details of each corruption scandal differed, in so many cases, there was a certain sameness to what occurred—reflecting perhaps some universal flaws in human nature—a sameness that meant that apart from the personalities involved and the particularities of the challenges of uncovering the corruption, the stories often were not as engaging as one might have hoped.

I could have edited several volumes of investigative reporting from around the world, but I hope this one volume is at least an inspiration for what can be done. What are the lessons for today? It can take years for journalism to make a difference; many of the most important outlets were not sustainable, they didn't make money, and they were run by passionate crusaders who seized the moment, wrote the stories, and then moved on. But the legacy they left behind is still worth studying, not just for how they did their work and the causes they exposed but for the possibilities that remain in a world still filled with injustice.

LABOR ABUSES

1

E.D. MOREL

THE THIRD TEST OF CONGO STATE RULE—MILITARISM, MURDER, MUTILATION, AND THE TRAFFIC IN ARMS (1904)

from *King Leopold's Rule in Africa*

INTRODUCED BY ADAM HOCHSCHILD

Congo

The first great international human rights campaign of the twentieth century had its birth on the docks of Antwerp. A British shipping firm, Elder Dempster of Liverpool, had the monopoly on all traffic between Belgium and the Congo Free State—the vast colony in Central Africa that belonged not to Belgium, but privately to the country's monarch, King Leopold II. Only later would it become the Belgian Congo, and then the Democratic Republic of Congo.

Antwerp was Belgium's major port, and in the late 1890s, every few weeks Elder Dempster would send a young official to the city. Edmund Dene Morel would supervise the unloading of each company ship as it arrived from the Congo, and the loading of cargo as it prepared for the return voyage. Morel, then in his midtwenties, began to notice something odd. Every time one of these ships docked at Antwerp, it was filled to the hatch covers with enormously valuable cargoes of ivory and, above all, rubber. But when the ships sailed back to the Congo, they carried almost no merchandise. Instead, they were filled mainly with soldiers, guns, ammunition, and other military supplies.

Morel gradually realized something that thousands of other people working at that dock over the preceding decade had chosen to ignore:

Excerpt from E.D. Morel, "The Third Test of Congo State Rule—Militarism, Murder, Mutilation, and the Traffic in Arms," in *King Leopold's Rule in Africa* (London: William Heinemann, 1904), 102–4.

nothing was being sent to Africa to pay for the ivory and rubber. He was looking at evidence of a forced labor system thousands of miles away. He went to the head of his shipping company to say that he thought they should not be taking part in such an enterprise. His boss, dismayed at the prospect of losing his best contract, offered Morel a higher-paying job in another country. When that didn't work, he tried to buy Morel's silence with an annual retainer as a consultant. That failed also. In 1901, Morel quit his job and in short order turned himself into one of the greatest investigative journalists of his time.

Over the next dozen years, he worked ten or twelve hours a day to put the scandal of forced labor in King Leopold's Congo on the world's front pages. He wrote three books on the subject, several dozen pamphlets in both English and French, and hundreds of articles, and he started a newspaper whose principal cause this became. Within a few years he founded the Congo Reform Association, which staged hundreds of protest meetings, primarily in Britain and the United States, but as far away as Australia and New Zealand as well.

As with any journalist who exposes something, people with more stories to tell sought Morel out. Hezekiah Andrew Shanu, a Nigerian working in the Congo Free State government, smuggled incriminating documents to him. So did Belgians returning home with a sense of guilt or horror at what they had seen. The most important witnesses were missionaries: British, American, and Swedish Protestants who had gone to the Congo expecting to save souls and had found themselves instead in the middle of a human catastrophe. When they returned from Africa, John and Alice Harris, British Baptists, worked with Morel in the Congo Reform Association. Photographs by Alice Harris and Daniel J. Danielson, a missionary from the Faeroe Islands, provided stunning graphic evidence of what forced labor looked like in practice.

The dawn of the automobile age had sent rubber prices soaring around the world. The Congo's rubber was in wild vines that twined their way upward around palms or other trees in search of sunlight. A contingent of King Leopold's private army—nineteen thousand strong, black conscripts under white officers—would march into a village and hold its women hostage in order to force the men to go into the rain forest and tap a monthly quota of wild rubber. But the vines were scattered only sparingly, and as those near a village were drained dry, men would have to travel for days to find vines with rubber. Sometimes, in this search, they would be gone for several weeks out of each month. Meanwhile, their chained-up wives were often subject to rape by soldiers.

Morel deals with a further refinement of the system in the excerpt below. When Leopold's white officers issued bullets to their men to enforce this regime, they demanded that for every bullet fired, a soldier bring back a hand from the person he had killed—whether a villager resisting the system, or someone taking part in an uprising, of which there were many. This would be proof that the bullet had not been saved for use in hunting or a mutiny—and there were many of these also. But often soldiers fired at someone and missed, and then satisfied their officers by returning with a hand chopped off a living person.

The forced labor system took its toll in different ways: rebels killed in revolts, rubber gatherers worked to death, hostages starved, and people who, weakened by the near-famine caused by the system's disruption of subsistence farming, died of diseases they might otherwise have survived. And, with women held hostage and their husbands desperately searching for rubber deep in the forest, the birth rate plummeted. Demographers estimate today that, from all these causes, the number of people in the Congo dropped from approximately 20 million in 1880 to roughly half of that in 1920.

Morel's campaign lasted for more than a decade, and forced some reforms—although bigger changes came only in the 1920s, when Belgian colonial authorities realized that the system's toll was shrinking the population so drastically that they would eventually have no workforce left. Morel, meanwhile, had become a brave, outspoken voice against the madness of the First World War. For this, the British government sent him to prison for six months at hard labor in 1917 and 1918. He had some vindication after the war, being elected to Parliament and becoming the Labor Party's chief spokesperson on foreign affairs. But prison had shattered his health, and he died of a heart attack at the age of fifty-one.

The first intimation that Congo State troops were in the habit of cutting off the hands of men, women, and children in connection with the rubber traffic reached Europe through the Rev. J. B. Murphy, of the American Baptist Missionary Union, in 1895. He described how the State soldiers had shot some people on Lake Mantumba (Tumba), "cut off their hands, and took them to the Commissaire." The survivors of the slaughter reported the matter to a missionary at Irebu, who went down to see if it were true, and was quickly convinced by ocular demonstration.

Among the mutilated victims was a little girl, not quite dead, who subsequently recovered. In a statement which appeared in the Times, Mr. Murphy said, "These hands, the hands of men, women, and children, were placed in rows before the Commissary, who counted them to see that the soldiers had not wasted cartridges." The second intimation was conveyed in the diary of Glave (one of the fine type of Englishmen connected with the Congo in the early days), and published in 1896 after his death, in the Century Magazine. Glave wrote that the Rev. J. Clarke, a missionary at Mantumba, reported that he had seen "several men with bunches of hands, signifying their individual skill. These, I presume (Glave), they must produce to prove their successes, . . . I have previously heard of hands, among them children's, being brought to the stations. . . ."

Mr. Sjoblom, a Swedish missionary, confirmed, in 1897, the statements of Murphy and Glave. He reported having seen a native shot by a soldier before his eyes. After the murder the soldier "told a little boy . . . to go and cut off the right hand of the man who had been shot. . . . after some labour (the native was not quite dead) cut the hand off and laid it by a fallen tree. A little later the hand was put on a fire to smoke before being sent to the Commissary, . . . If the rubber does not reach the full amount required, the sentinels attack the natives; they kill some and bring the hands to the Commissary, . . . The sentinels, or else the boys in attendance on them, put these hands on a little kiln, and after they have been smoked, they by-and-by put them on the top of the rubber baskets. I have many times seen this done. . . . From this village I went to another, where I met a man, who pointed to a basket, and said to me, 'Look, I have only two hands.' He meant there were not enough to make up for the rubber he had brought. . . . When I reached the river, I turned 'round and saw that the people had large hammocks in which they were gathering the rubber to be taken to the Commissary. I also saw smoked hands and prisoners to be taken down to the Commissary. That is only one of the places. . . . When I crossed the stream, I saw some dead bodies hanging down from branches in the water. As I turned my face away from the horrible sight, one of the native corporals who was following us down said, 'Oh, that is nothing; a few days ago I returned from a fight, and I brought the white man 160 hands.' . . . Two or three days after a fight, a dead mother was found with two of her children. The mother was shot, and the right hand taken off. On one side was the elder child, also shot, and the right hand also taken off. On the other side was the younger child with the right hand cut off, but the child still living was resting against the dead mother's breast. This dark picture was seen by four missionaries. On December 14 a sentinel passed our mission station and a woman accompanied him, carrying a basket of hands. Mr. and Mrs. Banks, beside myself, went down the road, and they told the sentinel to put the hands on the road that they might count them. We counted eighteen right hands smoked, and from the size of the hands we could judge that they belonged to men, women, and even children." [. . .]

Personally, I had always thought, until the early part of 1901, that these mutilations were carried out upon dead people only—natives slain in connection with the odious raids upon villages, for not bringing in a sufficiency of rubber, and that the idea was at once to strike terror into the hearts of other villages, and to justify, in the eyes of the Congo State officer, the expenditure of the cartridges by soldiers whom he had sent out upon the work of slaughter, to prove to the satisfaction of their superiors that a village behindhand in its tribute of rubber or food-stuffs had been really and effectively wiped out.

But it was only towards the end of 1901 that I ascertained, by receiving photographs and letters from the Upper Congo, that mutilations were frequently practised by the Congo soldiery upon the living, upon men, upon women, upon poor little innocent children of tender years. The information I then received has been, alas! but too amply corroborated since from various sources, and notably by Mr. Roger Casement. Consul Casement's evidence is abundant and precise. In the Lake Mantumba District he saw two mutilated natives, whose cases, authenticated beyond doubt, proved the committal of the deed by Government soldiers "accompanied by white officers." [. . .]

Comment is needless.

2

BENJAMIN SALDAÑA ROCCA

THE WAVE OF BLOOD (1907)

from *La Sanción*

INTRODUCED BY JORDAN GOODMAN

Peru

Iquitos was then, as it still is today, Peru's main Amazonian city. Though its population in 1907, the year in which Benjamin Saldaña Rocca published his shocking revelations, had not yet reached ten thousand, and was therefore small by comparison with Peru's cities on the other side of the Andes, Iquitos played a major role in the Peruvian and Amazonian economy as the center of the rubber industry. Based on the extraction by gangs of indigenous labor of latex from rubber trees growing wild near rivers feeding into the Amazon, the Iquitos rubber industry attracted men with an appetite for uncertain but possibly huge profits. Though Iquitos had several rich men, none had as much wealth and power as the Peruvian business-man Julio César Arana: his rubber empire was concentrated in a substantial area on the north bank of the Putumayo River—on lands whose ownership was claimed by both Peru and Colombia. The area was accessible only by motorized ships, about one week's sailing time to the north of Iquitos. No one could go into or come out of the Putumayo rubber operation without Arana's permission.

Why Benjamin Saldaña Rocca decided to take on Arana is unclear: he certainly believed he had a mission in telling the truth and exposing

Excerpt from Benjamin Saldaña Rocca, "The Wave of Blood," in *La Sanción*, August 22, 1907. Translated by Walter Hardenburg in Iquitos in 1908.

immoral and illegal acts, but what more was in his mind we can no longer know. Yet that is precisely what he did.

Though he began his career as a highly decorated soldier, at some point in his life Saldaña Rocca traded in the rifle for the pen and became a journalist. When, around 1906 and aged in his midforties, he arrived in Iquitos, he found a town whose politics ran to Arana's beat.

On August 9, 1907, not long after settling in Iquitos and while Arana was away in London registering his company as a British concern—the Peruvian Amazon Company—Saldaña Rocca pounced on his prey when he petitioned the judge of the criminal court to proceed with charges against eighteen employees of Arana's company. The petition, supported by eyewitness reports, alleged that Arana's company used brutal methods of physical violence, torture, and murder to force the local people to collect rubber. Saldaña Rocca urged the judge to act quickly, "as the bones of thousands of Indians who have been murdered lie scattered around the houses." But instead of action, all Saldaña Rocca got was silence.

Possessed of a deep sense of moral outrage, Saldaña Rocca did not let matters rest and two weeks later he printed the first issue of his own newspaper, *La Sanción*, a four-page title with snippets of local and regional news, book reviews, a little poetry, and advertisements for local services. But the newspaper also had a mission. "Enough of mysteries and cover-ups," Saldaña Rocca declared in his first editorial on August 22, 1907, explaining that he was on a crusade to clean up Iquitos. "In such a noble and worthwhile task nothing nor anyone can stop me: I will fight undaunted and without respite, scorning the switchblade of the assassin and the pistol of the thug." If anyone had any doubts about what Saldaña Rocca meant by "mysteries and cover-ups," then the answer was on the paper's third page—a public denunciation of Julio César Arana's methods.

This piece, which is reproduced for this book, was a letter written to Saldaña Rocca by Julio Muriedas, who had worked for Arana's company in one of its regional headquarters to the north of the Putumayo. It was one of the eyewitness accounts that Saldaña Rocca presented in his court petitions, and became the first eyewitness account to be published of a reign of terror heretofore hidden from public gaze. Each kilogram of rubber that arrived at Arana's wharf in Iquitos was soaked in blood.

From this point on, Saldaña Rocca published further revelations of the labor regime of his enemy in every one of *La Sanción*'s issues, using eyewitness accounts of brutality and murder by former employees of Arana's company. But, apart from an article in the *Jornal do Commercio* [a Manaus-based newspaper], in September 1907 and another in Lima's *La Prensa* in December 1907, Saldaña Rocca's accusations attracted no attention.

Arana fought back and had the last word. In February 1908, less than six months after its first issue was published, *La Sanción* closed down. Soon afterward, Saldaña Rocca was tipped off that the police were on their way, and he quietly and quickly left town for the relative safety of Lima.

Silence now filled the space previously occupied by Saldaña Rocca, his newspaper, and his denunciations of Arana. And it would have remained so had it not been for Walter Hardenburg, a young engineer with an adventurous spirit. Hardenburg had stumbled into Arana's Putumayo territory and had been ill-treated by some of Arana's employees. When they let him go, he was shipped to Iquitos, where he remained for a year, during which time he discovered the details of Saldaña Rocca's single-handed campaign. He believed that the story of Arana's brutal and violent methods had to get out of the Amazon. So he left for London, where Arana's company was registered.

When, in early September 1909, Hardenburg arrived in London, he shared the copies of *La Sanción* he had collected with the Anti-Slavery and Aborigines' Protection Society, a major campaigning organization founded in the 1830s to protect the rights of indigenous people worldwide. The society's secretary urged Hardenburg to get his story into the press. A few weeks later, on September 22, 1909, an article appeared in a popular London muckraking magazine, *Truth*, with the arresting headline: THE DEVIL'S PARADISE: A BRITISH-OWNED CONGO. Saldaña Rocca's revelations about Arana had left the closed atmosphere of the Amazon. The story of the devil's paradise now spread around the world, bringing, in its wake, investigations by the British, American, and Peruvian governments.

Saldaña Rocca, however, never got the credit he deserved for first exposing Arana and his brutal regime in his own lifetime. He died in 1912, just days before the publication of Roger Casement's report for the British government on the Putumayo atrocities. Everything Saldaña Rocca had reported, Casement concluded, was true.

Despite the confirmation of the truthfulness of Saldaña Rocca's allegations, not only by Casement but also by the American State Department and a Peruvian judicial enquiry, both in 1913, no one connected with Arana's business was ever charged. Arana continued to produce rubber from his lands until 1933 when, after a short war between Peru and Colombia, all of the territory on the north shore of the Putumayo, including Arana's, was ceded to Colombia.

Iquitos, July 31, 1907
Sr. Benjamin Saldaña Rocca, City

Dear Sir and Friend,

   I left this place for the Putumayo in November of last year, having been offered, once there, a position. In El Encanto [one of the two operational headquarters of the company], I was detained three months, for my servant fell in of small-pox. Though Señor Loayza was generous to me throughout this time he could not offer me a position since it was then occupied by another person; for although it is true Señor J. C. Arana gave me a letter to Señor Loayza, in which he told him to give me a position, it is also true that Pablo Zumaeta, with the meanness that characterizes him, wrote to Señor Loayza another letter, disauthorizing what his chief and brother-in-law had promised me.
   Such undignified conduct as this is not uncommon: unfortunately, I became aware of this farce only upon my return here.
   Seeing that there was no position for me there, I went to La Chorrera [the other operational headquarter of the company], of which Victor Macedo is Manager, to whom I brought letters of recommendation from Señor Loayza. At this place, I stayed three months more, awaiting, not only the promised employment, but also, at the end of my time there, a steamer in which to run to Iquitos, as I did at last in the "Cosmopolita."
   If what is said can be believed, we shall have to consider true the report, so well known in the Putumayo, that Carlos Zumbiaur, the Captain of the "Liberal," in a moment of a drunken rage attacked the young Limanian, Juan Juárez, with a club and with such fury that he left him for dead. Juárez, seeing himself lying there completely crippled and with blood gushing from his mouth, ears and nose, shot himself with his revolver and this put an end to an existence, painful and unfortunate.
   But what is indeed true and which I certify, is that in one of the dependencies of La Chorrera, in the section called Matanzas, the chief, Armando Norman, applies two hundred or more lashes, which are given with rough halters of crude leather, to the unhappy Indians, when they—to their misfortune—do not deliver punctually the number of rolls of rubber with the weight that the soulless Norman desires. At other times, when the Indian, fearful of not being able to deliver the required amount of rubber, flees, they take his tender children, suspend them by their hands and feet and, in this position apply fire, so that under this torture they will tell where their father is hiding.

On more than one occasion, always because their rubber deliveries fall short of the required weight, they are shot, or their arms and legs are cut off with machetes and the body is thrown around the house, and more than once the repugnant spectacle of dogs dragging about the arms and legs of one of the unfortunates has been witnessed.

In Fort Tarma, four hours from La Chorrera, section Oriente, of which Fidel Velarde is Chief, the Colombian Aquileo Torres is held prisoner with an enormous chain around his neck. This unhappy wretch lives in a dying condition in the cellar of the house and was taken there from the Caquetá for they accused him of having rounded-up Indians for himself: a horrible crime in the Putumayo for all the Indians who live in this region are the sole and exclusive property of the feudal J. C. Arana & Hermanos Company by the grace and will of the same and by the acts of their model employees. When the higher employees of the company get drunk—which occurs with great frequency—they make the unfortunate Torres the target of their cowardly attacks, spitting on him, beating him and abusing him vilely.

I have also witnessed another scene, excessively inhuman and repugnant. Juan C. Castaños embarked in the "Liberal" for this place and wished to take along with him his Indian woman, Matilde, which was not permitted for Bartolomé Zumaeta [Arana's brother-in-law] had taken a fancy to the beauty of this unhappy woman. Castaños, seeing that they refused to let him take her with him, in spite of all Matilde's pleadings to be allowed to accompany him, had to abandon her, and, in his presence, the unfortunate woman was given to Zumaeta. The Indian woman fled from this repugnant and diseased wretch, who continued his journey to El Encanto. Upon her return to La Chorrera, she went to sleep on board one of the vessels anchored in that port, where, it is said, all kinds of excesses were committed upon her, and, not content with what they had already done to the unhappy woman, they delivered her to the company; here she was inhumanly whipped with twenty-five lashes and her body was almost cut to pieces by the effects of the lash. She was shut up in a warehouse where she remained at the time of my departure from La Chorrera.

Finally two employees whipped three Chiefs of the Yaquebuas tribe and the Chief of the Nuisayes. The first was whipped to death and the others were kept chained up for several months, all for the "crime" of their people not delivering the number of kilos fixed by the company. Just before this happened, one of the employees involved murdered three Indians, stabbing them with his own hands.

These are the actual deeds that are carried out constantly in the

Putumayo, and for the lack of one kilogram in the weight of their quota of rubber, they murder, mutilate and torture the people.

The relation which I have made of some of the many crimes of the Putumayo is made only for the sake of the suffering and defenceless Indians in the hope that a stop will be put to these crimes. It is inconceivable that within two steps of Iquitos, where there are political authorities and a superior court of justice, crimes of the class I have described are committed.

(Signed) Julio F. Muriedas[1]

On September 29, 1909, *Truth* published an abridged version of this letter. It appeared in this same form in Hardenburg's book, *The Putumayo: The Devil's Paradise*, London, 1912. For reasons that are unknown, Hardenburg's original dedication to Saldaña Rocca, with which he began his manuscript, was left out of the published work.

3

DWARKANATH GANGULI

SLAVERY IN THE BRITISH DOMINION (1886)

from *The Bengalee*

INTRODUCED BY JAYEETA SHARMA

India

During the years 1886–87, Dwarkanath Ganguli, a Bengali schoolteacher–cum–social crusader, transfixed Indian newspaper readers with reports on the "Slave Trade in Assam" that exposed the indentured "coolie" system then prevalent in the British Empire. This system was similar to the private indentured contracts with which nineteenth-century Spanish planters imported Chinese laborers to grow sugar and mine guano in Cuba and Peru. But it was the British slave emancipation of the 1830s that provided indenture with lasting historical significance. It was then that the British government began recruiting a cheap, dislocated workforce to grow lucrative commodities such as tea, coffee, sugar, and rubber on plantations in India and overseas.

From 1838 to 1920, indentured contracts took more than two million laborers from India, China, and Southeast Asia to British colonial plantations across Assam, Natal, Ceylon, Malaysia, Fiji, Mauritius, Surinam, and the West Indies. The term *coolie*, at the time across Asia and the Indian Ocean to mean a laborer who performed manual work, became a racially charged term used to denote Asian proletariats across the world.

The importance of Dwarkanath Ganguli's reportage came from his difficult fact-finding mission, during which he investigated firsthand the

Excerpt from *The Bengalee* XXVII, no. 39 (September 25, 1886): 461. Reprinted in Dwarkanath Ganguli, *Slavery in the British Dominion* (Calcutta: Jijnasa, March 1972), compiled by Professor K.L. Chattopadhyay, edited by Sris Kumar Kunda.

lives of indentured workers on Assam plantations that produced tea, the British nation's favorite beverage. His journey was arduous, despite Assam's geographical closeness to Bengal. Assam lacked proper transportation infrastructure—only what was necessary to ship tea to London via Calcutta.

Ganguli spent days travelling, first by train from Calcutta, next by a slow steamboat, and then a lengthy trek, since the plantation region had neither roads nor vehicles. This was all done in secrecy, since he ran considerable risk if his mission went prematurely public. Assam was colloquially called "Planters' Raj" (Kingdom), where British managers held almost absolute dominance, and strongly discouraged visitors who might discover the inhuman conditions under which tea's indentured workers, recruited from indigenous communities of Central India, lived.

Ganguli's reports, published in Calcutta newspapers, effectively contested British emancipation claims, since the immobility and exploitative conditions of Assam coolies seemed strikingly akin to those of African American slaves. Previously, British abolitionist campaigners such as John Scoble had amassed evidence on indenture's abuses on sugar plantations when Indian coolies were first introduced in the wake of Caribbean slave abolition. But Ganguli's reports were the first widely circulated in British India. They depicted the hundreds of thousands of men, women, and children who were lured onto Assam's plantations and defrauded into believing that they would earn a living wage in salubrious surroundings.

British annexations and commercialization of agriculture caused an increase in rural poverty that in turn produced a flood of footloose labor across the nineteenth century, and these desperate workers became easy subjects for recruiters. Once on the plantations, state-enforced penal provisions meant that coolie laborers could not leave until their contracts expired on threat of imprisonment, no matter how much conditions diverged from what employers promised.

Born in 1844, Dwarkanath Ganguli had a name in social-reformist circles as a campaigner for women's equality and emancipation that led him to become the headmaster of one of India's first girls' schools. A few years before his Assam journey, he married Kadambini Basu, who, with his support, became a pioneering woman doctor despite conservative opposition. The couple were members of the Brahmo Samaj, an important modernizing sect influenced by Unitarianism that sought to reform Hindu social practices across India.

Most Brahmos were highly educated, held progressive views on political and economic questions, and were active in nationalist organizations such as the Indian National Congress. From the late nineteenth century a lively circuit of small newspapers in India's cities, despite the obstacles of insufficient capital and state censorship, provided an alternative forum for writings critical of colonialism that would never see the light of day in establishment giants such as the daily *Statesman* in Calcutta. Such newspapers also operated in local languages such as Bengali, Hindi, or Tamil, enabling them to reach an audience beyond the small English-reading one. Ganguli, for instance, published his pieces in English in the *Bengalee* newspaper, and in Bengali in the *Sanjivani*.

Ganguli's journalistic writings on indentured labor exploitation received wide publicity in nationalist circles. More evidence mounted against the coolie system when Totaram Sanadhya, a former indentured laborer on Fiji's sugar plantations, published his own account. The impact was so great that the Indian National Congress sent fact-finding missions to plantations to amass more evidence.

Middle-class Indians such as Gandhi had already discovered that all Indians suffered racial abuse as coolies—such was the negative association of race with servile work. By the early twentieth century, coolie indenture abolition became an important plank for Indian nationalist agitation against colonial rule. Unlike slave abolition, it never became an important political cause for British liberals. But a combination of Indian nationalist pressure and economic unviability led the British government to finally end the imperial indenture system in 1920.

Recent historical research on Asian diasporas asserts that despite the indenture system's abuses, it provided opportunities for socioeconomic mobility outside of rural India's semifeudal structures and caste discrimination. For instance, many laborers in Fiji and Mauritius were able to establish small businesses after completing contracts. Despite the danger of sexual exploitation, many women workers led freer lives outside of restrictive caste and village structures. But others did not benefit then or later, as in the case of the Assam and Ceylon (Sri Lankan Tamil) laborers. These groups largely remained racially stigmatized proletariats with limited access to education and alternative employment. For them, the exploitation of "coolitude," of which the Mauritius poet Khal Torabully writes, exists as a lived condition even in the twenty-first century.

Coolie trafficking was a historical process that indentured contracts promoted in the era of plantation agro-industry and colonial empires. Its successor, the human trafficking of vulnerable women and children, often affects coolie descendants whose labor services today's world economy. As *The Guardian*'s Gethin Chamberlain recently reported, Assam workers producing world-renowned brands of tea earn only 40 percent of India's minimum wage, and their daughters are prime targets for traffickers who sell them into the urban sex trade or the modern quasislavery of forced domestic labor.

Tea-cultivation in Assam is a grand industry and it has largely contributed to the material prosperity of the province. It has converted a vast wilderness into a prosperous and smiling garden; it has opened out means of communication with the far interior of the country; it has increased the population and has added to the wealth of the province by giving employment to nearly 3 lakhs of emigrants including their children. If in securing all these advantages the emigrant labourers were subjected to such hardships as were not beyond human endurance, we would not probably have raised our voice. But the position of the labourers in many tea-gardens is almost as bad, if it is not worse than the condition of the American Negro slaves before their emancipation. [. . .] It is not mere sentiment that leads us to write in this strain. We have before us stubborn facts, collected from the records of Criminal Courts and other unimpeachable sources to support us in the position that we have taken. [. . .] The latest published report on the labour emigration into Assam shows that in 1884, there were 180,831 adult laborers in the tea-garden; of which 102,557 were men and 78,274 women. Of this labour force, Assam supplies only 5.5%.[1] [. . .] The emigrants as a rule were recruited from the lowest and most ignorant class of the people. The recruiters do not always deal fairly with the lowest class of emigrants. It is to be deeply regretted that they are too often entrapped into the snares of the recruiters either by fraud or misrepresentation and when once caught are never allowed to escape. It is doubtful whether these emigrants who come willingly understand the real nature of their contract. [. . .] The law provides that an emigrant "should understand the contract as regards locality, period and nature of service and the rate of wages and the price at which the rice is to be supplied to him, that the terms thereof are in accordance with law, that he has not been induced to agree to enter thereunto by any coercion, undue influence, fraud, misrepresentation and that he is willing to fulfill the same." Before registering the laborer under the Inland Emigration Act of 1882, it is necessary that the Registering Officers should satisfy himself to these points [. . .] the Registering Officer begins to examine them and they are examined *en masse*. This no doubt saves much labour and trouble on the part of the Registering Officer, though at considerable sacrifice of the interests of the emigrants.[. . .] Here the first chapter of [the coolie's] life ends. But his evil days have not yet begun. He still thinks that he is going to

Indra's Paradise where many a blessing and many a comfort are eagerly awaiting him. Alas! As soon as he reaches that place of his labour he finds to his great disappointment that the picture which had been so skillfully painted for him in all its glory, had now suddenly disappeared. He rises from a dream; the enchantment has left him; and when too late, he curses the unhappy fate which had torn him away and had brought him to Assam.

4

HENRY WOODD NEVINSON

PART VI—THE ISLANDS OF DOOM (1906)
from *Harper's Monthly Magazine*

INTRODUCED BY CATHERINE HIGGS

São Tomé and Príncipe

In late 1884 and early 1885, representatives of Britain, France, Portugal, Spain, Belgium, and Italy met in Berlin at the invitation of Germany to discuss Africa. All the invited parties had banned their citizens from trading in slaves and had outlawed slavery in their colonies, though they often ignored its persistence. In almost every part of Africa that Europe had occupied or wished to colonize, Africans, Arabs, Afro-Arabs, and Afro-Europeans continued to trade slaves and to practice slavery. This situation gave the delegates in Berlin the rationale for colonizing the African continent. They pledged to end slavery in Africa and to replace it with the civilizing effects of free labor and commerce, but this moral agenda masked the more prosaic motive of the 1885 General Act of the Berlin Conference—the desire of European colonizing powers to clarify their territorial claims and to redraw the map of the African continent in order to best exploit its economic potential. Among the claims made by Portugal were to the islands of São Tomé and Príncipe, located near the equator on the West African coast, and to the larger territory of Angola, further south along the coast. To some outside observers, it appeared that Portuguese agents continued to trade in slaves,

Sections of this introduction are excerpted with the permission of the Ohio University Press from Catherine Higgs, *Chocolate Islands: Cocoa, Slavery, and Colonial Africa* (Athens: Ohio University Press, 2012), 9, 10, 22, 23, 40, 42, 52, 86–87, 114, 145, 159–60. Excerpt from Henry W. Nevinson, "The Islands of Doom," part VI of "The Slave Trade of To-day," *Harper's Monthly Magazine*, February 1906, 327–37.

sending men and women contracted in Angola to labor on lucrative cocoa plantations on the islands, from whence they never returned. In 1904, this trade caught the attention of the English journalist Henry Nevinson, who set out to expose its abuses.

In October 1904, Nevinson wrote to William Cadbury, a director of the British chocolate manufacturer Cadbury Brothers, offering his services to the company and asking for introductions to planters in Angola and on the islands of São Tomé and Príncipe in Portuguese West Africa. Like Edmund Morel, who used his *African Mail*—backed financially by Cadbury—to expose atrocities on the rubber plantations in the Congo Free State claimed by Belgium's King Leopold II, Nevinson was an activist journalist. He had been an organizer and advocate for the working class in London and a teacher before becoming a war correspondent. He reported from Madrid during the Spanish-American War and on the siege of Ladysmith during the South African War. In September 1904, he signed a contract with *Harper's Magazine* to write a series of articles about the slave trade in Portuguese West Africa.[1]

The rumors that laborers contracted in Angola were being forced to harvest cocoa in São Tomé and Príncipe first reached William Cadbury in April 1901. The firm imported about 55 percent of its cocoa from São Tomé and Príncipe, the world's third-largest exporter after Ecuador and Brazil. The company would not knowingly use slave-harvested cocoa in the manufacture of its chocolate. The Quaker Cadbury family had been active in the abolitionist movement and supported worker's rights. Labor, including in São Tomé and Príncipe, should by definition be dignified, and a worker free to leave his or her job.

To clarify the labor situation on the islands, Cadbury met with British and Portuguese colonial officials. Workers on the islands were paid and under a 1903 Portuguese law, 40 percent of their wages placed in a fund to repatriate them after they completed their five-year contracts. Less clear was whether any contracted workers had ever returned home. In July 1904, Cadbury hired a fellow Quaker, Joseph Burtt, to investigate conditions on the islands, sending him first to Porto to study Portuguese. Cadbury answered Nevinson's October 1904 letter politely, and gave him the name of A.G. Ceffala, who ran the telegraph station in São Tomé. Cadbury doubted the journalist's seriousness, noting that he spoke no Portuguese, had no contacts in Portugal, planned a brief tour, and intended to publish an account of his journey. To a colleague, Cadbury worried that Nevinson's "impressions will be all from the surface, and I hope what he publishes will not be of such a sensational character as to injure Joseph Burtt's chance."

Nevinson and Burtt met in São Tomé in mid-June 1905. To Burtt, Nevinson admitted that the workers "seem comfortable" but he disliked how much power the planters had. Nevinson recalled their conversation rather differently. Burtt, he concluded, was "about the youngest man of 43 that could live—the mind of a youth, confused and interesting and full of dreams and theories." Burtt's yearlong stay at the communist Whiteway Colony in England had apparently left him "despising the working man" and convinced that the "slave system" in São Tomé was good for Africans. "All very crude and youthful stuff," the forty-nine-year-old Nevinson thought; "full of contradictions and very astonishing." On a whim, he joined Burtt on a visit to the model *roça* (agricultural estate) of Boa Entrada. The owner, Henrique Mendonça, had built individual apartments for workers and their families, a hospital, and a primary school. Boa Entrada, however, was located in the low-lying and swampier region of the island, five miles inland and without the benefit of prevailing winds from the south. Mortality rates were high, ranging from 12 to 25 percent.

Nevinson left São Tomé on July 1, 1905, after a two-week visit. He wrote to William Cadbury, and contradicting his harsher diary entries, assured him that Burtt was "a thoroughly good fellow [who] will be able to tell you all that you want to know." Cadbury remained concerned about what "Nevinson intends to do with his notes." Nevinson published them, in a six-part series in *Harper's* from August 1905 through February 1906 (which he later edited as *A Modern Slavery*). The first five installments chronicled his journey to Angola and along the slave route that stretched from Kavungu deep in the interior near the border with the Congo Free State and ended at Benguela on the west coast. Readers of *Harper's* were left with no doubt that a slave trade continued.

After six months on the islands, Burtt headed to Angola in December 1905. There he read the final installment in Nevinson's series, the evocatively titled "Islands of Doom." Burtt found the article "so unfair" that he could barely contain his irritation. "On page 328," he complained to Cadbury, "the guest who says 'The Portuguese are certainly doing a marvelous work for Angola' must have been myself." Burtt was outraged at the implication that he supported slavery. When he met Nevinson in June 1905, however, Burtt had just arrived on São Tomé. He was naive, but it seems unlikely—given his mission for Cadbury Brothers—that he would have supported slavery. Nevinson had just spent five months trekking through Angola. Physically and emotionally spent and convinced that slave trading continued in Angola, he arrived in São Tomé equally convinced that the islands of doom were the place Angolan slaves went to die.

That Burtt made the journey in reverse, first spending six months on the islands before going to Angola, shaped his own view of conditions on São Tomé and Príncipe, as well as his reaction to Nevinson's article. The average death rate, he reminded Cadbury, was 11 percent, not the 20 percent claimed by Nevinson. Burtt also rejected the journalist's assertion that "the prettiest girls are chosen by the agents and the gangers as their concubines." White men did forge relationships with black women, but they were "almost exclusively" São Toméan, rather than *serviçaes* (literally, servants), as the Portuguese called the contract workers. Nevinson's claim that children were encouraged to engage in bestiality for the amusement of planters deeply perturbed Burtt. To the contrary, he recalled that one boy had been "severely flogged" for his outrageous behavior. Flogging, however, was rare, and Burtt found no evidence that runaways were hunted and killed. For him, the final article in the *Harper's* series was an abomination that pointed "clearly to this; that Nevinson writes authoritatively on matters of which he knows practically nothing." Despite the six months Burtt spent on the islands, he still struggled "to get at the truth amongst strangers, and if I found it difficult in six months it is quite impossible for Nevinson to have learnt much in as many hours, which was about the time he spent at the roças."

Burtt spent a year in Angola, and like Nevinson, he followed the slave route into the interior. Ultimately, his December 1906 report to Cadbury placed him firmly in the journalist's camp. Africans were enslaved in Angola in a still-active trade. Shipped to the islands of São Tomé and Príncipe, they found themselves "doomed to perpetual slavery." In 1908, William Cadbury went to West Africa; Burtt accompanied him to the islands, to Angola, and to the British Gold Coast (modern-day Ghana), where free African farmers grew cocoa. Just before their departure, an editorial in the *Standard* questioned the company's concern for the "African hands, whose toil . . . is so essential to the [firm's] beneficent and lucrative operations." Cadbury Brothers, stung by the suggestion that it had done nothing to try to improve conditions, sued for libel. In a surprising turn, Nevinson wrote to the *Standard* to defend William Cadbury's efforts to expose labor abuses. In March 1909, the company announced that it would no longer buy cocoa from the islands. In December, the courts decided in Cadbury Brothers' favor, awarding one farthing (¼ of a penny) in damages, widely interpreted as a criticism of the eight years it had taken the firm to boycott cocoa from São Tomé and Príncipe. In 1913, a new Portuguese governor-general succeeded in ending the slave trade in Angola; by 1916, workers were regularly returning carrying severance payments from the repatriation fund. Yet as Nevinson notes in the extract below, "the great contest with capitalism" continued. Despite the boycott, the islands remained a major supplier of cocoa to other firms until 1918, when an outbreak of thrips devastated the cocoa trees and largely removed São Toméan cocoa from the international market.

They stand in the Gulf of Guinea—these two islands of San Thomé and Principe where the slaves die—about 150 miles from the nearest coast at the Gaboon River in French Congo. San Thomé lies just above the equator, Principe some eighty miles north and a little east of San Thomé [. . .]. The population [. . .] may now be reckoned considerably above 40,000 [. . .]. It is difficult to say what proportion [. . .] are slaves. The official returns of 1900 put the population of San Thomé at 37,776, including 19,211 serviçaes, or slaves [. . .]. But the prosperity of the islands is increasing with such rapidity that these numbers have now probably been far surpassed. It is cocoa that has created the prosperity [. . .]. The islands possess exactly the kind of climate that kills men and makes the cocoa-tree flourish.

One early morning at San Thomé I went out to visit a plantation which is rightly regarded as a kind of model—a showplace for the intelligent foreigner or for the Portuguese shareholder who feels qualms as he banks his dividends. There were four hundred slaves on the estate, not counting children, and I was shown their neat brick huts in rows, quite recently finished. I saw them clearing the ground under the cocoa-trees, gathering the great yellow pods, sorting the brown kernels, which already smelt like a chocolate-box, heaping them up to ferment, raking them out in vast pans to dry, working in the carpenters' sheds, superintending the new machines, and gathering in groups for the midday meal. I was shown the turbine engine, the electric light, [. . .] the clean and roomy hospital with its copious supply of drugs [. . .]. To an [outsider], [. . .] the Decree of 1903 for the regulation of slave labor had been carried out in every possible aspect [. . .]. Then we sat down to an exquisite Parisian déjeuner [. . .] and while I was meditating on the hardships of African travel, a saying of another guest kept coming back to my mind: "The Portuguese are certainly doing a marvelous work for Angola and these islands. Call it slavery if you like. Names and systems don't matter. The sum of human happiness is being increased."

The doctor had come up to pay his official visit to the plantation that day. "The death-rate on this roça," he remarked casually, during the meal, "is twelve or fourteen percent a year among the serviçaes." "And what is the chief cause?"

I asked. "Anemia," he said. "That is a vague sort of thing," I answered; "what brings on anemia?" "Unhappiness [tristeza]," he said frankly.

[. . .] This cause, however, does not account for the high mortality rate among children. On one of the largest and best-managed plantations of San Thomé the superintendent admits a children's death-rate of 25 percent, or one-quarter of all the children, every year [. . .]. No wonder the price of slaves is high and that it is almost impossible for the supply from Angola to keep pace with the demand, though the government calls on its agents to drive the trade as hard as they can, and the agents do their utmost to encourage the natives to raid, kidnap, accuse of witchcraft, press for debts, soak in rum, and sell.

The common saying that if you have seen one plantation you have seen them all, is not exactly true [. . .]. High up in the hills we came to a filthy village, where a few slaves were drearily lying about, full of the deadly rum that hardly even cheers [. . .]. The buildings are arranged in a great quadrangle, with high walls all round and big gates that are locked at night [. . .]. In the centre of the square at regular intervals stood the whity-brown gangers, leaning on their long sticks or flicking their boots with whips. Beside them lay the large and savage dogs which prowl around the buildings at night to prevent the slaves from escaping in the darkness.

About once a month the slaves receive their wages [. . .]. By the Decree of 1903, the minimum wage for a man is fixed at 2500 reis (something under 10 shillings) a month, and for a woman at 1800 reis [. . .]. According to law, only two-fifths of the wages are to be paid every month, the remaining three-fifths going to a "Repatriation Fund" in San Thomé [. . .]. They never send the slaves home, and they do not deduct the money for doing it.

[. . .] I am inclined to think that for business reasons the violent forms of cruelty are unlikely and uncommon. Flogging, however, is common if not universal, and so are certain forms of vice. The prettiest girls are chosen by the agents and gangers as their concubines—that is natural. But it was worse when a planter pointed [. . .] out a little boy and girl [. . .] and boasted that [. . .] they were already instructed in acts of bestiality [. . .]. Sometimes the runaways are hunted and shot down. For the most part they live a wandering and hard, but I hope not an entirely unhappy existence in the dense forest [. . .]. Every now and again the Portuguese organize manhunts to recapture them or kill them off.

[. . .] In 1885, by the Berlin General Act, England, the United States, and thirteen other powers, including Portugal and Belgium, pledged themselves to suppress every kind of slave-trade, especially in the Congo and the interior of Africa.

[. . .] If anyone wanted a theme for satire, what more deadly theme could he find? To which of the powers can an appeal now be made? Appeal to England is no longer possible. Since the rejection of Ireland's home-rule bill, the abandon-ment of the Armenians to massacre, and the extinction of the South African republics, she can no longer be regarded as the champion of liberty or justice [. . .]. It might be better for mankind that the islands should go back to wilder-ness than that a slave should toil there. I know the contest is still before us. It is but part of the great contest with capitalism, and in Africa it will be as long and difficult as it was a hundred years ago in other regions of the world. I have but tried to reveal one small glimpse in a greater battlefield, and to utter the cause of a few thousands out of the millions of men and women whose silence is heard only by God.

5

CHRISTIAN PARENTI

CHOCOLATE'S BITTERSWEET ECONOMY (2008)

from *Fortune*

INTRODUCED BY ROBERT FRIEDMAN

West Africa

The seeds of the cocoa tree, from which chocolate is produced, are bitter. So too is the story of how this sweet confection gets to our mouths.

Much of the world's cocoa is picked by tiny hands, those of children as young as seven or eight, in places like Ivory Coast, which supplies more than 30 percent of the global harvest. An estimated six hundred thousand children work in cocoa fields there, wielding machetes, handling dangerous pesticides, often toiling far from home and rarely going to school. Some are sold or bonded into slavery.

In the fall of 2007, six years after the world's biggest chocolate makers agreed to rid the industry of child labor, I sent writer Christian Parenti and photographer Jessica Dimmock to West Africa to see what progress had been made. The answer, as Parenti's piece and Dimmock's pictures showed: not much.

"Chocolate's Bittersweet Economy," published in *Fortune* in February 2008, is one of those classic exposés of globalization—reporting that pierces the veil of ignorance or indifference to the suffering that lies behind a highly valued and widely sold product. I had assigned and edited similar pieces about how children were exploited in the stitching of soccer balls in Pakistan and in diamond mining in Sierra Leone. Other journalists have made us aware of horrendous working conditions in factories where mobile

Excerpt from Christian Parenti, "Chocolate's Bittersweet Economy," international editions of *Fortune*, February 4, 2008.

phones and undergarments are produced. In some cases, multinational corporations such as Nike and Apple have been shamed into taking action to better police their supply chains. In others, little has changed.

Chocolate, sadly, is in the latter group. In 1906, *Harper's Monthly* published a series of articles by British journalist Henry Nevinson about the use of slaves in the cocoa industry in São Tomé, an African island then a Portuguese colony. He chronicled conditions so severe that, he said, 20 percent of the workforce died each year. In 1998, almost a century later, the United Nations Children's Fund, UNICEF, documented abuses by cocoa farmers in Ivory Coast who were enslaving children from neighboring Burkina Faso and Mali. It was the UNICEF report and a subsequent BBC documentary that spurred U.S. Senator Tom Harkin and Congressman Eliot Engel to push through legislation that led to voluntary industry standards certifying that cocoa was being produced without child labor.

The problem, as Parenti and Dimmock found during their two-week trip to Ivory Coast, was that no one—not the manufacturers, not the government, not the middlemen who buy beans from farmers and sell them to exporters such as Cargill, Archer Daniels Midland, and Barry Callebaut, not even the organizations set up to help implement the reforms—was enforcing the voluntary code. In villages without electricity, running water, or schools, Parenti and Dimmock found boys working with machetes, exposed to pesticides and carrying heavy loads, conditions not unlike those Nevinson found last century.

There has been some progress since the story was published. In 2012, the European Union passed a resolution calling for full implementation of the Harkin-Engel Protocol. Nestlé, one of the the world's biggest chocolate manufacturers, is working with the Fair Labor Association to ensure that its supply chain is free of cocoa from farms that employ children. Still, political instability in Ivory Coast and a failure to provide education and social services has slowed the pace of change. The industry has pushed back the deadline to 2020.

We'll need more journalists like Nevinson and Parenti to keep those companies to their word. And for chocolate to lose its bitter taste.

———————————

Outside the village of Sinikosson in southwestern Ivory Coast, along a trail tracing the edge of a muddy fishpond, Madi Ouedraogo sits on the ground picking up the cocoa pods in one hand, hacking them open with a machete in the other, and scooping the filmy white beans into plastic buckets. It is the middle of the school day, but Madi, who looks to be about 10, says his family can't afford the fees to send him to the nearest school, five miles away. "I don't like this work," he says. "I would rather do something else. But I have to do this."

Sinikosson, accessible only by rutted jungle tracks, is a long way from the luxurious chocolate shops of New York and Paris. But it is here, on small West African farms like these, that 70% of the world's cocoa beans are grown—40% from just one country, Ivory Coast. It's not only the landscape that is tough. Working and living conditions are brutal. Most villages lack electricity, running water, health clinics, or schools. And to make ends meet, underage cocoa workers like Madi and the two boys next to him spend their days wielding machetes, handling pesticides, and carrying heavy loads.

This type of child labor isn't supposed to exist in Ivory Coast. Not only is it explicitly barred by law—the official working age in the country is 18—but since the issue first became public seven years ago, there has been an international campaign by the chocolate industry, governments, and human rights organizations to eradicate the problem. Yet today child workers, many under the age of 10, are everywhere.

The big cocoa exporters—Cargill, Archer Daniels Midland, Barry Callebaut, and Saf-Cacao—do not own plantations and do not directly employ child workers. Instead, they buy beans from Ivorian middlemen called *pisteurs* and *treton*. These middlemen own warehouses and fleets of flatbed trucks that travel deep into the jungle to buy cocoa from the small independent farmers who grow most of the crop. But labor and human rights activists charge that Big Chocolate has an obligation to improve working conditions on the farms where so many children toil. They argue that the exporters and manufacturers bear ultimate responsibility for conditions on the farms because they exert considerable control over world cocoa markets, essentially setting what is called the farm gate price.

The controversy reached a zenith in 2001, when U.S. Congressman Eliot Engel (D-N.Y.) and Senator Tom Harkin (D-Iowa) introduced legislation mandating a labeling system for chocolate. Industry fought back, and a compromise was reached establishing a voluntary protocol by which chocolate companies would wean themselves from child labor, then certify that they had done so. [. . .] To turn up the heat, the U.S. Department of Labor contracted with Tulane University to monitor progress.

Tulane recently released its first report, and though the tone is polite, the picture isn't pretty. [. . .] The report criticized the governments of Ivory Coast and Ghana for lack of transparency. And it said the industry's certification process "contains no standards."

In some respects the situation only got worse after Harkin-Engel. From 2002 to 2004, Ivory Coast was gripped by civil war. [. . .] Like diamonds and timber, cocoa became a so-called conflict resource. "Blood chocolate" was providing fast cash for armed groups and creating misery for common people. Since 2004, Ivory Coast has settled into an armed peace, with French and UN troops keeping the warring factions apart. But chocolate exporters and manufacturers say the war and its aftermath have hampered their efforts to eradicate child labor. [. . .]

Outside Sinikosson, El Hadj Sankara cultivates 27 acres of cocoa, from which he usually harvests ten tons of beans, earning about $9,000 a year but remaining deeply in debt. Sankara and his 11-year-old son, Ibrahim, are preparing a large mound of cocoa pods for processing. "I want to help my father," says Ibrahim, standing on a pile of pods, toying with his machete. "I need to learn how to be a farmer." His sentiment captures the complexity of the child-labor issue here: Typically it is poverty that compels child labor, not greedy overseers. [. . .]

Cocoa prices have been declining in recent years—currently about 90 cents a kilo—because of corruption and a poorly planned economic liberalization. President Felix Houphouët-Boigny, who ran Ivory Coast from the late 1950s until the mid-1990s, borrowed heavily against his country's assets and wasted the money on megalomaniacal vanity projects like the world's largest basilica, built in the country's desolate interior. During his reign, Houphouët-Boigny invited in hundreds of thousands of Muslim farmers from neighboring Mali and Burkina Faso to grow cocoa. [. . .]

When the bills on Houphouët-Boigny's squandered loans came due in 1999, the government imposed fiscal austerity and liberalized the economy. Its marketing board, Caistab, was defanged, prices were deregulated, and new oversight agencies and development funds were created to support the market and aid farmers hurt by lower farm gate prices. According to European Union and World Bank audits, these new government bodies now collect three times as much money from the cocoa sector, much of it from exporters, as did the old system, but they spend little on infrastructure or subsidies. In short, not much money gets past corrupt officials and down to the farmers.

Economic hard times followed, and many native Ivorians turned against the immigrants from Burkina Fao and Mali. Demagogues preached a xenophobic creed that they called *Ivorité*, and in 2002 ethnic tensions exploded into civil war. Now, with the front lines frozen and the armed peace holding, the many non-Ivorian cocoa workers, like those who live in Sinikosson, are trapped on remote farms. [. . .] "I've not been into the main town for four years," says Aladji Mohamed Sawadogo, the chief of Sinikosson. "The last time I tried to go I did not have enough money to pay all the bribes at the checkpoints. I am just stuck. These are the conditions in which we live." [. . .] Adds Sawadogo: "We are not happy that we ourselves live and work like this. Of course we don't want it for our children. But there is no choice." What would make a difference? "Better prices." [. . .]

Hershey, like other major chocolate firms, signed the Harkin-Engel protocol and maintains it is working. "The protocol's value is seen in measurable progress on the ground," says Kirk Saville, a Hershey spokesman. "It has created greater community awareness of child welfare issues and increased incomes for family farms and access to education."

But Hershey has no direct role in implementing reforms in Ivory Coast. Instead, the protocol required the industry to create a foundation to oversee certification. That body is the International Cocoa Initiative, or ICI, headquartered in Geneva, and funded by the chocolate industry to the tune of about $2 million a year.

The foundation began its work in Ivory Coast in 2003, and it claims to have six pilot projects underway there. [. . .]

But the foundation has only one staff member in Ivory Coast, Robale Kagohi, and his activities appear limited. [. . .] He explains that the anti-child-labor campaign has so far favored "sensitization"—workshops with local officials, police, and farmers to explain that child labor is wrong and that if it continues Ivory Coast will be shut out of world cocoa markets. On the roads there are billboards urging people to say no to child labor.

Farmers describe these efforts as more akin to intimidation than to education. "People are worried that America will not buy our cocoa anymore," says Julien Kra Yau, director of a farmers' cooperative in Thoui. "That would be very bad." [. . .] The industry's evident lack of compliance with Harkin-Engel puts everyone involved in a difficult position. New coercive legislation requiring "child-labor-free" labeling could cause trouble for the large cocoa exporters and chocolate manufacturers if there were boycotts of non-labeled chocolate. But impoverished Ivorian farmers say loss of markets would also hurt them and their children. Since the idea was first floated in 2001, the chocolate industry has taken the same position: Labeling "would hurt the people it is intended to help," says Susan Smith, a spokeswoman for the Chocolate Manufacturers Association and the World Cocoa Foundation.

There is fair-trade chocolate on the market, but it accounts for no more than 1% of global supply, and the movement has little traction in Ivory Coast. A more effective way to combat child labor would be for the government of Ivory Coast to invest some of the revenue it gets from high taxes on cocoa exporters in education and social services to help poor farmers. But the government of Ivory Coast is ranked among the most corrupt in the world by Transparency International, a non-governmental watchdog group. And it seems happier making excuses than changes.

[. . .] Congressman Engel, for one, isn't happy with the lack of progress. He and Senator Harkin plan to travel to Ivory Coast soon on a fact-finding mission of their own. "We have given the industry plenty of time," Engel says. "I am not prepared to give another extension."

6

TAUFIK ULHADI AND USMANDI ANDESKA

ANALYZING THE ADDED VALUE OF THE SHOE INDUSTRY FOR WORKERS (1991)

from *Media Indonesia*

INTRODUCED BY JEFF BALLINGER

Indonesia

The struggle against Nike and other major U.S. footwear and clothing brands that underpaid their workers in factories throughout the developing world led to the major consumer boycott of the 1990s. Although Indonesians had long been aware of the terrible conditions and low wages in garment and footwear factories, it was in the 1990s that the U.S. media began to intensively cover the problems. As the outrage grew, it led to the formation of anti-sweatshop organizations on U.S. campuses, massive consumer boycotts, greater scrutiny of textile and garment companies manufacturing in South America, a State Department investigation, and, eventually, to companies developing corporate codes and an infrastructure for monitoring and reporting on conditions. To some extent, the more recent scrutiny of conditions in China at the factories of companies like Foxconn/Apple has its roots in the earlier campaigns against exploitation by Nike and its suppliers.

Indonesia was the epicenter of this struggle. As light manufacturing aimed at promoting export-led growth became the pattern of development in much of Asia, sweatshops spread all over the region. In Indonesia, workers took to the streets to protest the conditions, encouraged by local unions and international NGOs. To some extent, they succeeded. The mass protests at factories in Indonesia, China, and, to a lesser degree, Vietnam have pushed up wages. It is worth noting that this alliance and the resulting protests

Excerpt from Taufik Ulhadi and Usmandi Andeska, "Analyzing the Added Value of the Shoe Industry for Workers," *Media Indonesia*, March 5–6, 1991.

came a decade before political scientists Margaret Keck and Kathyn Sik-kink started writing about transnational advocacy movements and the development of global civil society and unionists spoke of "global labor solidarity."

The campaign against Nike was helped by media coverage in Asia and around the world. Foreign publications—especially the now-defunct *Far Eastern Economic Review*—and U.S. television and newspapers covered the story in great detail in Vietnam as well as in Indonesia.

Of the local coverage in Indonesia, the best example of the increased sophistication of reportage came in 1991 in the following excerpt from a multipart exposé that ran in the Jakarta daily *Media Indonesia*. Previous local coverage of Nike contractors' depredations was limited to reports on mass strikes, beginning in 1988, and reports on factories which ran afoul of the Manpower Ministry's minimum wage enforcement efforts. The latter stories appeared in tabloids and even the English-language dailies and regional publications. But the excerpt below focuses on the economic explanation of why wages were so low and how little the Indonesian workers were benefitting from the foreign companies they worked for. With its solid attention to detail and reliance on facts and figures, as well as the comprehensive information the article supplies about working conditions and the corporate pricing and profit structure, the *Media Indonesia* exposé reads like a report rather than a news feature. Although the plight of the workers is mentioned often, this is not a tug-at-your-heartstrings human-interest story. Rather, it is a forceful and sophisticated argument for better wages and conditions at the shoe factories.

Analyzing the Added Value of the Shoe Industry for Workers

The rapid growth of the sports shoe industry is unique in [. . .] Indonesian industrial history. Until 1986 there were only three active companies, producing 6.8 million pairs of sports shoes. Four years later there are 205 companies with an estimated production capacity of 581.5 million pairs. The growth has been heavily influenced by foreign investment, especially from South Korea, Taiwan and Hong Kong.

In the last three years, Nike has used Indonesia as one of its production centers. Nike doesn't actually own a factory, but uses the facilities of other companies with factories here. To guarantee that quality doesn't drop, in every factory there is a Nike employee observing production and examining quality. Most of the factories are Korean-owned, and the connection between Nike and the factories is that between licensor and licensee.

The license is for 2–3 years and is bought at a high price from Nike Inc. But factories holding a license are not guaranteed orders. Nike only gives orders to those factories whose production costs are low and quality high. Factories unable to compete can easily have their license revoked.

The factories can buy raw materials and components from any factory. But, according to Nike itself, 80% of components used are imported from South Korea. The reason being that Indonesian factories are unable to make the components according to Nike standards. Given the amount of components and raw materials that are imported, it is almost certain that the positive impact on local industry is minimal.

As most production components are fixed costs, the only component that can be depressed is the cost of labor. And Indonesian workers are cheap. The retail price of Nike shoes in the US is between $50 and $175, on average $75. But the production cost in Indonesia is $5.60 a pair. The labor component of this is Rp 418 (US$0.22) or 0.3% of the retail price.

Nike-licensed factories employ over 24,000 but it is questionable whether these workers benefit from Nike's presence in Indonesia. Take for instance Siti (not her real name), a worker in one of the Nike-producing factories in Tangerang. She starts work at 7.30am and cannot leave the factory for at least 10 hours. All day she does the same repetitive work. It is simple and boring, but she does it six days a week. At mid-day she can rest for half an hour provided that she does not leave the factory canteen. According to the factory, Siti's labor is worth Rp 986 a day. [. . .]

Before we ask the question whether the wages are sufficient, we need to state that factories paying less than Rp 1,600 are breaking national labor law. But every Nike-licensed factory pays some or all of its workers at less than this rate.

But even supposing that workers are paid a wage based on the legal minimum, this is not enough. In 1988 the minimum physical needs standard for West Java was Rp 60,000 for a single person. Two years later the average wage for new male workers in West Java sports shoe factories was Rp 42,672. In other words, the male wage in sports shoe factories is not sufficient to meet the minimum physical needs from three years ago.

The only way workers can bridge the gap between the minimum wage and basic needs is by working [overtime]. In each factory there is the practice of compulsory overtime. Most workers work between 40–42 hours a week. But on top of this, they are compelled to work two extra hours per day.

By paying a basic wage that forces workers to take overtime, Nike-licensed factories are hampering one of the government's aims in developing the industrial sector. If workers did not have to work overtime to meet their basic physical needs, this would open 6,000 new employment opportunities in Nike-licensed factories. Such a raise would have little effect on the retail price of a pair of Nikes abroad. The retail price would rise (on average) from $75 to $75.13.

The extent to which Nike-licensed factories take their workers for granted was most evident when the glue storeroom at the Hasi factories caught fire in January 1991. Looking at the thick smoke and firemen running back and forth in the factory compound, management took the decisions to allow workers to go home at 1.00pm with a full day's pay. But come the following Saturday workers who normally knock off at 1.00 were forced to work until late afternoon to make up for the time lost. Two workers died in that fire. [. . .]

In every Nike-licensed factory, workers have stories about others whose fingers have been severed by unsafe machines. Moreover, in one other South Korean factory—Starwin—a health care employee said he was so used to seeing fingers cut off that he no longer saw it as an unusual occurrence. Sometimes, fingers were thrown on the garbage bin. [. . .]

It is most clear that Nike makes great profit from Indonesia, especially those working in their licensed factories. But those people do not enjoy any benefit from Nike's presence. The public needs to know the customs and practices in the factories. The workers need to know their rights and the violations by the factories.

7

ALAN BUTTERFIELD AND JIM NELSON

SHOCKING REPORT FROM EL SALVADOR (1999)

from the *National Enquirer*

INTRODUCED BY IRA ARLOOK

El Salvador

In the midnineties most Americans, if they thought about it at all, remembered the sweatshop as a relic of early twentieth-century history. By then, however, American apparel brands and retailers had been re-creating the conditions that infamously prevailed almost a century earlier in New York City's garment industry by moving their clothing production to factories throughout much of Central America and Asia. Two events alerted journalists to the new reality. In August 1995, California and federal investigators discovered seventy Thai immigrants imprisoned in a two-story apartment complex that the media described as a "fortified sweatshop complex" in the Los Angeles suburb of El Monte. There they sewed garments seventeen hours a day, seven days a week, for $1.60 an hour. To prevent escape, the owners surrounded their makeshift factory with razor wire and fences, plus inward-facing spiked bars. Less than a year later, labor rights activist Charles Kernaghan inadvertently discovered daytime television star Kathie Lee Gifford's use of a Honduran sweatshop, also surrounded by razor wire and fences, to produce her Walmart clothing line.

In a meeting convened weeks later by Kernaghan at the New York City residence of Roman Catholic Cardinal John O'Connor, Kathie Lee met with fifteen-year-old Wendy Diaz, one of the Honduran workers who sewed the star's clothing line. Kathie Lee agreed to join efforts to end sweatshop

From Alan Butterfield and Jim Nelson, "Shocking Report from El Salvador," *National Enquirer*, October 13, 1999.

practices and promised Diaz, "I had no idea what was happening but now that I know I will do everything I can to help you." She then added that she would never do it again. This promise would prove to be impossible to keep while continuing to work with Walmart or other major brands and retailers, whose profit margins required keeping wages to a minimum and squeezing suppliers on all other costs in what came to be known as the "Walmart model."

By the time Kernaghan and his National Labor Committee for Human and Labor Rights in El Salvador (NLC, now the Institute for Global Labor and Human Rights) happened upon Gifford's clothing label again, this time in a Salvadoran sweatshop almost two years later, journalists had honed their approach, telling the story primarily through the eyes and voices of the workers themselves. Alan Butterfield and Jim Nelson wrote their *Enquirer* story from the perspective of one of the Salvadoran women, a single mother of two young children. They made the story more vivid than any of the sweatshop stories that preceded it by combining the *Enquirer*'s sensationalist approach with accurate reporting that, in this case, lived up to the hype.

Sweatshops in El Salvador and other Central American countries had become the focus of Kernaghan's work at the end of the Salvadoran civil war. He and his staff were among the first to investigate and publicize the human toll being taken by Walmart, Gap, and other household brand names as they moved their manufacturing operations abroad. Kernaghan and his colleagues contributed to the rebirth of a movement that had begun nearly a century earlier, in large part as a response to the March 1911 Triangle Shirtwaist factory fire in New York City, in which 146 mostly young immigrant women died, trapped in an eight-story building. Nearly one hundred years later, in December 2010, a factory fire in Bangladesh killed 29 apparel workers and injured another 100. Dhaka replaced Manhattan, but otherwise it was a repeat performance: young women who were paid below-subsistence wages working long hours under criminally negligent conditions, sewing clothing destined for American women, died from inhaling smoke and jumping out windows of a factory where exits were locked.

Another factory fire followed, and then the worst garment industry disaster ever, the collapse in December 2012 of the Rana Plaza, just outside Dhaka, an eight-story building housing five thousand apparel workers. Over eleven hundred died. By then, the second-generation global anti-sweatshop movement, inspired by the NLC's work and the stories it generated, were able to bring about some institutional changes. A global coalition of union federations and labor rights organizations forced over seventy major apparel companies (including PVH, owner of Tommy Hilfiger and Calvin Klein; Abercrombie & Fitch; Sean Jean; American Eagle; and H&M) to sign a legally binding building and fire safety accord that gave promise of preventing future tragedies.

Kernaghan's seminal work was the starting point. The *Enquirer* article amplified it by communicating with precisely the readership targeted by Gifford's Walmart marketers, with a style and content that resonated. As newsroom budgets tightened over the last decade, many journalists found it difficult, if not impossible, to do the initial investigations. But they were willing to follow up on the research done by labor rights organizations, using networks of contacts in developing countries. So the *Enquirer* article would become a blueprint for labor reporting for decades to come.

———————

"Kathie Lee's sweatshop is killing my kids!" That's the anguished cry of Norma Elizabeth Alvarez, who works as a seamstress at Caribbean Apparel, the factory in Santa Ana, El Salvador, that produces a Kathie Lee Gifford clothing line.

The ENQUIRER traveled to the Central American nation to uncover the truth about the working conditions—and we were shocked by what we discovered.

An exhausted Norma works an unspeakably grueling six-day, 60-hour week for a pitiful 60 cents an hour in a true sweatshop where the temperature soars above 100 degrees. She barely subsists in a squalid two-room shack with a mud floor that she and six relatives call home.

"Because I don't make enough money to feed my children properly, they are very sickly," Norma told us. "I have no medical insurance for them and money for a doctor. My worst nightmare is one of these days, sickness will take one of my youngsters.

"I pray to God for my children's sake that Kathie Lee will see that we are treated properly."

Tragically, Norma's desperate plea will almost surely fall on deaf ears.

Despite the multimillionaire entertainer's public expressions of sympathy with the workers, she is willfully turning a blind eye on horrifying abuses, charges a top labor leader.

"I have a signed agreement by Kathie Lee saying that she would never again tolerate sweatshop conditions and that she would open them up for inspection by local religious and human-rights leaders," a furious Charles Kernaghan told The ENQUIRER. "None of these promises has been kept!

"We had a long discussion with Kathie Lee in 1996. She apologized to the workers. She said, 'I didn't know these sweatshops existed.' She said she would make sure the conditions were O.K. There were very few changes after all the promises."

Kernaghan—whose 15,000-member nonprofit human rights organization fights sweatshops worldwide—said: "The conditions are still disgusting!"

Norma—a 29-year-old mother of two—is incredibly courageous to issue her open appeal to Kathie Lee.

Attempts to bring a union to the factory resulted in workers receiving terrifying death threats. And The ENQUIRER interviewed a co-worker of Norma, Blanca Ruth Palacios, who told us she lost her job at the sweatshop for her involvement in the union organizing!

"I hope I don't lose my job over this interview, I am only telling the truth," says Norma, who prays for a better life for her children—Iris, 6, and Jonathan, 4.

Indelibly etched on this devoted mother's mind is the day a malnourished Jonathan became so weak, he could barely walk. The condition persisted for a week but she couldn't afford a doctor.

[. . .] "After the doctors tested him, they found he had rickets—a bone disease, because I don't have enough money to buy milk and vegetables rich in calcium and vitamin D.

"A doctor told us it was a matter of life or death. He said that in severe cases, rickets can be fatal. I was panic-stricken.

"I decided there was only one thing to do: I would go without food every other day in order to buy him some dairy products.

"I lost weight and felt faint at times, but I managed to get through each day at work. Gradually, over several months, the pains in Jonathan's legs eased—although he still walks with a bit of a limp.

"I am not the only one suffering. I know other women in the factory who have had miscarriages because they couldn't afford to eat well or go to the doctor. Some have lost children to illnesses that should have been treated by a doctor."

[. . .] Norma's family lives in a tin-roofed "house" with mud walls and no indoor plumbing or refrigeration. With no windows, it is as dark and dank as a tomb—and filled with mosquitoes that carry the threat of malaria.

Norma's life of misery begins at 5 a.m. as she gets ready for work which starts at 7 a.m.

The hellish factory has no air-conditioning and the temperature soars above 100 degrees beneath its metal roof, says Norma. During each sweat-drenched day in this human oven, she is allowed just one break—40 minutes to stuff down lunch and relieve herself.

"[. . .] Officially our work hours are from 7 a.m. to 3:40 p.m., but there is mandatory overtime and the earliest we leave work is 5:40 p.m.—six days a week.

"We don't have sick days, and the only vacation is when the factory closes for two weeks around Christmas."

On her TV show, Kathie Lee told fans, "I spend an enormous amount of money every year monitoring factories . . . I want to make sure that anything that's made in my name, as much as I possibly can, is done in an ethical and moral and righteous way."

But a destitute and desperate Norma responds: "I know Kathie Lee is making millions of dollars from the clothes we sew. I'm asking her to come to El Salvador and see firsthand the conditions we work and live in.

"Kathie Lee and her family are more than welcome to spend the weekend at my house. Her two kids can play with mine. I just pray that my kids make it to adulthood."

8

LIU ZHIYI

YOUTH AND DESTINY SPENT WITH MACHINES— 28 DAYS UNDERCOVER AT FOXCONN (2010)

from *Southern Weekend*

INTRODUCED BY BEIBEI BAO

China

Many countries in Asia developed their economies through "export-led growth," first by growing commodities such as rice, rubber, and cotton, then moving up the chain to textiles, garments, footwear, and finally technology. Assembling electronics for famous international brands like Apple was supposed to be a step up the ladder, providing better-paid jobs that required more skills. But it turned out that the new "electronic sweatshops" had many of the same shortcomings as the old low-tech factories we read about in that groundbreaking Nike coverage.

International organizations, along with the Western press, had been investigating conditions in factories since about 2003. Even before the Foxconn scandal, many of the major media outlets ran a number of long stories about the high price paid by Chinese workers—the foot soldiers of the country's consistently high economic growth. But China's media are government-controlled and, although there were many journalists and outlets that pushed hard on the limits, it was not until Chinese teenagers and twenty-something males and females began committing suicide, or attempting suicide in early 2010, that local media began covering the story. These incidents produced a rash of new coverage, and the fact that Foxconn was the biggest supplier to American electronic brands such as Apple and

Excerpt from Liu Zhiyi, "Youth and Destiny Spent with Machines—28 Days Undercover at Foxconn," *Southern Weekend*, May 13, 2010, www.infzm.com/content/44881. Translated by Beibei Bao.

Hewlett-Packard made the story irresistible to the Western press. It was this second tidal wave of press coverage that helped to bring about changes in conditions.

So what was the turning point?

At 4:30 a.m. on January 23, 2010, a nineteen-year-old male worker named Ma Xiangqian was found dead at one of Foxconn's largest factories in China. In the six months that followed, nine deaths and three other suicide attempts occurred at the two factories run by the Taiwanese electronics manufacturer in the same southern city, Shenzhen. Including Ma, twelve of the thirteen workers who had attempted suicide had apparently jumped from high-rise buildings. The first few deaths didn't attract much attention locally, partly because of prevalent poor labor conditions in the world's second-largest economy. Chinese audiences have grown accustomed to news of deaths in mines, factories, or construction sites. The tragic circumstances of Ma Xiangqian's death were also obscured by China's most popular holiday, the Spring Festival, and the joy of family-gathering time soon washed away any sense of sadness or alarm over the death of an unknown boy. In fact, the news lingered in the local papers for all of ten days before dying down.

If that had been the only factory suicide in 2010, most Chinese people wouldn't have known what Foxconn was. A major producer of parts for the most famous technology companies in the world, including Apple, Dell, and Hewlett-Packard, each year Foxconn contributed more than 20 percent of Shenzhen's exports and generated more than 5 billion yuan ($680 million) of tax revenue for the city.[1] Before the deaths in the spring 2010, the Chinese media hailed Foxconn as the "favorite company" of this booming southern city.

However, eight suicides and two failed suicide attempts followed Ma's in four months. It was a disturbing trend, and both Chinese and foreign media sensed something unusual about the frequency of these events, but there was a lack of unique, exclusive stories. The public began to question whether Foxconn was in fact a sweatshop, and if so, what spurred those workers' suicides? On May 13, 2010, a front-page story in the *Southern Weekend*, an investigative newspaper based in the nearby city of Guangzhou, grabbed national media headlines for its bold and enterprising journalism. Liu Zhiyi, an intern reporter at the *Southern Weekend*, arguably the nation's best paper, had gone undercover at a Foxconn factory in Shenzhen for twenty-eight days, working as an assembly worker and collecting firsthand information from fellow workers. He filed the front-page story excerpted here, as well as a few other side stories. Through his reporting, Liu concluded that what he discovered at Foxconn was not just some "inside scoop," but the desperate fate that awaited an entire generation of Chinese workers. After describing many cruel facts about conditions at Foxconn, such as low wages and the common use of demeaning language, Liu realized that the equipment and operation standards at Foxconn were better than at its mainland Chinese counterparts. As a Taiwanese corporation, it seemed much more concerned about its international image and reputation than local Chinese factories, most of which were subject to neither Chinese labor laws nor the scrutiny of labor NGOs because of their lesser prominence and closer relationship with local governments.

In less than two weeks after the publication of Liu's report, when major Western media stepped up their coverage, the chairman of Hon Hai/Foxconn Technology Group, Terry Gou, flew from Taiwan to Shenzhen and held an unprecedented press conference at the factory, bowing ninety degrees three times and apologizing in front of cameras. Even though there was no evidence that the press conference was directly linked to Liu's report, the story undoubtedly played a critical role in drawing the attention of the Chinese public to Foxconn's conduct, as well as to broader labor topics such as China's Labor Law and minimum wage. The article also inspired foreign media to follow suit, which helped shape the global agenda to pressure Foxconn to make improvements. Within one year, Foxconn more than doubled the base pay for its workers and adopted other measures to increase care for its workers, who were largely in their twenties.

At the time of the undercover reporting, Liu was a twenty-two-year-old college student in Wuhan, a central Chinese city known for its sizzling temperatures. He returned to college after the internship and made his way to the Graduate School of Journalism at Tsinghua University, one the most prestigious universities in China. In an interview in 2013, Liu said that he had been offered a full-time job at the *Southern Weekend*. When asked about what he thought of all the notoriety he received, Liu said, "It's a good thing that people can recognize your reporting and writing, but it may not be so good that they recognize you, unless you are Oriana Fallaci. . . . I hope my reporting will overshadow myself as an individual."

I know two groups of young people. One group is college students just like me, living in an ivory tower and spending their time in libraries or in a landscape of mountains and lakes. The other group is those living with gigantic machines and containers at factory complex housing numerous advanced workshops. The second group always calls their supervisors *lao ban*, or boss, and they call each other, insultingly, even when they don't know each other well, *diao mao*, pubic hair, which is an increasingly popular reference among grassroots in China.

My undercover reporting was triggered by the investigation of six consecutive suicide attempts at the Foxconn factory.[2] All the other reporters at the *Southern Weekend* were too old to pass Foxconn's interviews [for workers], but as a twenty-two-year-old I was accepted immediately. The twenty-eight days I spent there left me in complete shock, not because I understood why they wanted to kill themselves, but because I began to understand how they lived.

The day they felt the richest was the tenth of each month: payday. People lined up in front of the ATMs and restaurants where special dishes were offered. Their salary consisted of the minimum pay of 900 RMB and a floating overtime compensation. Every worker has signed to a "Voluntary Overtime Work Agreement," so their overtime hours were not limited by the thirty-six-hour cap designated by law.

In their eyes, working beyond the legal overtime limit was not a bad thing at all. Many of them believed that factories requiring a lot of overtime hours were good factories, because otherwise the workers wouldn't be able to make money. For them—workers eager to make money even though overtime work was "pain with each breath"—days without money were suffocation.

At new electronics stores, salespeople proudly showcased the new iPhone to workers standing around, everyone's eyes glued to the phone's new functions. Foxconn produces the parts for iPhones, iPads, and many other popular digital products, but assembly workers would never imagine owning the final product. At those stores, the phone was sold at 2,198 RMB, advertised as a "shockingly low" price but slightly higher than the workers' salary for one month.

During the many conversations I had with them, I was often left speechless. I felt my life was excessively happy in comparison to theirs. Some workers even envied those injured on the job because they could get days off. They joked with each other while chatting about how toxic their work was. And, when they discussed the suicides, they looked unbelievably calm, even disdainful, and sometimes even joked about that too. It seemed to me that everyone saw himself as an outsider.

Those workers produced the most cutting-edge electronic products in the world but accumulated their own wealth at the slowest pace. The public account password for their office system was set up ending with 888 ("8" is pronounced like *fa*, "becoming rich" in Chinese). Workers approved of this number and firmly believed in the homonym. These people were rarely aware that their hands were the source of the 8 percent economic growth of their country, and when it came to them, even though they went to work and worked hard every day, they could hardly find their own "8." They bought lottery tickets and even gambled on horse races, all to no avail.

The most hardworking worker in my workshop, Wang Kezhu,[3] always complained about his meager salary, but when he tried to get some after-work training, he said he "couldn't understand a thing." He gave up. Wang admitted that with his limited knowledge, he could only handle the most basic and tough jobs. It was his destiny.

Sometimes, he said, he suffered from severe headaches, but other times he felt reborn. When he picked up goods, he always pulled the cart ahead rapidly, like flying, as if those twenty-four boxes of goods had no weight. Each and every day, he climbed up the packing boxes—as high as two to three meters—to check if the account was correct, and sometimes squeezed himself in the narrow gap between boxes to check the tags. When I asked him why he would dedicate his life to this job, he didn't answer. One day I saw him standing in front of a pillar, yelling "Help!" At that moment he may not have been conscious of what he had just screamed out, but I thought I heard his soul.

Factory buildings stand firmly in the complex, indistinguishable from each other except for English letters and numbers marked on the top. Machines, storage boxes, and uniformed assembly workers in this factory all lose their characteristics. Early one morning, I saw two faces poking out of the window of a workshop, completely unmoving, eyes staring at the flow of pedestrians on the street. I was too far away to see their expressions; I couldn't hear their voices either. Seen from my position, those faces were only two black dots. And to them, it was the same: people walking on the street resemble nothing more than black dots. Against the backdrop of giant white factory buildings, everyone is negligible, yet uniform.

When Shenzhen, formerly a small, sleepy coastal village, leapfrogged to become the most prosperous metropolis in China's Pearl River Delta, behind its ever-shifting skyline was a population of young people dwelling on confusion and anxiety. When *Time* magazine named Chinese workers as the "Person of the Year" in 2009, the editor commented that those workers brightened the future of humanity by "leading the world to economic recovery." In reality, their sweat, youth, and even life have been all but sucked out by the capital, which uses up its people to churn out computers, cell phones, and automobiles.

This Foxconn factory where more than four hundred thousand workers worked and lived was not quite the sweatshop most people would imagine. It provided food and dorms within a space the size of a mid-tier city. Assignments flew down in an orderly fashion to the assembly lines. Among all factories in China, Foxconn stood out because of its relatively high standards, superb equipment, and well-regulated labor treatment. Day after day, tens of thousands of people flooded to the factory just to find a position for themselves, seeking a dream that may never come true.

What I found during my undercover reporting days was not an inside scoop about a factory, but the fate of an entire generation of Chinese workers.

9

E. BENJAMIN SKINNER

THE FISHING INDUSTRY'S CRUELEST CATCH (2012)

from *Bloomberg Businessweek*

**INTRODUCED BY GLENN SIMMONS,
CHRISTINA STRINGER, AND HUGH WHITTAKER**

New Zealand

Most academics want to avoid controversy and, consciously or unconsciously, choose research topics that will not make their lives difficult. Occasionally, however, they stray into controversy, a minefield where they face a dilemma of beating a careful retreat versus going forward. Such was the case with our research on the fishing industry in New Zealand, which started in 2008 with a study of business practices of New Zealand fishing companies. This led us to look at the foreign-charter-vessel business model, which involved New Zealand companies chartering foreign trawlers to fish their quota in New Zealand's exclusive economic zone. The vessel owners sourced crew from countries such as Indonesia, the Philippines, and China. And this led to controversy. Benjamin Skinner's article "The Fishing Industry's Cruelest Catch" followed our research into the abuse of foreign crew working on board South Korean trawlers fishing in New Zealand's waters with largely Indonesian crew, as well as investigations by Michael Field, a *Sunday Star Times* journalist.[1]

Our interest—and concern—was piqued when, in August 2010, the *Oyang 70*, a South Korean trawler fishing in New Zealand's waters, sunk with the loss of six lives. The surviving crew members told of exploitative and abusive working conditions. In 2011, crew members from another two South Korean fishing trawlers walked off their vessels—first in Auckland and then

Excerpt from E. Benjamin Skinner, "The Fishing Industry's Cruelest Catch," *Bloomberg Businessweek*, February 23, 2012.

in Christchurch, citing widespread physical and sexual abuse, as well as the nonpayment of wages. Interviewed by New Zealand television and print media journalists, crew members detailed their oppressive and inhumane working conditions. This led to a public outcry. Motivated to discover the extent of the problem, we undertook extensive research into what was happening aboard these fishing vessels. Our research findings led to a public seminar and the publication of "Not in New Zealand's Waters Surely? Labor and Human Rights Abuses Aboard Foreign Fishing Vessels" as a working paper through the University of Auckland's New Zealand Asia Institute.[2]

The research gained international media exposure and Skinner, an award-winning journalist specializing in modern-day slavery and a fellow of the Schuster Institute for Investigative Journalism, realized its importance. For years the United Nations Office on Drugs and Crime and the International Labour Organization has been calling for research into what is described as a secretive industry. Building on our research, Skinner aptly answered that call in a remarkable piece of investigative journalism. Following his six-month, three-country investigation, Skinner vividly described the modern-day enslavement of foreign fishing crew in New Zealand waters. What he found was Indonesian men indentured into servitude aboard Korean trawlers fishing in New Zealand's waters.

Skinner took us on a journey through the eyes of one of the victims—Yusril. His narration followed Yusril and others from their initial desperation for work until their return home. They hoped that working in a first-world country would provide a better future for their families. Instead their rights were stripped and they were forced to live and work in floating sweatshops. They were deceived, coerced, verbally demeaned, physically and sexually abused, and forced to work up to thirty-hour continuous shifts under the threat of violence and financial penalty. Many were raped repeatedly. Skinner highlighted the plight of migrant fishing crews in a first world country that prides itself on decency, fair play, and human rights.

Skinner's article helped give the crew a very public voice. For over three decades, New Zealand authorities have largely ignored the plight of the crew, treating crew complaints as wage disputes and workplace bullying. Skinner's exposure invoked an immediate reaction from businesses and governments. Major international retailers including Walmart and Safeway moved swiftly to launch investigations into their supply chains. Some shipments were halted while audits were undertaken. In 2011, the New Zealand government announced a Ministerial Inquiry into the foreign charter sector. Skinner's article was timely as it was published nine days before the March 2012 release of the Inquiry's findings. Skinner's article most probably influenced the Inquiry's fifteen far-reaching recommendations to crack down on exploitative labor practices.

Two months later in a surprise move amidst ongoing controversy, the New Zealand government announced that all foreign fishing vessels chartered by New Zealand companies must fly the New Zealand flag by 2016. This means that these vessels will be fully captured by New Zealand vessel safety, employment, and fisheries management laws—necessary to protect the human rights of crews. The New Zealand charterers oppose the law, arguing that some foreign vessel owners will not reflag and hence will no longer fish on their behalf. The Fisheries (Foreign Charter Vessels and Other Matters) Bill was introduced into Parliament to give legislative effect to reflagging and other recommendations outlined by the Ministerial Inquiry. The bill unanimously passed its first reading in February 2013. Similarly the Korean government passed new laws to protect migrant fishing crew following an interagency investigation in Korea, Indonesia, and New Zealand.

Skinner's journalism helped galvanize two governments to take action. For us, his research was an important affirmation of our findings; Skinner brought the journalistic dimension to expose the horrendous practices. His research generated support for our own research, which had not been without incident. Attempts had been made by third parties to question our findings, intimidate us, and threaten our translators and informants. In fact, during our research, we were subjected to surveillance by private investigators and accosted by industry thugs after meeting crew members. Ultimately, Skinner has made and will continue to make the world a better place for many voiceless people.

On March 25, 2011, Yusril became a slave. That afternoon he went to the East Jakarta offices of Indah Megah Sari (IMS), an agency that hires crews to work on foreign fishing vessels. He was offered a job on the *Melilla 203*, a South Korea–flagged ship that trawls in the waters off New Zealand [. . .]

Yusril is 28, with brooding looks and a swagger that belies his slight frame. (Yusril asked that his real name not be used out of concern for his safety.) He was desperate for the promised monthly salary of $260, plus bonuses, for unloading fish. His wife was eight months pregnant, and he had put his name on a waiting list for the job nine months earlier. After taking a daylong bus ride to Jakarta, he had given the agent a $225 fee he borrowed from his brother-in-law. The agent rushed him through signing the contracts, at least one of which was in English, which Yusril does not read.

The terms of the first contract, the "real" one, would later haunt him. In it, IMS spelled out terms with no rights. In addition to the agent's commission, Yusril would surrender 30 percent of his salary, which IMS would hold unless the work was completed. He would be paid nothing for the first three months, and if the job were not finished to the fishing company's satisfaction, Yusril would be sent home and charged more than $1,000 for the airfare. The meaning of "satisfactory" was left vague. The contract said only that Yusril would have to work whatever hours the boat operators demanded.

The last line of the contract, in bold, warned that Yusril's family would owe nearly $3,500 if he were to run away from the ship. The amount was greater than his net worth, and he had earlier submitted title to his land as collateral for that bond. Additionally, he had provided IMS with the names and addresses of his family members. He was locked in.

What followed, according to Yusril and several shipmates who corroborated his story, was an eight-month ordeal aboard the *Melilla 203*, during which Indonesian fishermen were subjected to physical and sexual abuse by the ship's operators. Their overlords told them not to complain or fight back, or they would be sent home, where the agents would take their due. Yusril and 23 others walked off in protest when the trawler docked in Lyttelton, New Zealand. The men have seen little if any of what they say they are owed. Such coerced labor is modern-day slavery, as the United Nations defines the crime.

The experiences of the fishermen on the *Melilla 203* were not unique. In a six-month investigation, *Bloomberg Businessweek* found cases of debt bondage on the *Melilla 203* and at least nine other ships that have operated in New Zealand's waters. As recently as November 2011, fish from the *Melilla 203* and other suspect vessels were bought and processed by United Fisheries, New Zealand's eighth-largest seafood company, which has sold the same kinds of fish in the same period to distributors operating in the U.S. (The U.S. imports 86 percent of its seafood.) [...]

Yusril's story and that of nearly two dozen other survivors of abuse reveal how the $85 billion global fishing industry profits from the labor of people forced to work for little or no pay, often under the threat of violence. Although many seafood companies and retailers in the U.S. claim not to do business with suppliers who exploit their workers, the truth is far murkier.

Hours after Yusril arrived in Dunedin, New Zealand, the *Melilla 203* officers put him to work unloading squid on the 193-foot, 26-year-old trawler. The ship was in bad shape, and the quarters were musty, as the vessel had no functioning dryer for crew linens or work clothes. [...] The ship trawled for up to two months at a time, between 12 and 200 miles offshore. The boatswain would grab crew members' genitals as they worked or slept. When the captain of the ship drank, he molested some of the crew, kicking those who resisted. As nets hauled in the catch—squid, ling, hoki, hake, grouper, southern blue whiting, jack mackerel, and barracuda—the officers shouted orders from the bridge. They often compelled the Indonesians to work without proper safety equipment for up to 30 hours, swearing at them if they so much as asked for a coffee or bathroom break. Even when fishermen were not hauling catches, 16-hour workdays were standard.

New Zealand authorities had plenty of prior evidence of deplorable working conditions on foreign vessels like the *Melilla*. On Aug. 18, 2010, in calm seas, a Korean-flagged trawler called the *Oyang 70* sank, killing six. Survivors told the crew of the rescuing vessel their stories of being trafficked. A report co-authored by Christina Stringer and Glenn Simmons, two researchers at the University of Auckland Business School, and Daren Coulston, a mariner, uncovered numerous cases of abuse and coercion among the 2,000 fishermen on New Zealand's 27 foreign charter vessels (FCVs). The report prompted the government to launch a joint inquiry. After eight months aboard the *Melilla 203*, Yusril and 23 other crew members finally protested their treatment and pay to the captain. Their move came after a Department of Labour investigator, acting independently, visited the ship in November 2011, when it was docked in Lyttelton. The official gave Yusril a government fact sheet stipulating that crew members were entitled to certain minimum standards of treatment under New Zealand law, including pay of at least $12 per hour. When deductions, agency fees, and a manipulated exchange rate differential were subtracted, the fishermen were averaging around $1 per hour.

The captain dismissed the document and threatened to send them home to face retribution from the recruiting agency. Believing that the New Zealand government would protect them from such a fate, Yusril and all but four of the Indonesian crew walked off the boat and sought refuge in Lyttelton Union Parish Church. Aided by two local pro bono lawyers, they decried months of flagrant human rights abuses and demanded their unpaid wages under New Zealand's Admiralty Act.

[. . .] When I found him last December, Yusril was back in his in-laws' modest home, tucked well off a side road. He was out of work and brainstorming ways to scratch out a living by returning to his father's trade, farming. IMS, the recruiting agency in Jakarta, had blacklisted him and was refusing to return his birth certificate, his basic safety training credentials, and his family papers. It was also withholding pay, totaling around $1,100. In total, Yusril had been paid an average of 50¢ an hour on the *Melilla 203*. [. . .]

Two of the 24 men who walked off the *Melilla 203* returned to work on the ship rather than face deportation. The ship's representatives flew the remaining

22 resisters back to Indonesia. When they returned to Central Java, they say, they were coerced by IMS into signing documents waiving their claims to redress for human rights violations, in exchange for their originally stipulated payments of $500 to $1,000. Yusril was one of two who held out. On Jan. 21, when I last spoke to him, I asked why he had refused to sign the document.

"Dignity," said Yusril, pointing to his heart.

ANTICOLONIALISM

10

FIDEL A. REYES

BIRDS OF PREY (1908)

from *El Renacimiento*

INTRODUCED BY SHEILA CORONEL

Philippines

The United States emerged from the Spanish-American War a world power, inheriting from a defeated and humiliated Spain a clutch of islands in the Caribbean and the Pacific. Till then untutored in the ways of global empire, the world's newest colonial sovereign now had the task of pacifying and governing far-flung possessions—Puerto Rico, Guam, and the Philippines—that were oceans apart.

At the dawn of the twentieth century, as the United States fought a brutal pacification campaign in the Philippines and struggled to justify its expansion overseas to its own people, it did not seem that empire was writ in America's stars. In the words of William Howard Taft, the Philippine governor-general who would later became president, "We've blundered into colonization."

It took three years for U.S. troops to establish control over the Philippines. During that period, up to 22,000 Filipinos were believed to have been killed in battle. Many more—anywhere from 200,000 to 500,000—died from famine and disease.

Pacification involved torture (waterboarding had its origins in the U.S. campaign in the Philippines) and the forced evacuation of villages sympathetic to the *insurrectos*. But its next phase had U.S. soldiers setting up local schools, which had been long denied by Spanish colonialists. It also involved

Excerpt from Fidel A. Reyes, "Birds of Prey," *El Renacimiento* (1908). Translation from donfidelreyes.com/aves-de-rapina/.

transporting to the Philippines mirror images of American institutions—courts, a legislature, U.S.-style elections. And the press was allowed a measure of freedom.

In 1901, some prominent Filipinos founded *El Renacimiento* (Rebirth), a Spanish-language daily. Some of them had fought in the revolution against Spain and had opposed the U.S. occupation. The paper was the voice of the native intelligentsia and reflected their aspirations for self-rule, even as they had, by then, accepted the reality of American sovereignty.

The newspaper took on the Philippine Constabulary, or the PC, a paramilitary force that assisted the U.S. army's subjugation of the islands. In 1906, the paper reported that hundreds had been crammed into a filthy compound in a town near Manila on suspicion that they were helping *insurrectos*.

The PC sued for libel, and the paper pounded on the abuses as the trial was taking place. *El Renacimiento* won nine months later and celebrated by hosting a banquet for Manila's Filipino aristocracy. Emboldened, it aimed at bigger targets. In 1908, it published "Aves de Rapina" ("Birds of Prey"), an editorial that lashed out at Dean C. Worcester, then the secretary of the interior of the U.S. colonial government.

Worcester was not named, but there was no doubt in the readers' minds who the target of the editorial was. There was reference to a U.S. official's travels around the country, ostensibly for scientific exploration. Worcester, who had been trained as a zoologist, had gone around the Philippines on scientific excursions. His real interest, the editorial suggested, was not in science but in land speculation and gold mining.

Worcester sued and was in court every day. Locals jammed the courtroom, many of them just to catch a glimpse of him. This time, the paper lost, its editors were sentenced to prison, and the owners were ordered to pay a fine of 35,000 pesos. Faced with the hefty penalty, the owners sold the presses in a public auction. Worcester took possession of the paper's name, and in 1910, *El Renacimiento* published its last issue.

In the meantime, the editor, Teodoro M. Kalaw, who was celebrated for his defense of free speech, was elected to the Philippine Assembly. Then, in 1913, a new Democratic president, Woodrow Wilson, took office in the United States. A new Philippine governor-general was named, and he pardoned all the accused before they could be jailed.

"Aves de Rapina" showed the assertiveness of the Filipino elite and their tug-of-war with U.S. power. But it also reflected their ambivalence toward their new colonial masters: unlike the peasant remnants of the revolution who staged guerrilla attacks or millenarian uprisings, the native elite fought their battles in the arenas designated by the American sovereigns.

The case bared the contradictions of U.S. colonial rule. In the country-side, American troops were burning villages and waterboarding rebels. But in the capital, U.S. colonialists thought themselves in charge of the Filipinos' democratic tutelage and so allowed the most privileged among them a taste of freedom.

On the surface of this globe, some people are born to eat and devour, others to be eaten and devoured.

Now and then, the latter bestir themselves endeavoring to rebel against an order of things which makes prey to, and food for, the insatiable voracity of the former. Sometimes they are fortunate in successfully putting to flight the eaters and devourers; but in the majority of cases, the latter only gain a new name of plumage.

This situation is the same in all phases of creation: the relationship dictated between the one and the other is that dictated by too keen an appetite, the satisfaction of which must always be at another fellow creature's expense.

Among men, it is easy to observe the development of this daily phenomenon. Likewise, for some psychological reason, nations who believe themselves powerful take the fiercest and most harmful creatures to be their symbol. Such as the lion, or the eagle, or the serpent. Some have done this on a secret impulse of affinity; others, because it has served them as some sort of stimulant to an inflated vanity, the wish to make themselves appear as that which they are not nor ever will be.

The eagle, symbolizing liberty and strength, has found the most admirers. And men, collectively and individually, have even desired to copy and imitate this most rapacious of birds in order to succeed in the plundering of their fellow men.

But there is a man who, besides being like the eagle, also has the characteristics of a vulture, the owl and the vampire.

He ascends the mountains of Benguet ostensibly to classify and measure Igorot skulls, to study and to civilize the Igorot; but, at the same time, he also espies during his flight, with the keen eye of the bird of prey, where large deposits of gold are located, which is the real prey concealed in the lonely mountains, in order to appropriate them for himself afterwards, thanks to the legal facilities he can make and unmake at will, always, however redounding in his own benefit.

He authorizes, despite laws and ordinances to the contrary, the illegal slaughter of diseased cattle as to make a profit from its infected and putrid meat, which, in his official capacity, he himself should have condemned.

He presents himself on all occasions with the wrinkled brow of a scientist who has spent his life deep in the mysteries of the laboratory of science; when

in truth his only scientific work has been the dissection of insects and the impor-
tation of fish eggs, as though fish in his country have so little nourishment and
savouriness that they deserve replacement by species from other climes.

He gives laudable impetus to the search for rich lodes in Mindanao, in Min-
doro, and in other virgin regions of the archipelago, a search undertaken with the
people's money and with the excuse of it being for the public good when in strict
truth, his purpose is to obtain data and discover the keys to the national wealth
for his essentially personal benefit, as proved by the acquisition of immense
properties registered under the names of others.

He promotes, through secret agents and partners, the sale to the city of
worthless lands at fabulous prices, which the city fathers dare not refuse for their
own good for fear of displeasing him.

He sponsors concessions for hotels on filled-in lands with the prospect of
enormous profits at the expense of the people.

Such are the characteristics of this man who is also an eagle, who surprises
first and then later devours, a vulture who gorges himself on dead and putrid
meats, an owl who affects a petulant omniscience, a vampire who silently sucks
his victim bloodless.

Birds of prey always triumph; their flights and aim are never thwarted. For who
can dare stop them?

There are some who share in the booty and the plunder, but the rest are
merely too weak to raise a voice in protest. Some die in the disheartening destruction of their own energies and interests. Yet at the end, there shall appear, with terrifying clearness, that immortal warning of old: *Mene Mene Tekel
Upharsin!*

11

ALBERT LONDRES

THE COURT OF MIRACLES (1924)

from *Au Bagne*

INTRODUCED BY MARK LEE HUNTER

French Guiana

A colony serves, among other things, as a warehouse for the people whom one doesn't want at home, from wastrel sons to paupers, prostitutes, and criminals. Folks like these are at best an embarrassment in the mother country—to their families, as well as to good citizens who are otherwise proud of their society. The treatment reserved for them creates further embarrassment, especially for authorities, who are inevitably accused of cruelty by the same populace that demands justice for miscreants. How convenient, then, to export one's riffraff to a place where nature, with a minimum of human assistance, will discreetly dispose of them. Their fate was Albert Londres's subject in *Au Bagne* ("At the Penal Colony"), excerpted here.

Londres's 1924 exposé about Devil's Island sparked an official investigation, fed a reform movement, and spawned an entire genre of journalism about the brutality of the penal colonies.[1] Dumping grounds for political detainees as well as criminals, they were an essential element of the nation's colonial project overall. They were as reviled then as Guantánamo Bay is today.

When Londres (b. 1884) began his career as a journalist in 1906, France, after losing Quebec, Louisiana, and Mexico, still held colonial territories in West and North Africa and Southeast Asia, plus some major outposts in the South Pacific, the Caribbean, and South America. This global empire was

Excerpt from Albert Londres, "The Court of Miracles," *Au Bagne* (1924). Translated by Vanessa Pope.

not Londres's first interest. When he began to establish his reputation as a foreign correspondent—a *grand reporter*, as the French put it—he traveled first to the Balkans, Greece, Italy, and the nascent Soviet Union, following the news and wreckage of the First World War. In a second career phase, he served up exotica from China and Japan, in a time when newspapers were their publics' main and cheap window on the world. Only in the last decade of his life, beginning in 1923, did he turn his attention to the colonies.

Beginning with *Au Bagne* (pronounced "ban-ya"), Londres repeatedly chronicled how France's colonies had become instruments of torture—not only for convicts in the hideously misnamed Salvation Islands off the coast of Guiana, but for African conscript labor. He took sides, especially for the victims. He wrote as if he were highly educated, but he mainly taught himself; he was the son of a provincial working-class widow. Before he became a foreign correspondent, he published four books of poetry. One of his models appears to have been Dante Alighieri, whose *Divine Comedy* might well have provided Londres with the structure for *Au Bagne*.

In the opening chapter, we ride with him across water that could be the River Styx, pulled by silent oarsmen. In successive vignettes we descend deeper and deeper into a world where, like Dante's *Inferno*, every space is occupied by someone with an astonishing and dreadful tale to tell. But unlike Dante, the shocks of this narrative are not rooted in the collective or individual imagination. They come from a reality that was unimaginable until Londres shoved it in France's face. He couldn't imagine it, either. The place continually surprises his expectations in ways large and small, and thus humbles him. Walking around what passes for a hospital in this Hell, he notes that the inmates call him Mr. Inspector, and shares the thought that hits him like a slap in the face: "In these camps, nobody ever, ever comes to visit." The reporter's job, he said, is not "to precede parades with one hand in a basket of rose petals," it is "to stick the pen in the wound." It is not to display one's own wounds, either. When Londres evokes an emotion, he depersonalizes it: not "It hurts me," but "It rips you up." Thus he speaks not for himself, but for his reader.

His chief rhetorical device is irony—a very French way of expressing, in a single moment, disgust, disdain, and amazement: "This is just a very little bit too much." It goes well with his subject. Everyone in the Bagne is ironic, insane—"I'm not crying, this is joy!"—or both, like the doctor whose absurd, torturous mission is to watch men die. For the *bagnards* (pronounced "ban-yar," the convicts) irony, which Isak Dinesen identified as the property of aristocrats, provides them with some small if not superior distance from their condition. For Londres, it becomes an instrument of revolt, a way to see through the horror by surmounting it. Ultimately, he abandons the device and speaks plainly, delivering verdicts that can't be appealed: "This is a factory of suffering that works without plan or pattern. You search in vain for the template that shapes the convict. It smashes him, period."

One thinks of Kafka's "In the Penal Colony," published in 1914, which likewise contains a machine that tears people apart in order to rehabilitate them. Maybe Londres read that story, maybe not. But he certainly saw a place where it was not fiction. Like Kafka, he had to find a way to persuade his audience to suspend disbelief that such things can occur. Unlike Kafka, he had to sustain that effect until reform could occur.

For a modern investigative reporter, Londres seems at once primitive and fundamental. He doesn't offer statistics. Even more striking to a contemporary reader, he doesn't name names. In our era this would be considered laziness, or a lack of professional courage: if you have the proof, you use it. But something else is going on here, and it's one of the sources of Londres's power.

He isn't looking for someone to blame. Unlike much contemporary investigative reporting work, in which the "results" that win prizes often include putting people in jail, his target isn't a corrupt individual. Certainly, in another passage he shows us a guard who extorts money from a convict at the end of a gun, and other guards who take a cut on the prisoners' various traffics, their *camelote*. (Londres has a very good ear for the words that define a world.)

But they are merely illustrations of a larger point: the system he's describing would corrupt anyone whom it did not destroy. This, too, may be something he learned from Dante. The individuals trapped inside the *Inferno* embody facets of a wider logic, of divine punishment. Similarly, the characters—not "sources"—whom Londres encounters in the *bagne* embody the inhuman madness of a system that destroys men because it doesn't know what else to do with them: "He's a maniac, a drunk, he stole . . . he always gave these things back a few days later. But he did it more than six times and they deported him."

What Londres *is* looking for is how to end this horror. This is another place where he differs from the investigative reporters of my generation, and where I'm not ashamed to say I learned from him. As a reporter I was taught and expected not to take sides—quite like Woodward and Bernstein, who even at the end of *All the President's Men* did not dare to say flat out that Richard M. Nixon had to go. Londres passes judgment. He calls his last report on the *bagne* "An Open Letter to the Minister of Colonies," and he says: "I'm done. The government has to start." He then sets out four urgent and doable reforms. He justifies them in France's self-interest: the colony will never be profitable like this, France's reputation suffers. He does not demand an end to colonization. He is no revolutionary. But he wants the world to change, and he tells you how.

He got his reforms—not all before he died in 1932—but some of them, and the others followed. Devil's Island, opened in 1852, closed in 1946.[2] Some pointless suffering disappeared. Perhaps, someday, someone will do the same for Guantanamo, another penal colony that throws innocents in with the wicked, and smashes them all. Londres said having such a place was a terrible mistake. He was right then, and he's still right.

This is just a very little bit too much.

"This" is two camps that are both called The New Camp. One is for deportation, the other for transportation. Four hundred and fifty dogs in the former, 450 in the latter. Truth be told, they are not dogs, but men! But these men have been reduced to nothing more than mangy, snivelling, pared-down, anxious, abandoned beasts.

When, shocked by this spectacle, stiff as a board, you've spent an hour in these two shameful zoos, you feel surprised that these creatures don't walk on all fours.

Another surprise is that, when questioned, these men speak rather than bark. The one-armed, one-legged, hernial, skeletal, blind, those riddled with tuberculosis, the paralyzed, all brought together in these two infernal witch's cauldrons.

The penal colony is a dumping ground. These two camps are the dumping ground of the penal colony.

"We're all gonna *die*, man! And you too, if you stay!"

This one is an Arab. I can't really say that he's coughing his lungs up—it's already happened. [. . .]

There isn't a hospital, then? There is. There's a big one at Saint-Laurent-du-Maroni. But you don't become game for the hospital at the penal colony just like that! It's not enough to be condemned to step through the delightful doorway of this luxurious establishment. You have to have a limb that requires amputation, or, just as good, to be able to prove that you'll die within the next eight days.

And what about the doctors?

The doctors are disgusted. The most violent critics of the penitentiary administration can be found among them.

The doctor sees a man. The administration sees a convict. Trapped between these two perspectives, the inmate sees only death.

A thousand inmates die a year. These nine hundred will die.

"But it's slow, sir," says one, born in Bourges, "it's slow . . . ! Slow . . . !"

At the camp for the deportees, the doctor comes by every Thursday; at the transportation camp, it's every ten days.

"We're sick to our stomachs when we go there," they say, "but what can we do? We have no say, no medication. Our medical visits? A sinister farce! With heavy hearts we feel as if we're mocking these poor creatures." [. . .]

Nothing. There is nothing to give to these nine hundred patients, plagued with all sorts of illnesses.

"All I can do," says the doctor, "and not always, is to bring in a few skeletons that are still twitching to kick the bucket in a bed."

The central pharmacy in Saint-Laurent only just received—*in July 1923*—the medicines that were ordered *in 1921*. They hoard cotton like gold, and here iodine solution is a precious liquid. [. . .]

They hung on to my canvas jacket. Their words were always the same: "Get us out of this horrific hellhole, however you can."

"Look," the doctor said to me, "at the transportation camp there's one inmate who promises to sink six inches of steel in my stomach every time I'm there. He's right! He's sick. He's in pain. I'm a doctor, I should treat him and I don't!"

These camps are well turned out: twin cells, triangular roofs covered with banana leaves. It makes for a pretty picture. As long as you don't get any closer.

The dying groan on hard planks. [. . .]

One speaks to me. But there's too much coughing, I can't hear him.

"What did you say?"

"It's hard, Mr. Inspector!"

Of course, what else could they think? In these camps nobody ever, ever comes to visit. It goes without saying, for these cloistered men, that I am Mr. Inspector, Mr. Director, Mr. Delegate. Of what, they don't know, but there must be a very important reason for me to be here. One tells me: "You're the good Cyrenean, helping us carry the cross!" and the other: "Give me your hand." It tears you up.

And Jeannin, the photographer Jeannin, has just recruited some troops to "set the scene."

"No! No, Jeannin!"

But they come with their crutches. They collaborate with good grace. In front of the camera—they remember those—you must smile. *They smile.* [. . .]

But someone comes toward me at a run, he's afraid he won't reach me in time. He's just a fellow man, a poor guy racked with sadness and regret. I remember him clearly. Oh! He didn't kill anyone. He's a maniac, a drunk, he stole a parcel from a station, a chicken from the market; once, he took a package containing old newspapers, two candles, and a knife from the bench of a café. And he always gave these things back a few days later. But he did it more than six times and they deported him.

He cries. Emotion makes him stutter. He wants to get on his knees in front of me. [. . .] He says: "Look! Look!"

He says: "I'm not crying, this is joy!"

He begs me: "Tell them everything! Everything! So things might change a little . . ." [. . .]

12

NGUYỄN AN NINH

IS A REVOLUTION POSSIBLE? (1924)

from *La Cloche Fêlée*

INTRODUCED BY PHILIPPE PEYCAM

Vietnam

This article was written by the twenty-three-year-old Saigon-based intellectual and activist Nguyễn An Ninh (1900–1943). Ninh belongs to the generation of French-educated urban middle class Vietnamese who grew up in the cosmopolitan city of colonial Saigon and was, from an early age, exposed to French culture and politics as well as to the oppression of foreign rule in his country.

The largest urban center and economic hub of French Indochina, Saigon, in the heart of the southern part of Vietnam, then called Cochinchina, had a population of three hundred thousand. In many ways, the port-city and the Mekong Delta region within which it lay represented a unique socioeconomic environment for the development of a new medium of public expression brought in by the colonizers: print journalism. After nearly fifty years of French rule, a growing number of Vietnamese had become used to reading and buying newspapers published in the romanized transcription of Vietnamese, *quốc ngữ*, or in French. In the first two decades of the twentieth century, the application of metropolitan republican laws of press freedom in the Colony of Cochinchina, though restricted to French language and subjected to numerous procedural and extralegal restrictions by the colonial administration, enabled the development of an original political space that the Vietnamese called *làng báo chí*, or "newspapers' village," of which

Excerpt from Nguyễn Tinh (pen name of Nguyễn An Ninh), "Is a Revolution Possible?," *La Cloche Fêlée*, May 19, 1924. Translated by Vanessa Pope.

Nguyễn An Ninh was one of the most brilliant representatives. Saigon's Vietnamese political press thereafter became the main force of public opposition to French rule. Newspapers aimed at the Vietnamese were initially encouraged by the colonial government that, particularly during World War I, hoped it could rely on elements of the emerging middle class. Such an act of political weakness on the part of the French administration echoes that of ancien régime Western European monarchies, which Habermas identified as the origin of an autonomous public sphere that preceded the French revolution.[1]

Of all the Vietnamese intellectuals who confronted French colonial occupation, Nguyễn An Ninh is perhaps one of the most complex and compelling figures. Born in 1900, he was the son of an author of Chinese literature and a political activist, Nguyễn An Khương. While conversant in Chinese characters thanks to his father, Ninh completed his Franco-Vietnamese secondary studies at the prestigious Collège Chasseloup-Laubat. Dissatisfied with the education he received at the so-called Hanoi "university," he left for France in 1920, where he studied at the Paris Faculty of Law and obtained his *licence*. While in Europe, Ninh, who was economically independent, enjoyed the intellectual life of the French capital. He participated in some intellectual groups including anarchist and anticolonial circles. An avid reader, he showed great curiosity about Western culture. He traveled to Germany, Italy, Switzerland, and the Netherlands.

La Cloche Fêlée (Broken Bell) was launched in December 10, 1923, upon Ninh's return from a second trip to France. Although other newspapers had circulated in French and in Vietnamese before, none captured the popular imagination as did Ninh's *La Cloche Fêlée*. In just a few issues, the newspaper revolutionized the way political journalism was done in Vietnam. Its circulation was remarkable for a publication that was written in French and overtly oppositional. Encouraged by the public reception, *La Cloche Fêlée* became a weekly. It increased its print run from one thousand copies to fifteen hundred and later to two thousand, accounting for just under 10 percent of the total turnover of the whole Saigon press. Each of the nineteen issues that appeared until July 14, 1924, represented a step in Ninh's effort to mobilize—and challenge—his reader compatriots into action.

As a journalist, Nguyễn An Ninh's impact upon his readers was due to his precocious political intelligence and his engrossing style as an articulate writer endowed with a wide range of intellectual references. As an activist it was his numerous roles, of which leading a newspaper was one, that made him popular both among the educated urbanites but also among the rural populations whom he reached by resorting to traditional grassroots modes of communication and mobilization.

Ninh targeted primarily the educated youth whose sense of social and political responsibility against what he described as the likelihood of the "death of the [Vietnamese] race" he sought to raise. He asserted that they, as individual social agents, as citizens, were morally responsible for their fate. This gave him the right to criticize them for their passivity whilst sharing his own personal doubts over his actions.

Ninh's short life was entirely devoted to the liberation of his country, for which he died prematurely in a French colonial jail. A free-minded individual, strongly influenced by the anarchist traditions of his home, southern Vietnam, and France, his adopted cultural realm, he never fit into a simple category of militant or intellectual tradition. Although a communist sympathizer, he never joined the party. His spiritual inclination led him to incorporate influences from India and other thinkers of his period: Rabindranath Tagore, Mohandas Gandhi, Leo Tolstoy, Jean Jaurès, or Romain Rolland, among others. As he grew older, in a fast-transforming social and political scene, affected by numerous long stays in prison, Ninh's message became less iconoclastic. He realized that an organized mass–based movement was necessary in order to break the "modern form of oppression" represented by colonialism.[2] He even expressed doubts as to whether contradictory debate and public inquiry alone could achieve freedom. Yet until the end, he remained a brilliant polemicist whose anticonformism and cosmopolitanism would have made it difficult for him to fit into the tight mold of Vietnamese communism as it was shaped by Ho Chi Minh and his followers had he lived after 1945 and the outbreak of the Vietnamese revolution.[3]

The article chosen here was written after Ninh's return from a trip to the Mekong Delta to collect unpaid subscriptions to the newspaper. The paper ceased to appear for a month. Ninh's financial situation was becoming dire. He was subjected to numerous forms of harassment by the *Sûreté*, the colonial police, from intercepted mail to forced changes of printing houses, while his readers suffered from intimidation.[4] It is in this context that Ninh set out to summarize many of the points he had previously raised in his editorials. The title, with its reference to "Revolution," was a provocative stand against the colonial state and an attempt to bolster the determination of his readers. Beyond the prose, there are a few fundamental points highlighting Ninh's political concepts at a time when the young activist was reviewing his own political role.

The article "Is a Revolution Possible?" is a good example of Nguyễn An

Ninh's political generosity and courage. His voice resonates beyond the article's original period and the world of Vietnamese nationalism.

A few days ago on a Chinese sloop that goes between Trà Vinh and Mỹ Tho,[5] I overheard a group of Annamites[6] chatting about how Japan was transformed through its contact with Europe, comparing Annam to Japan, attacking the selfishness of their rich fellow countrymen, demonstrating what Annamites could achieve if each accepted a little sacrifice, and insisting on a method of resistance similar to India's Non-Cooperation.

[. . .] Their chatter differed very little from the nattering of old women passing the time and their dreams smacked of powerlessness. In Cần Tho',[7] three days prior to the meeting of this group of Annamites with revolutionary ideas (revolutionary is the official term to denote ideas of this type), I heard a chauffeur respond "Keep your insults for the French" to the rudeness and vulgarity of one of his countrymen, who belonged to the class of naturalized [Vietnamese] French citizens whose biggest pleasure is to impose their *European superiority* on their fellows, a privilege which extends to brutish policemen and a viceroy-like administrator.

A little before these two encounters, a very famous Annamite in this country told me of a *tiên* consultation (where spirits are attracted with fasting and purity and respond through a brush held by two children) requested by himself and a group of friends. Their *tiên* confirmed that within three of four years an important social event will take place that Annamites could use to make their hopes reality.[8]

These three expressions of Annamite patriotism encountered within a small time frame and in very different circles of the native society in Cochinchina prove that, despite the love of peace touted by officials, despite the relative calm reigning in Cochinchina over the last few years while plots in favor of independence still take place in the North, a feeling of nationalism stirs in the country.[9] [. . .]

Annamite patriotism is not xenophobia. The awareness of a superiority based exclusively on the rights of conquerors, the obstacles to intellectual development of the defeated race, the brutal censorship that suffocates the people, the ignorance that offends a civilization not founded on violence, the social inequalities based on ridiculous and silly premises, the reign of incompetents, of sharks, of piano and candelabra thieves, the waste of public funds on maintaining the princely families that succeed one another on the thrones of Indochina—is that not enough to revolt a vanquished people?[10]

Either way, Annamite patriotism is an undeniable fact. The hope of seeing the country one day liberated and caring for its own people stirs within every

Annamite who has not been corrupted by gold or the symbolic titles of the current masters of Indochina. [. . .]

Yes, occasionally a popular movement, disorganized, exasperated, is easily crushed by a mere hundred guns, one or two machine guns. A month later the silence has erased the memory of the powerless people's anger.[11]

But what does all this lead to? To exhaustion, to the waste of the race's energy.[12] [. . .] Is the current lull in Cochinchina not a sign of exhaustion?

I've said it many times before: an order must be opposed by an order, a force by a force. If India was able to rattle British powers, it is because India pitted the moral force of unarmed Hindu masses against the brutal force of the British and their cannons; it is because India opposed the powerful organization of the British Empire with the organization of Non-Cooperation.[13] [. . .]

India has given us a model of the only revolution possible in Asia under the yoke of European colonizers. Are the Annamite people capable of this kind of revolution? Is there an elite that can, despite *all* obstacles, prepare the people for this revolution? The answer to this question, affirmative or negative, is the same as the answer to this question:

Is revolution possible in Indochina?

However, whether revolution is possible or not, one thing is certainly possible: to fight the crudeness and the violence rooted in colonial habits and that contribute significantly to render the atmosphere here suffocating, that spark and activate hate for the victors in the vanquished.

For example, Annamites could form a league with no political goal, but whose members' strength would be put to the service of those weaker, threatened or hit by a colonial brute [. . .] Prison? We'll bear it because, I can assure you, a few healthy lessons of this kind will be enough to calm the *violence* of enraged colonisers, violence that Mr. Léon Werth rightly calls *cowardice* because it stops, he says, in Marseille.[14] [. . .]

Annamites could pinpoint the injustices and attacks that they have been victims of, the various ways colonizers have exploited the colonies, for example how a governor rigs a colonial election in Bạc Liêu.[15] The facts, specified and compiled, will be revealed to the public.

Let us forget the prejudice that it is naïve for the conquered to call for justice from the conquerors, or for compensation and punishment for the injustices and scurrility of the conquerors themselves.

Let us trust the French law. La Cloche Fêlée that the barbarous colonials fight against by any means possible owes its existence to a French law. Let us trust France, trust in others, as Gandhi trusted Britain until the day when, confronted by the mounting lies and treachery of the British Empire, he preached revolt.

13

A PRIME EXAMPLE OF BRITISH CIVILIZATION (1943)

from *Biplabi*

INTRODUCED BY MADHUSREE MUKERJEE

India

On August 8, 1942, the Indian National Congress, the predominant political party in India, adopted a "Quit India" resolution demanding independence from British colonial rule. If granted independence, the Congress asserted, India would support the Allied cause in World War II; if not, the party sanctioned a nonviolent struggle "on the widest possible scale" against the colonial regime. Early the next morning, Mahatma Gandhi and all the Congress leaders were swept off to jail, and the country erupted in protest. Over the next years, more than ninety thousand protesters would be arrested and ten thousand killed by British Indian forces.

In a corner of Midnapore, a coastal district in Bengal in eastern India, a small group of Congress leaders managed to establish a secret, independent administration called the Tamluk National Government. The government, whose functionaries received only food as payment, collected funds from willing villagers and recalcitrant landlords, ran courts to settle civil disputes, had an intelligence service, and published a Bengali newsletter, *Biplabi*. Although the senior leaders of this organization were all Gandhians, following the mass rapes described in this extract they gave up on nonviolence; the Tamluk government also acquired a military of sorts, which eliminated informers and other enemies.

Colonial authorities had shut down Gandhi's *Harijan* newsletter and

Excerpt from "A Prime Example of British Civilization," *Biplabi*, January 25, 1943. Translated by Madhusree Mukerjee.

forbidden the publication of any news about the Quit India movement or its repression. *Biplabi*'s main courier, Krishna Chaitanya Mahapatro, recalled that when he handed copies of the newsletter to editors of Bengali newspapers in Calcutta, the commercial and administrative capital of Bengal, he could see "agonized helplessness printed on their faces" from learning so much more than they could publish. As historian Paul Greenough observes, "*Biplabi* became something of a 'newspaper of record' in the matter of official oppression." The leaflet disseminated news, such as of police atrocities and deaths from the famine that broke out in early 1943, instructed villagers on forthcoming actions, and strove to bolster their revolutionary spirit. Although the prose is often flaming—the journal's title means "rebel"—my interviews with villagers who remembered the same events turned up remarkably few inaccuracies or exaggerations.

Couriers, mainly Mahapatro, brought global news from the city, while runners carried in reports from around Tamluk subdivisions sent by Congress sympathizers. (Because their work was so laborious, during the famine the runners were allowed all the rice they could eat—a luxury not permitted anyone else.) Ajoy Kumar Mukhopadhyay, one of the two heads of the Tamluk government, edited the news and also supplied the editorials, including this one. Radhakrishna Bari, a precocious teenager with beautiful handwriting, wrote the text onto silk-screen paper, also smuggled from Calcutta, and printed 500 copies using an old Italian Roneo duplicator.

Since there were only two presses in Tamluk, both under police surveillance, Bari had to print at night on the attic floor of a mud house, by the light of a kerosene lamp. (The region had no electricity and virtually no brick houses.) If a stencil tore in the course of printing, he would hurriedly inscribe a fresh one. Special issues demanded one thousand copies and two stencils. In October 1942, a massive cyclone killed some thirty thousand people in coastal Bengal and washed away thousands of homes, including that of Bari's family. To his relief, though, the house sheltering the duplicator survived.

After Mukhopadhyay's arrest in September 1943, Bari became the editor and often also wrote the editorials. The other head of state, Satish Samanta, was already in prison, so Sushil Dhara, a lapsed Gandhian who as the secret government's military chief assassinated many informers, stepped into Mukhopadhyay's shoes as the de facto head. Dhara was a gifted poet and writer and also penned editorials.

On the back of each copy of *Biplabi*, Bari would write, "Read and pass on to others." The morning after printing, volunteers would separate the copies into bundles and send some to merchants from Midnapore who supplied vegetables to Calcutta. Secreted between betel leaves, the bundles would find their way to the city. Mahapatro, who posed as a college student engaged in cyclone and famine relief, would hide the leaflets until he could distribute them personally to editors, political leaders, and other individuals.

At one point Mahapatro realized that either the Intelligence Bureau or the police were watching a building, in one apartment of which he had secreted copies of *Biplabi*. Fearing a search, he staged a move. He recruited a male friend and two streetwalkers and asked them to pose as family, hid the copies in a bedroll, placed it on a cart, and piled pots, pans, brooms, and pillows on top. Posing as a householder, his wife, sister, and brother, they talked and cursed loudly about water supply and other domestic matters until they were well past the guards. The sex workers then asked what it had all been about. "When we explained who we were, they were in tears, so thrilled were they at having been able to help," recalled Mahapatro. "They wouldn't take any money."

On other occasions, sex workers in Midnapore hid bundles of *Biplabi* under the bed or fugitives on them, as feigned customers. Local support for the insurgency was overwhelming. Rebels could always find shelter in the homes of villagers, and police informers were often double agents who warned them when the authorities were about to stage a raid. In frustration, the police, aided by soldiers on "internal security" duty (Muslims from northwest India were posted in predominantly Hindu Midnapore, divide-and-rule being the principle by which armed forces were assigned to different parts of the colony), burned down homes and stores of rice, beat villagers, and perpetrated many rapes, including those this item describes. Six decades later, my interviews confirmed the allegation. On January 9, 1943, police and soldiers in uniform surrounded three villages in turn; they took away the men at gunpoint and raped all the women they could find: forty-six, according to testimonies subsequently collected by Congress workers.

In August 1944, after Gandhi was released from prison, he ordered all the insurgents around the country to surrender, and Dhara complied. The Tamluk government wound down and *Biplabi* stopped publication. That December Gandhi traveled to Midnapore to investigate allegations that some of his most ardent followers had taken to violence; informed about the mass rapes, he sent female aides to interview the survivors. On the night before he was to leave, Bari and others asked how they were supposed to defend women from assault without using violence, and Gandhi confessed that he did not know how he himself would have reacted in such circumstances.

On January 9, 1943, the superintendent of Geokhali police station, Houseburning Nalini Raha (who earned this title from villagers after burning down many homes) surrounded the villages of Masuria, Chandipur, and Dihi Masuria with six hundred soldiers. *Biplabi* has already presented an account of the beatings, looting, and other atrocities committed on that day. Below we describe the circumstances in which these beasts in human form also committed mass rape in Masuria and Chandipur. We do not yet have full knowledge of the events in Dihi Masuria.

Almost two months ago, when a minister of Bengal described to the governor of Bengal and the inspector general of police the atrocities being perpetrated in Midnapore, in particular the arson and rapes, the two white chiefs completely denied their occurrence. Determined to prove his case, the minister demanded an inquiry—upon which they loudly announced that the police chief would himself investigate and, should even one of the alleged incidents prove to be true, would punish the culprits. But not only did they fail to investigate, they also did not allow the minister or anyone else to make enquiries. Why should they? It is on the orders, and with the encouragement, of these two civilized Englishmen (admittedly backed up by the viceroy and the secretary of state for India) that the Punjabi civilian and Muslim flag-bearer Khan (the district magistrate of Midnapore) and the son of Sheikh (the sub-divisional officer of Tamluk) have been engaging their subordinates in these atrocities. [. . .]

We need not be ashamed that the Khan-Sheikh-Raha triad and their camp followers are Indians. In this enormous India there is no dearth of dangerous forests; in order to accomplish his ends the British lion has searched out these beasts from the jungle. There is no reason to think of them as human Indians.

Still, we die of shame when we consider the conduct of our village men. How indeed do we consider as human those men who, when enemy soldiers attack, abandon their mothers and sisters and try to save themselves . . . ? If there was no other means to protect the women, then our men could at least have injured the lust-crazed soldiers while they were engaged in rape. Indeed, the Mahatma, the votary of nonviolence, has himself directed as such. The Congress directives forbid killing, and we have always obeyed this and asked others to do so as well. But in such cases even the killing of such beasts is scarcely blameworthy. [. . .] As long as he has life, protecting a woman's chastity is the duty of a man. Nonviolence is not cowardice. True nonviolence requires courage, heroism, and self-sacrifice.

We have repeatedly instructed village women that if their cowardly husbands and sons abandon them to the enemy, they have to protect their own honor. [. . .] The moment they hear of the impending arrival of the enemy, the women must pick up knives, shovels, and whatever other weapons they can find, gather in a room, and hit out at any miscreants who seek to attack. Should one or two of the beasts die as a result that is of no consequence. [. . .]

People of Midnapore! If you don't defend the honor of your mothers and sisters, who will? In one blow you have paralyzed this regime, with another you will vanquish it. Only then will you find peace.

CORRUPTION

14

LIU BINYAN

FROM *PEOPLE OR MONSTERS?* (1979)

INTRODUCED BY PERRY LINK

China

Fall 1979 was an exhilarating time for writers in mainland China. They were emerging from the straitjacket of the Mao Zedong years, and excitement was in the air. They felt a special energy and—if not quite freedom—at least a sense that there was suddenly much more space to explore. A year earlier Deng Xiaoping, the new man at the political top, had urged them to "look forward" and to "liberate thought."

Yet shadows remained. Deng's current counsel to "harbor no fears" could almost seem a gentle reminder that a reasonable person might want to harbor some. As if to underscore the point, in mid-October 1979, the Deng regime sentenced Wei Jingsheng, an electrician who a few months earlier had "liberated his thought" sufficiently to issue a public call for democracy, to fifteen years in prison.

Liu Binyan (1925–2005) was at one time China's most famous journalist. Like many writers, though, his fortunes rose and fell with political campaigns ordered by the country's rulers. He was expelled from the Communist Party and sent to the Chinese countryside in the 1957 Anti-Rightist Movement, "rehabilitated" in the late 1970s, expelled from the party a second time in 1987, and lived in forced exile from 1988 until his death.

In 1979, when he wrote *People or Monsters?*, which is excerpted here, Liu was a special correspondent for *The People's Daily*, the Communist Party's

Excerpt from *People or Monsters?* November 9, 1979, 15–67.

national newspaper. The piece examines a major corruption case in Bin County in his native Heilongjiang Province. A report on the case had already appeared in the official press five months earlier, and Wang Shouxin, the main culprit, had been detained and was awaiting trial. She would be executed, and her case held up as an example. But Liu set out to find something deeper.

People or Monsters? is "reportage" (*baogaowenxue*), a modern Chinese genre that falls between literary art and news reporting. Good reportage differs from ordinary news reporting in several ways: it normally is longer and more carefully written, and while it may begin from an event in the news, its author seeks to uncover aspects of social or political life that are more basic and enduring than the news event itself.

The outlines of the story of Wang Shouxin's corruption were already known before Liu set out to do *People or Monsters?* His contribution—which was formidable, given the barriers and risks involved—was patiently to gather and check facts, and then to piece them together into a single mosaic whose unity lies not only in the logical coherence of the whole, but also in the steady moral presence of the author. He traveled to Bin County, did extensive interviews, and wrote a detailed account not just of how one big boss had been corrupt but how a system of corruption had grown to include many people—*some of whom were still in power.* He observed that all of the corrupt actors were Communist Party members and dared to ask: "What does this fact tell us?"

He could easily have treated Wang Shouxin as an isolated case or as a scapegoat for the larger problem, but he chose to do basically the opposite. He used the case to illuminate the general conditions that allow corruption in China's authoritarian system to grow. And after he published his results, readers all across China recognized his analyses as applying, to a greater or lesser degree, in their own environments. They wrote letters to Liu and his editors praising him for pinpointing *our* problems, *right here.* This fact, in turn, generated anger at Liu not only from party leaders at the national level, who feared national "instability," but from many provincial leaders who feared that the malfeasance Liu had revealed too closely resembled their own. Liu received threat-ladened warnings from the governors of seven provinces he had never visited.

On November 9, 1979, shortly after *People or Monsters?* had appeared, Liu delivered a major speech in Beijing to a congress of the All-China Association of Literature and Art Workers. The speech was repeatedly interrupted by applause, not least for these lines:

I have awoken to a hard fact: in today's China, if one speaks or writes and *does not* incur somebody's opposition, one might as well not have spoken or written at all. One has no alternative. The only alternative is to cower in a corner and fall silent.

Liu was not recommending contrariness for its own sake. He was advising his fellow writers to tell the truth as they saw it and just let the effects be what they will be. His point was that if you tell only certain truths, only the approved or "safe" ones, you are doing something that any writer can do and that in fact many others will always be doing. You can almost gauge whether you have written something worthwhile by seeing whether anyone objects.

Liu suffered colon cancer for most of 2005 and died on December 5 of that year in a New Jersey hospital. In China, news of his passing was blocked. Ever since his exile in 1988, state media in China, and all textbooks, were barred from mentioning his name. A writer who in 1985 had been one of the most famous in China by 2005 was almost entirely unknown to young Chinese.

Wang Shouxin began as the [coal] company's cashier. [. . .] When the great billows of the Cultural Revolution rolled along, they stimulated God knows which ones of Wang Shouxin's animal desires, but in any case brought out in her political urges that had lain dormant for years. At first she tried to establish herself in commercial circles, but no one would have her. She tried the students, but no luck there either. She finally got some support when she reached Commissar Yang of the Munitions Ministry; then she returned to the coal company and tried to build an organization.

[. . .] One day in August 1968, Commissar Yang strode briskly and boldly into the planning office of the Bin County Commercial Revolutionary Committee. He looked around the room at the committee members, all of whom had risen out of respect. Then, in his customarily firm voice, he shocked everyone by saying, "Wang Shouxin must be allowed to join you on this committee." [. . .] This was an order, and as such it was adopted immediately and unanimously by the committee, who did not bother to wait for a referendum among the commercial workers of Bin County. For those days, this was normal. [. . .] After that Commissar Yang again ordered the Commercial Revolutionary Committee to "receive" Wang Shouxin into the Party. [. . .] In the end, despite the opposition of 70 percent of the Party members, Wang Shouxin joined the Party as a member "specially endorsed" by Commissar Yang. This happened in September of 1969. [. . .] Ten years had to pass before anyone could even raise questions about this massive inversion of justice.

[. . .] Over the years Wang Shouxin had come to know this tiny coal company [later fuel company] thoroughly, and to become thoroughly bored with it. Yet once she became boss, all that changed; everything now seemed to take on a strange radiance. Jet black coal piles, glistening lumps of coal—how delightful! No longer was she bored with those who were busy unloading the coal, weighing it or collecting payment for it. Everything now belonged to her, and everybody belonged to Wang Shouxin's orders.

[. . .] The first reform she carried out was to sell coal according to a person's position. She arranged to have the top-grade coal picked out and packed in waterproof straw bags for delivery by truck directly to the doors of the County Party secretary and the members of the Standing Committee. This was coal that caught fire quickly and burned well—just right for cooking dumplings at New Year's. And payment? "What's the rush? We'll discuss it later . . ."

[. . .] Wang Shouxin was deeply concerned about the difficulties of people in Bin County. The county's cadres' wages hadn't risen for over ten years, and every family felt the pinch. Many had borrowed anywhere from several hundred to nearly a thousand dollars of public funds. In 1975 the County Committee, on instructions from above, insisted on a deadline for the return of the public funds. Enter Wang Shouxin, the "goddess of wealth." She always carried with her a passbook for an unregistered bank account, and she could produce ready cash just by reaching into the drawer of her office desk.

[. . .] A new relationship arose from the transfer of the proletarian state's money: first, Wang Shouxin, rather than the state, assumed the creditor's role; second, Wang Shouxin's money did not necessarily have to be returned. In fact, she preferred that it not be returned, because then people would owe her their loyalty and future favors. But even if the money was returned, the debts of favor would remain. The favorite method of repaying these obligations was for the debtor to use his own power for Wang Shouxin's convenience. This caused the debtor no material loss, and for Wang Shouxin it was more than she could buy for a thousand pieces of gold. So why not do it this way, since it had such benefits for both sides?

At bottom, all this was an exchange of goods that was effected by trading off power. One form of this barter involved the direct handling of goods. For example, Wang Shouxin raised a large number of pigs, pork being another item in her power-broking. But where could she get fodder for the pigs? Just seek out the vice-director of the Grain Bureau, of course! More than five tons of corn, bran, soybeans, and husks were sent right over. [. . .] In return the vice-director could "borrow" money or bricks from Wang Shouxin, or "buy" complete cartloads of coal on credit. Payment was never required, and in fact no payment was made. [. . .] For years this trading of influence went on between Wang Shouxin and dozens of officials—perhaps a hundred—on the County Party Committee, County Revolutionary Committee, and at the district and even the provincial level.

[. . .] After 1970, Bin County suddenly began to build all sorts of factories; the use of coal increased dramatically, while coal production remained the same. This phenomenon set the stage for Wang Shouxin to display her talents.

[. . .] But there was one question: her money. Where did it come from?

There were two kinds of coal. Coal produced by the state-run coal mines had a sale price fixed according to the cost of producing it, and was supplied "under the state plan." Coal supplied "outside the state plan" was small-pit coal, and transport and miscellaneous charges were added to its price. From 1972 onward, Wang Shouxin hit upon an extremely simple scheme for making money: take a portion of the state coal and charge small-pit coal prices for it. This would net from three to nearly ten dollars per ton.

[. . .] The fuel company was only 220 yards away from the headquarters of the County Party Committee. [. . .] What about the letters of complaint relayed down to them several times from the provincial and prefectural Party Committees? Had they never seen or heard any of these things? [. . .] Did this reluctance to speak up come from everyone's having been bought out by criminals such as Wang Shouxin? Of the eleven members of the Standing Committee of the County Party Committee, nine had accepted Wang Shouxin's gifts—this was a fact.

[. . .] The exposure of Wang Shouxin's case shocked the entire country. How could such a crude, shallow woman muster such boldness and such ability? How could such brazen criminal activity go uninvestigated for so many years? From their common sense and intuition people naturally focused their attention on Bin County Party leadership: they were at the root of this, they were her accomplices, it was they who had protected Wang Shouxin!

This is, to be sure, the impression one gets when one views Wang Shouxin's case in isolation from the economic, political and social life of Bin County. But if one looks a the whole living organism, with Wang Shouxin and her criminal activity organically linked by a maze of arterial connections to the rest of life, then the situation appears very different.

Viewing the situation organically, one discovers the following: were it not for the illicit treasury in which she held cash amounting to over a third of a million dollars, Wang Shouxin and her activities would never have aroused the attention, or caused the shock, that they did when the full extent of her corruption was exposed. [. . .] Her party-throwing and gift-giving were carried out on a grand scale. But what officials were *not* throwing parties and giving gifts? The maxim "Without proper greasing, nothing works" is as true today as ever. [. . .] Wang Shouxin may indeed have been the Coal Queen of Bin County, but she most certainly was not alone. Bin County also had an Electricity King, the head of the electricity board, who was also called "the millionaire." This man's gift-giving and lavish parties cost in the neighborhood of $10,000 each year. Just as did Wang Shouxin's fuel company, the electricity board had to pay tribute to higher-ups.

[. . .] Where was the borderline between legitimate gift-giving and the offering and accepting of bribes? Was using public funds for wining and dining or for converting public property to one's own use (as in requiring a "test use," or a "test wearing," or a "taste test") any different from corruption and robbery?

[. . .] The case of Wang Shouxin's corruption has been cracked. But how many of the social conditions that gave rise to this case have really changed? Isn't it true that Wang Shouxins of all shapes and sizes, in all corners of the land, are still in place, continuing to gnaw away at socialism, continuing to tear at the fabric of the Party, and continuing to evade punishment by the dictatorship of the proleteriat?

15

PANG JIAOMING

FAMILY PLUNDERING (2011)

from *Century Weekly*

INTRODUCED BY VINCENT WEIFENG NI

China

Five years ago, when investigative reporter Pang Jiaoming first attempted to pitch a story about a child trafficking scandal in China's central Hunan Province, his newspaper editor's reply was delivered in no uncertain terms: the one-child policy is a basic national policy. Hands off. Pang kept collecting material and eventually joined Caixin Media in late 2010, where he was able to publish his exposé.

When it appeared in Caixin Media's *Century Weekly* in May 2011, the detailed revelation brought a public outcry so tremendous that even a top party official in Hunan stood up and demanded what he called a "thorough investigation." China's state-run *People's Daily* also followed up and criticized the local government's involvement in human trafficking.

Unprecedented in its detail, Pang's exposé drew upon four years of painstaking and perilous research documenting widespread abuses by local family planning authorities in Longhui County, Hunan Province, the birthplace of Chairman Mao. There the Yang family spent years searching for their nine-month-old daughter, Yang Ling. Local cadres abducted the girl while Yang and his wife, Cao Zhimei, were working far from home. After Yang failed to pay 6,000 yuan in "social support fees" for violating the one-child policy, his daughter disappeared. Behind the scenes, authorities declared the girl an orphan and she was sold for adoption in the United States. During the author's investigation in 2009, Yang Ling's adoptive

Excerpt from Pang Jiaoming, "Family Plundering," *Century Weekly*, May 2011.

parents were found. But since then, they have moved home and disappeared due to what they called "privacy concerns."

As China becomes more capitalist, the state has receded in many aspects. But in the provinces, local authorities, particularly in little-known cities like the one in the story, have extended their institutional power into nearly every facet of family life. From the destruction of homes to the indeterminate detention of one-child policy offenders, couples with hopes of having a bigger family can be faced with a family torn apart. Although giving up on the policy is widely discussed at the national level, in the thirty years since the one-child policy was first implemented, the provincial family planning bureaus have expanded exponentially in offices and personnel.

In 2005, local and international media first revealed that employees in the Hunan family planning bureau worked with orphanages to sell at least one hundred children for adoption by American parents. But despite the widespread reporting both domestically and overseas, little action was taken.

Although the policy itself is often not strictly enforced in remote areas to counter the impact of prenatal sex selection, family planning authorities discovered they can extort money from families by taking a broad interpretation of the policy. In this case, Hunan officials were engaged in fraud, abduction, unlawful use of force, and other crimes for personal profit.

Such practices in Longhui came to an end only in 2006 when an eight-month-old boy fell from the family planning office's second-floor balcony as the boy's mother tried to stop the kidnapping of her son.

According to the U.S. State Department, the number of Chinese children adopted in the United States is far larger than in any other country at 64,043 adoptions between 1999 and 2010. Yet perhaps few American parents know where their new family members are actually from.

Pang's story also revealed an entrenched resistance held by local officials toward acknowledging abuses of power. When Caixin published the report, authorities visited Mr. Yang several times. Soon Yang and his neighbor Zhou Yinghe, another father of a missing child, were detained for fifteen days on false charges. At around the same time, Longhui authorities started to hack Pang's e-mail in an attempt to stop his investigative work. Indeed, journalists in China face harassment and worse if they expose corruption and government misdeeds.

But the outcry, especially from China's Twitter-like Weibo, had been enormous since the publication of the investigation. Three months after Caixin's exposé, twelve local officials involved in the wrongdoing were sacked from their jobs and expelled from the Communist Party. Weibo has been particularly instrumental in exposing government corruption in recent years but, for obvious reasons, print media are able to delve more deeply into stories and provide detail and solid evidence. The story below appeared in *Century Weekly* magazine but documents and videos Pang collected during the four years of investigation were uploaded to Caixin's bilingual websites.

This story is a part of author Pang Jiaoming's ongoing effort to chronicle the villagers' tragedies and bring clarity to one of the country's many controversial national policies that hold limited relevance to a changing society. Adopting a new name every time his writing has been banned, Pang has just completed a book, *Orphan of Shao*, on human trafficking in China under his real name.

Families in a poor mountainous region have had children seized, and apparently sold, in the name of China's one-child policy.

On a long journey in search of his lost child, Yang Libing carries a single photograph. It's a faded snapshot of his daughter Yang Ling, who this year turns seven years old. Family planning agency cadres in the poor mountain town where Yang Libing lived with his wife Cao Zhimei seized their daughter in 2005 and shipped her to an orphanage because they didn't pay a 6,000 yuan penalty—so-called "social support compensation"—for violating China's one-child policy.

The nearly three-decade-old policy limits parents to a single offspring with certain exceptions. Authorities decided that the family of Yang Ling had overstepped strict bounds imposed by family planners in their hometown Gaoping and Longhui County, near the city of Shaoyang in Hunan Province. Local officials decided to take a tough—arguably inhumane—stand for central government population controls by claiming rights to the toddler and, as the parents have argued since 2009, allowing her to be sold into adoption abroad. Not only did the decision to confiscate the little girl serve to punish the parents, leaving them with mere memories and a worn baby photo, but it also provided operating cash for the local government.

Indeed, a Caixin investigation found that children in many parts of Hunan have been sold in recent years and wound up, sometimes with help from document forgers and complacent authorities, being raised by overseas families who think they adopted Chinese orphans. The official China Center of Adoption says more than 100,000 orphans and disabled Chinese children were adopted by families abroad until last year. The largest number now lives in the United States.

In some cases, child-selling revenues as well as social support compensation fees paid by Hunan parents who break one-child rules have become important sources of income for local governments in poor parts of the province.

Money Machine

Family planning agencies received less than 20 percent of the fees paid by Hunan's violating parents in 2004 and '05, according to the provincial Family Planning Commission. Most of the money was used to cover general government expenses, government sources told Caixin.

Highlighting the importance of this income source—and the power of local family planning officials—was Longhui County Director Zhong Yifan, who addressed the issue at a public meeting last year. "Small town (Communist) party committees and governments have a deep relationship with family planning departments," Zhong said, adding that the committees "dare not offend" family planners. "As a result," he said, "the family planning team holds the party committee and government hostage."

At the same time, though, local government officials appear to be happy to accept funds from family planners that help supplement what have been relatively meager tax collections in recent years. In Gaoping, officials told Caixin that the local government's budget was sorely strained after the central government abolished agricultural taxes in 2006. At times, payrolls went unmet. Family planning violation fees, though, have boosted fiscal budgets ever since Gaoping, population 70,000, started penalizing parents in 2001. Initially, the fee was 3,000 to 4,000 yuan per child. A few years later, local officials said, the penalty rose to 10,000 yuan and sometimes more. In addition, for at least the past decade, family planners have been taking children from parents who failed to pay the fee and selling them to orphanages. [. . .]

Altogether between 2000 and '05, according to Caixin interviews with local residents, family planning authorities seized at least 16 children, including little Yang Ling, from Gaoping parents who broke the rules and couldn't pay fines. Twelve of these children were turned over to the Shaoyang Prefecture Orphanage in the city of the same name. A source told Caixin most of the 12 were adopted by families outside China. Not all these children were being raised by biological parents when they were removed from their homes. Caixin learned that some were being raised by grandparents, aunts and uncles.

Some parents, such as Yang Ling's, were working as migrants in distant cities when the seizures occurred. The government's efforts have been credited with bringing Gaoping's population under control. Lowering the birth rate is also seen as an important accomplishment for Longhui, which is on a central government list of China's most impoverished communities. China has been working on population control since the early 1970s, and the one-child policy took effect nationwide in 1982. [. . .]

Family Planning Office

[. . .] The adoption process can be a moneymaker for an orphanage as well as the provincial government. "Adoptees need to pay an adoption fee," Jiang said, which for a foreign family is usually US$ 3,000. Payments go through a provincial adoption center tied to a civil affairs department, which takes a cut. The largest chunk is then transferred to the orphanage. Hunan's system has been marred by underground trafficking in the past. Seeking cash through foreign adoptions, according to provincial media, three county-level orphanages around Hengyang bought 810 babies through traffickers and other sources between 2003 and '05. The scheme was uncovered and, after a clampdown, 10 people were sentenced to up to 15 years in jail in November 2005.

Parents in Gaoping whose children were seized by family planners likewise argued that they had been victims of injustice. So they formed a group in hopes of locating and reclaiming their children. In 2006, some of these parents started planning to travel to Beijing to petition central government authorities about the perceived wrongs of the family planning agency. But local government officials quickly thwarted the appeal effort. [. . .]

A *Los Angeles Times* story in 2009 brought the topic to the U.S. Through Americans who wanted to help the families, photos of possible children adopted in the United States who may have been from Gaoping made [their] way to the town. That year, a stranger met Yang Libing and his wife in a hotel in the city of Chengde. They were shown two photos of a little girl, and they recognized her immediately. "I was certain at first glance that she was my daughter," Yang Libing said.

Later, a translator who sent the photos and used the family name Ye told the parents that the girl "is living a happy life in the United States, and her adopted parents love her." Ye provided no further information. Local parents, including Yang, could only guess whether their children were in the photos. DNA tests were never conducted, nor did the Gaoping residents receive any further information about how to contact the families with adopted children.

Searching for Daughter

Yang Ling was born a year before Yang Libing and his wife migrated to Guangzhou for jobs. The daughter was seized from the home of her grandparents in Gaoping, who had been raising her while the parents worked far away.

[. . .] Yang Libing's case file at [the] family planning department includes statements supposedly signed by Yang Libing and his father. The documents claim the little girl was found on a street, and that the family had been willing to accept all of the government's decisions for her care. But no one in the family admits making such depositions. Moreover, the signature of Yang Libing's father in the documents was misspelled. Another file, supposedly signed by a now-retired local official named Wang Xianjiao, had similar problems. Wang said she never wrote nor signed such a document, and that her name was misspelled. Other local parents have similarly rejected government arguments that they wrote letters giving up custody rights. They claimed local government officials forged these files. Their claims go against a statement by Liu Shude, Gaoping's director of family planning five years ago, who said "it's impossible to fake" these documents.

Yang Libing's wife Cao Zhimei was happy to learn that her daughter apparently lives in the United States. She told her husband she wanted Yang Ling to come home, right away. But later it became clear that the family could not afford to pursue more than a local search for the daughter. So the mother abandoned Yang Libing, and moved away. "She left a note saying that since her daughter was abducted and could not be brought home, what's the use of living with me," said Yang Libing, as tears welled up in his eyes. "So as long as I'm alive, I'll continue trying to bring my daughter home."

16

JANIO DE FREITAS

THE NORTH-SOUTH RAILWAY BID IS A FARCE (1987)

from *Folha de S. Paulo*

INTRODUCED BY GUILHERME ALPENDRE
AND ANGELA PIMENTA

Brazil

On May 13, 1987, *Folha de S. Paulo*, one of Brazil's leading newspapers, published a story by Janio de Freitas, a well-known political columnist, illustrated by a magnifying glass zooming in on classified ads. Caught in the magnifying glass was an encrypted classified ad, planted in *Folha de S. Paulo* by Freitas, revealing which construction companies would win North-South Railway contracts five days before the supposedly closed bid envelopes were opened.

Mr. Freitas's series of stories on corporate malfeasance in the North-South Railway, a conspiracy involving both construction companies and government officials, are now considered a fundamental chapter in Brazilian investigative journalism. In the late 1980s, Brazil was a fledgling democracy struggling to overcome hyperinflation and to shore up the power of its legal institutions. The press had been cowed and controlled by years of a hard-line military government; after the 1985 end of the dictatorship, the first years of media freedom began and the press began to flex its muscles and try its hand at investigative reporting.

The plan to connect the impoverished north with the more prosperous south was an important one for Brazil's development. But the high cost has meant the project has stalled over the years. According to Mr. Freitas, it was the high cost ($2.5 billion in 1987) and some hazy information about

Janio de Freitas, "The North-South Railway Bid Is a Farce," *Folha de S. Paulo*, May 13, 1987. Translated by Angela Pimenta.

corruption involving the bidding construction firms that caught his attention. The first step in his news gathering was to publish a column on corruption in railway construction—a bait to hook possible whistle-blowers. It worked. After establishing indirect contact with sources and fact-checking, he decided to publish the information he gathered about bid results in the form of a disguised classified ad.

The first strategy Mr. Freitas considered was to hide the bid results in the racing section. But since horse racing was not a popular section in *Folha de S. Paulo*, he decided to publish a fake ad. The ad, headed "Lots," assigned a number to each construction lot (a subdivision of the proposed railway) and paired it with the initials of the winning company. All eighteen results matched when the official winners were confirmed five days later.

Besides Mr. Freitas, the only person who knew about the secret ad was the newspaper owner, Octávio Frias de Oliveira. Anticipating a backlash from the government, which came in the form of a Federal Police investigation and charges under the National Security Act, Mr. Freitas did not reveal his plan to the newsroom until the bid envelopes were opened.

Although initially denying any involvement with the North-South Railway scam after the exposé, president José Sarney's administration was forced to cancel twenty different bids. Ironically, the same railway was still under construction in 2013. But thanks to the higher degree of freedom currently enjoyed by reporters and increasing governmental transparency, similar stories continue to be published—and bids canceled—all over Brazil.

In 2013, millions of Brazilians took to the streets to protest against malfeasance, impunity, red tape, and substandard public services despite a high tax burden. These will be tough problems to tackle but president Dilma Rousseff and Congress say they are listening to the people and taking steps to fight corruption. However, even when convicted, businessmen, government officers, and politicians are seldom sent to jail. With the approval of the Anti-Corruption Law 12.846/2013, the administration at federal, state, and local levels will harden companies against corruption practices that may have civil and administrative penalties. Companies convicted of bribery will face fines of up to 20 percent of their gross annual revenue for the previous year or a maximum of BRL$60 million.

As for Mr. Freitas, at the age of eighty-two, he is an active and prestigious columnist who considers himself "just a journalist in a country flooded with corruption." He has received numerous awards, including the King of Spain Prize for Journalism.

The competitive public bid for construction of the Maranhão-Brasília (or North-South) railway, the results of which the government announced last night, was fraudulent and predetermined by corruption: *Folha* published the eighteen winners, covertly, five days before the state company, Valec, and the Ministry of Transportation even opened the envelopes containing the competing proposals.

The bid started with the opening of the envelopes at 9:30 a.m. last Friday, the 8th.

Folha had been circulating the results of the eighteen contested construction lots since the early morning of that same day. I could not post the results, in my possession since the eve of the announcement, in my column on page A-5 as that would have allowed time to postpone or tamper with the bid. Immediate publishing was essential, as the official results could come out on the same day as the comparison of the proposals. Hence, a coded announcement went out that same Friday 8th, amid *Folha*'s classified ads on page A-15, in the indicative section of "Business. Opportunities."

This announcement, as it was published, shows groups of letters where the L means the Lot (the part of the railroad); the number and the capital letter A or B identify the Lot; and the initials that follow identify the company that would be the winner. Now, compare this announcement with the bid's official results: Lot 1A, winner Norberto Odebrecht; 2A, Queiroz Galvão; 3A, Mendes Jr.; (Lot 4A does not exist); 5A, C. R. Almeida; 6A, Serveng; 7A, Egit; 8A, Cowan; 9A, Ceesa; 1B, CBPO; 2B, Camargo Correa; 3B, Andrade Gutierrez; (Lot 4B does not exist); 5B, Constran; 6B, Sultepa; 7B, Construtora Brazil; 8B, Alkyne Vieira; 9B, Tratex; 10B, Paranapanema; 11B, Ferreira Guedes.

Next to the names of the winning companies and the runners up for each lot, the official results show the discount offered by each one compared to the construction value, as budgeted by Valec and the Ministry of Transport. The discount is, with no difference between winners and losers of each lot, invariably of 10 percent. Immediately, this suggests that the price set by the government was so absurdly high that all companies were able to reduce it by 10 percent. As all the lots were budgeted by Valec and the Ministry of Transport for almost 2.5 billion dollars, it is clear that the government was willing to spend over US$250 million, or Cz$7 billion and 250 million.

As there was already an overall accord in the savings offered by the construction companies, it proves that there was not only a prior allocation of the construction contracts amidst the contractors: the collusion was pervasive because the tiebreaker, and therefore what decided the winners, was determined by Valec and the Ministry of Transport by assigning a score to each company. Scores and billions. Just out of patriotism, of course.

17

SHEILA CORONEL

ERAP AND FAMILIES (2000)

from iReport

INTRODUCED BY REG CHUA

Philippines

An observer of Southeast Asia's media landscape in the early 1980s would have gazed upon a field populated largely by timid pro-government organs, mindful of their relationship with power. But over the last three decades, a much more rambunctious collection of independent-minded newsrooms, unafraid to challenge officialdom, has also occupied the landscape.

Their numbers aren't large, but their impact has been. Southeast Asian journalism has never been freer or feistier.

To be sure, there are places where little has changed over the years, and continued progress toward more independent media isn't assured. Threats to journalists—physical and legal—are ever present, and the quality of journalism being practiced is uneven at best.

But what's noteworthy is how far and how fast the industry has changed, and how deeply such journalism has taken hold.

Credit the democratic transitions that have swept the region, spurred along in some cases by the Asian financial crisis of 1997–98, as well as the advent of the digital age, which offered a path around often-restrictive printing and licensing regulations. From the Philippines' "People Power" revolution to the fall of Suharto to the sudden liberalization of Burma, independent-minded journalists have seized the opportunities to expand their freedoms.

In Malaysia, the innovative online-only news organization Malaysiakini

Excerpt from Sheila Coronel, "Erap and Families," iReport, July–September 2000.

took advantage of the government's pledge to regulate the Internet with a light touch to establish its presence as an alternative to corporate media; in Indonesia and Thailand, journalists leapt on new asset-disclosure and freedom-of-information laws to uncover and expose official corruption; in Singapore, a small but vibrant circle of bloggers offered fresh perspectives on national issues.

The Philippines has been at the forefront of many of these trends. Ferdinand Marcos was swept out of office in 1986, a decade before Suharto; Filipinos were the earliest—and most enthusiastic—adopters of such communications technologies as SMS; and the Philippine Center for Investigative Journalism was one of the first of its kind—an independent, nonprofit newsroom focused on quality journalism—not just in the region, but in the world.

Founded in 1989, the center was a pioneer in many other ways, not least in its use of public records to ferret out official—and officials'—wrongdoing. Those techniques—along with old-fashioned shoe-leather reporting—were the cornerstone of a months-old investigation it undertook in 2000 of then-president Joseph Estrada's real estate holdings.

For three months, a team of a dozen reporters and interns retrieved and analyzed corporate filings to understand how the president had amassed undeclared properties and flouted government regulations in the building of a housing project. Armed with that information, they dug further, documenting the front men and dummies used to shield the transactions from public scrutiny. They even obtained floor plans of identical mansions built for each of his mistresses.

The first story in the series, published in July that year by a handful of small papers, initially didn't elicit much reaction. But it laid the groundwork for a second and third piece in subsequent months, carried this time by television stations as well, that prompted calls—unsuccessfully—for Estrada's impeachment. Still, momentum was building. In October, when yet another article was published, an erstwhile political ally of the president came forward with further allegations of corruption. A month later, the House of Representatives formally began impeachment hearings. And when those hearings were stymied, hundreds of thousands took to the streets in a second "People Power" demonstration that ultimately led to Estrada's removal.

That demonstration—of the power of information to galvanize public action—hasn't been lost on journalists in the rest of the region. In 2001, the Thai press showed how then–prime minister Thaksin Shinawatra registered his assets in names of, among others, his driver and maid; despite the outcry the story engendered, though, the constitutional court acquitted him later that year.

But regardless of the outcome, it's clear that readers around the region now expect a different—and higher—standard of accountability journalism from the media.

———————————

President Joseph Estrada has a weakness for grand houses. Many years ago, he built one for the First Lady, a sprawling mansion at 1 Polk Street in North Greenhills in San Juan. Expanded and renovated over the years, the official family home now covers three adjoining lots with a total area of 2,000 square meters. There, surrounded by his collection of expensive crystal, Estrada likes to hold court for his clan and cronies.

To mark his mother Mary's 95th birthday last May, the President had her Kennedy St., Greenhills home refurbished, a major renovation that converted the family matriarch's large, comfortable quarters into something close to palatial: high ceilings, a state-of-the-art kitchen, and a cavernous living room with a grand piano and exorbitantly-priced beige curtains.

Last year, the President's mother celebrated her birthday in a two-story villa owned by the Ejercitos in Laguna. Built in 1912, the house had fallen to neglect after the Second World War. On the President's orders, however, well-known architect Chito Antonio gave it a facelift, the results of which were featured earlier this year in the glossy architectural magazine BluPrint.

"Traditional elements were restored: capiz windows, the noble wooden floor, and decorative ceiling details," the magazine reported. The "Palace in Pagsanjan," as BluPrint called the villa, is apparently intended more as a "cultural landmark" than to be lived in. It boasts of a luxurious living room flooded with light from floor-to-ceiling windows and adorned with modern paintings. Estrada's bedroom, BluPrint noted, has an "exquisitely carved four-poster narra bed," billowing drapes, and French windows looking out to the garden.

Whether it is his own home or that of his mother or one of his wives, the President's architectural and design preferences tend toward opulence—heavy draperies, antiques, carved wood and crystal. All these of course add up to princely sums. But especially extravagant, say those who have seen them, are the more recent constructions attributed to either Estrada or one of his special women. These homes have been described consistently as being done in a style in which it was obvious that cost was not a concern. For instance, says an interior designer, a house supposedly for one of the presidential wives, in New Manila, Quezon City, features a swimming pool with real sand and a machine that churns artificial waves.

A two-story mansion being built on a 5,000-square-meter lot on Harvard Street in Wack Wack, Mandaluyong, has a mini-theater, a gym, a sauna and three kitchens on the ground floor and another upstairs. Until the furor over the construction made it too controversial, this house was supposedly designed especially for Laarni Enriquez, a long-time Estrada companion, and her three children.

As far as we can ascertain, Estrada was already a wealthy man before he assumed the presidency. The dimensions of his wealth, however, are not reflected in his asset statements, and the President seems to think it unnecessary to go into any detail on just where he is getting the money to indulge what looks like an edifice complex. Not even when it is already raising eyebrows in Manila's gossipy café society. [. . .]

If there is anything that characterizes Estrada's conduct of both his public and private life, it is a lack of discretion. The President flaunts his extravagance and his generosity to the women in his life. He believes that since he has been open about the complications of his private life—at least 11 children by six women and some other rumored mistresses—then he should no longer be held to account. That is why he gets really ornery when he is questioned about these matters.

Estrada may have been right earlier in his term, when he admitted to his extramarital indiscretions and retorted to those who had expressed unease about his multiple liaisons, "You seem to be more concerned than my wives." But the lavish lifestyle of those wives and the cost of maintaining those liaisons are now being widely discussed and fast becoming a public concern.

To begin with, Estrada does not explain how he can support four households in such grand style. Apart from the First Lady Luisa Ejercito, Estrada has long-term relationships with three other women: former actress Guia Gomez, with whom he has a son, 31-year old Jose Victor or "JV"; one-time starlet Laarni Enriquez, with whom the President has three children, the oldest of them 15 years old; and ex-model Joy Melendrez, a Pasig policeman's daughter who has borne Estrada a son.

On their own, these women are not independently wealthy. Yet Gomez is listed in records of the Securities and Exchange Commission (SEC) as an incorporator and shareholder of 33 companies ranging from real estate to trading and manufacturing. All but one of these companies were formed since Estrada was elected to the Senate in 1987; 15 were set up during his vice-presidency and four in the first two years of his presidential term.

In August, Gomez told a group of women journalists, "I have shares in more than 33 companies, but I don't have money in all of them." She also boasted that she employed thousands and that she planned to set up more enterprises.

Enriquez, meanwhile, has five companies to her name, among them Star J

Management, which manages a mall in Malabon. Incorporated in 1996, the company declared assets of P45 million in 1998. During Estrada's tenure as senator, Enriquez was living in a modest townhouse in Sunnyvale, San Juan; later, she moved to the penthouse of the Goldloop Towers in Pasig.

In the mid-1990s, after Estrada's election to the vice-presidency, Enriquez began living in posh Wack Wack, on a 1,000-square meter property registered in the name of businessman and presidential pal Jacinto Ng. The land alone, at current market values, costs about P40 million, while rental for a typical house in that neighborhood is about P100,000 a month.

When Estrada became president, preparations were made for even grander housing for Enriquez. That was when Ng bought the property on which the mansion supposedly being built for Wife No. 3 is being constructed. That piece of real estate is worth a fortune: At P40,000 per square meter, the going price for Wack-Wack property, its current value is close to P200 million.

Melendrez has no companies registered in her name and no known source of income but lives in a big house on Swallow Drive at the upscale Green Meadows in Quezon City.

It is not clear where these women—or the President, if he supports them—got the wherewithal to live in such style. According to JV Ejercito, the President was a successful movie actor and made substantial amounts from his films. No doubt he did. But there is a discrepancy between what Estrada declared in his statements of assets and his income tax return and what corporate records show are the rather vast holdings of his various families.

In July, the Philippine Center for Investigative Journalism (PCIJ) revealed the findings of a four-month research [effort] based on the records of 66 companies in which Estrada, his wives and his children are listed as incorporators or board members. Altogether, these companies—31 of which were set up during Estrada's vice-presidential term and 11 since he assumed the presidency—had an authorized capital of P893.4 million when they were registered. The President and his family members had shares of P121.5 million and paid up P58.6 million of these when the companies were formed.

It is difficult to estimate how much these businesses are now worth because of incomplete data at the Securities and Exchange Commission (SEC). But based on available 1998 and 1999 financial statements, 14 of the 66 companies alone have assets of over P600 million.

The President's official asset declarations over the last 12 years cannot explain where the funds to invest in so many corporations come from. In 1999, Estrada declared in his statement of assets a net worth of P35.8 million and in his income tax return, a net income of only P2.3 million.

Since the PCIJ's report was published, however, Estrada has declined to explain the obvious gaps in his asset and income tax declarations and the SEC records. JV Ejercito, who has taken up the President's defense, maintains that many of these companies no longer exist and that most of them were just small, "mom and pop" operations anyway. Ejercito, however, did not list which of the firms had been shuttered. More to the point, his argument does not explain the disparity in declared assets and income and the lifestyle and multifarious business activities of the First Families.

It is quite likely that some of the discrepancies can be explained by the carelessness of the President's accountants, who appear not to have bothered to prepare sufficiently credible declarations of assets and income that would explain the sumptuous lifestyles of the presidential women. But it is equally likely some of the funds in the President's possession are probably hard to explain, even by the most brilliant of accountants. [. . .]

18

KHADIJA ISMAYILOVA

AZERBAIJANI PRESIDENT'S FAMILY BENEFITS FROM EUROVISION HALL CONSTRUCTION (2012)

from Radio Free Europe

INTRODUCED BY LISA MISOL

Azerbaijan

Azerbaijan is an oil-rich and repressive state that has been ruled by the same family for twenty years. By the time President Ilham Aliyev succeeded his father, Heydar, in 2003, Azerbaijan had already started to experience tremendous oil-driven growth from deals struck during the 1990s. According to the World Bank, Azerbaijan's Gross Domestic Product increased more than tenfold in the decade from 2001 to 2011.

For Khadija Ismayilova, the explosion of business activity during the oil boom and the privatization of a number of state companies have provided fodder for her investigative reporting. Ismayilova hosts a talk show on U.S. government–funded Radio Free Europe/Radio Liberty's Azeri service and writes articles for the RFE/RL website. In both venues, she has frequently focused on opaque business practices and suspected governmental corruption, serving as the local reporter for the Organized Crime and Corruption Reporting Project. Although she insists that she did not set out to document the business interests of the president's family, the investigative leads she has pursued have led her there over and over again.

An August 2010 article she co-authored with Ulviyye Asadzade, "Aliyev's Azerbaijani Empire Grows, As Daughter Joins the Game," reported that one of the president's daughters benefited from state privatization deals under her father, becoming part-owner of a bank that formerly belonged to the

Excerpt from Khadija Ismayilova, "Azerbaijani President's Family Benefits from Eurovision Hall Construction," Radio Free Europe, May 9, 2012.

state-owned airline. Ismayilova followed up with a June 2011 story tying Ali-yev's two daughters, via offshore companies, to a telecommunications firm that benefited handsomely from a government-issued license. Next was a May 2012 article, co-authored with Nushabe Fatullayeva, that revealed that the president's two daughters had business interests, again via offshore com-panies, in a company that was granted the right to mine for gold without any tender process. That same month, she ran a story (excerpted below) about the hidden ownership of a major construction firm that has won tens of millions of dollars in state contracts. According to her investigations, it is owned via front companies by none other than the president's wife and daughters.

Ismayilova's research has earned her international recognition as an in-trepid reporter. It has also led to a blackmail attempt and a vicious smear campaign in retaliation for her investigations. On March 7, 2012, Ismay-ilova received an envelope from an anonymous sender containing explicit photos of her and her boyfriend with a note warning her, "Whore, behave. Or you will be disgraced." Ismayilova continued to pursue her investigative work, and on March 14 a secretly recorded video of Ismayilova having sex with her boyfriend was posted on the Internet. The day before the video was posted, a pro-government newspaper ran a long article attacking Ismayilova and criticizing her personal life. The government opened an investigation into violation of privacy but declined to investigate the threats.

Ismayilova has continued to be the focus of attacks intended to intimi-date her. On April 25, 2013, a pro-government website released a video fea-turing someone with her likeness engaged in sexual acts. This time, it was a fabrication designed to stir up additional controversy and to make her pay a price for her journalism.

Her investigative work continues in the face of a serious crackdown on freedom of expression in Azerbaijan as well as legislative changes that make her reporting more challenging. In apparent response to the publication of her series of articles that exposed the private business interests of the president's family, the Azerbaijani parliament adopted legislation in June 2012—a month after the piece below was published—that allowed Azer-baijani companies to withhold information pertaining to their registration, ownership structure, and shareholders. Parliament also granted the presi-dent and first lady lifetime immunity from criminal prosecution for acts during office. President Aliyev signed both bills into law.

BAKU—Later this month, the eyes of the world will be focused on a shimmer-ing glass-and-steel building newly erected on the shores of the Caspian Sea to welcome the pop stars and television crews from the more than 40 European countries that will broadcast the Eurovision Song Contest 2012 spectacle.

Azerbaijan won hosting rights to the popular extravaganza last year, when its pop duo of Ell and Nikki sang their way to victory in Eurovision 2011. The Azerbaijani government responded proudly with plans for a new $134 million concert showplace called the Crystal Hall, which seats 23,000.

Finished only a few weeks ago, it was a tense race to get the venue ready in time. Its importance was signaled by the frequent visits made by President Ilham Aliyev and First Lady Mehriban Aliyeva to the bold geometric structure as it rose amid the construction site.

But their interest was not just ceremonial and patriotic. An investigation by the Organized Crime and Corruption Reporting Project (OCCRP) and RFE/RL has discovered that the first family is personally profiting from the massive construction project through its hidden ownership in the Azenco construction company.

The company contracted for the work has long been identified in all official announcements as Germany's Alpine Bau Deutschland AG. Yet some of the equipment at the construction site is stamped with the company name Azenco. Rolf Herr, a representative of Alpine Bau in Azerbaijan, described Azenco as a subcontractor.

He would give no other details of its involvement. The Alpine Bau press office in Germany did not respond to questions about how subcontractors and vendors had been chosen.

Front Companies

Azenco is owned through a series of front companies that mask the real owners. The official newspaper of the agency for privatization of state property in Azerbaijan announced in 2010 that Baku-based Interenerji MMC acquired 97.5 percent of the shares of Azenco.

According to privatization records from March 2010, ADOR MMC, another Baku-based company, controls 70 percent of the ownership of Interenerji. Company registration documents list ADOR's legal address as "7 Samed Vurgun Street." The registered occupants of that address at the time were Mehriban Aliyeva, Leyla Aliyeva, and Arzu Aliyeva, the wife and daughters of the president, respectively.

In 2010, RFE/RL investigated the privatization of the State Aviation Company's infrastructure, including Azalbank (currently Silkwaybank), which also has as a registered shareholder Arzu Aliyeva, residing at the same address. Presidential spokesman Azer Gasimov at the time confirmed that the shareholder was indeed the president's daughter.

Gasimov did not respond to repeated phone calls and a written inquiry about the presidential family's connection to Azenco and the appearance of a conflict of interest if Azenco is profiting from state-funded construction projects. [. . .]

Very Expensive Flag

The Crystal Hall is the second project to raise conflict-of-interest questions about Azenco.

It also helped construct the grandiose $38 million State Flag Square near the Crystal Hall, which briefly held the "Guinness Book of World Records" title for tallest flagpole in the world.

A few months after it was put up, Azerbaijan's 162-meter flagpole was surpassed by an even taller flagpole in Dushanbe, Tajikistan.

Two-thirds of the cost of the square in Baku came from the Reserve Fund of the head of state by presidential Decrees 532 (October 26, 2009) and 1052 (August 3, 2010). The other one-third came directly from the 2011 state budget in accordance with a decree by the Cabinet of Ministers 260 S (August 25, 2011).

A spokesman for the cabinet, Akif Ali, refused to respond to questions about how Azenco came to be chosen as a partner in the project.

Looting State Coffers

Azenco has been employed on numerous state-funded projects less showy but possibly no less profitable than the Baku work. State Procurement Agency records show that in 2010 alone the company was awarded contracts worth $79 million. The company also recently gained control of Sumqayit Technology Park, a former state-funded enterprise started by Azerenerji, the government-owned energy producer.

Azer Mehtiyev, director of the Center for Assistance to Economic Initiatives, a politically independent think tank, says Azenco looks like a clear example of a scheme to "misappropriate" some of the country's oil wealth.

"With the big oil money flowing into the budget, a parallel process of monopolization of spheres of economy, redivision of state property . . . [made] way for the misappropriation of revenues," Mehtiyev said.

"Big infrastructure projects financed by oil revenues are mainly distributed to companies which belong to high-ranking officials. The government keeps the information about owners of the companies secret. The state contracts are assigned to companies established in offshore zones with unknown owners making public control over the process impossible," he added.

According to Mehtiyev, it is especially difficult to get information about the business interests of the president's family.

Anticorruption Talk, No Action

Azerbaijan adopted an Anticorruption Law in 2004 that obliges officials to declare the income and property holdings of themselves and their relatives.

In August 2005 (Order No. 278), the president ordered the Cabinet of Ministers to prepare a special form on which officials would give that information within two months. But the forms were never drafted and officials never provided the information. It is not clear if the president or the first lady, who is also a member of parliament, have submitted declarations in the past decade.

The presidential administration and the Central Election Commission will not respond to questions about their property. A written inquiry sent to the first lady's website was not answered.

In January 2011, President Aliyev declared that the government would take serious measures against corrupt officials.

The 2012 Eurovision event will have one other tie to the first family besides the new showcase auditorium: The president's son-in-law, singer Emin Agalarov, was chosen to entertain the crowd between acts.

OIL AND MINING

19

KEN SARO-WIWA

THE COMING WAR IN THE DELTA (1990)

from the *Sunday Times*

INTRODUCED BY CLIFFORD BOB

Nigeria

An activist and journalist from Nigeria, Ken Saro-Wiwa was a hero of the Western environmental movement and the charismatic spokesman of a major campaign against the Nigerian military government and Royal Dutch/Shell Oil in the 1990s. Outraged about the environmental damage caused in the Niger Delta by multinational oil companies and the way that oil revenues fed government corruption, citizens of the Niger Delta and shareholder activists and environmentalists in Europe and the UK joined together to push Royal Dutch/Shell to clean up its operations and to stop colluding with the brutal regime of General Sani Abacha. The execution of Saro-Wiwa by the Nigerian government in 1995 sent shock waves through the international environmental movement. The ensuing press coverage galvanized the corporate social responsibility movement worldwide and increased the pressure on oil companies to change how they operate. What follows here is an astonishingly prescient piece by Saro-Wiwa about the deterioration of the situation in the Niger Delta.

Originally interested primarily in the rights of the Ogoni minority who lived in the Niger Delta, Saro-Wiwa founded the Movement for the Survival of the Ogoni People (MOSOP) in 1990. However, he was media-savvy enough to understand that the group would not attract much-needed international support unless it shifted its focus to issues that the overseas NGO

Ken Saro-Wiwa, "The Coming War in the Delta," *Sunday Times*, November 25, 1990, reprinted in Ken Saro-Wiwa, *Similia: Essays on Anomic Nigeria* (London: Saros, 1991), 168–170.

community could understand and sympathize with. Saro-Wiwa's reframing efforts were successful, and by 1994 MOSOP had begun to attract international support. Although it began as a nonviolent movement for Ogoni political autonomy in Nigeria, MOSOP became known internationally for its campaign against Royal Dutch/Shell, the region's largest oil producer, demanding that it stop its environmental devastation of the Ogonis' indigenous lands. By late 1994, the Nigerian military government felt threatened both by MOSOP's call for autonomy and a halt to oil production and by the precedent that Ogoni mobilization seemed to be establishing for other Niger Delta minorities. Using military and paramilitary units, it began a crackdown, killing thousands of mostly peaceful protesters or bystanders. In 1995, Saro-Wiwa was imprisoned on trumped-up charges and hanged after a kangaroo trial. In the Delta, the Ogonis' nonviolent movement was crushed, and their demands largely ignored. Later in the decade, however, frustrated members of various Niger Delta ethnic groups took up arms against state repression in a bloody conflict lasting years.

Much of this was predicted in Saro-Wiwa's article, "The Coming War in the Delta," published before most of these events, on November 25, 1990, in the morning edition of Nigeria's government-owned *Sunday Times*. At the time, the military regime of General Ibrahim Babangida allowed some press freedoms, and Saro-Wiwa had become a regular columnist for the newspaper, writing scathing critiques of Nigerian politics and corruption. But unlike other articles he had written, "The Coming War in the Delta," with its emphasis on sensitive matters of minority rights and ownership of the country's petroleum reserves, struck a nerve with a government dependent on oil revenues and dominated by leaders of Nigeria's majority ethnic groups.

"The Coming War in the Delta" is an example of journalism that might have had an impact but did not. This is despite Saro-Wiwa's closing sentence: "Is anyone listening?" to the discontents of the minorities. One reason for this was that the newspaper suppressed the article, its editors pulling it from the evening edition. The article also failed to attract outside attention for another reason. At this time, Saro-Wiwa's focus was on critical issues for his own and other Niger Delta minority groups, their political marginalization and economic exploitation. The article says nothing of environmental matters and little of Shell. Tellingly, however, Saro-Wiwa's article predicts not only greater state violence but also an eventual turn to warfare in the Delta if the Nigerian government fails to meet minority demands. If the article had been heeded, despite the thorny political and economic issues it raised, all of that might have been avoided. In the event, Saro-Wiwa became a martyred hero in an international movement to improve operations of resource companies in repressive states. This had some success in convincing companies such as Shell to improve their environmental and human rights records. But the Ogoni remain marginalized in Nigeria.

———————

About three weeks ago, the smouldering war in the delta claimed its first lives. Six dead, twenty injured. I had foreseen it way back in 1988 and given ample warning. I fear that worse is to come if action is not taken promptly to diffuse the situation.

Before I go any further, I must warn the delta communities to abjure violence in the just struggle for their rights. I believe that history is on their side. But they are faced by a Company—Shell—whose management policies are racist and cruelly stupid, and which is out to exploit and encourage Nigerian ethnocentricism. And I am not sure that the Nigeria Police Force has the skills to handle the volatile situation in any but a brutal manner. Therefore, any violence will only lead to needless spilling of blood and waste of human life.

On the other hand, I believe that great political acumen will have to be displayed by the Government if a just settlement is to be reached, because the neglect of the past twenty years has been criminal and the wrong done the delta communities monumental. All past administrations from Gowon to the present one have a share of the blame.

The problem in the delta is not just an oil problem. It is political. The overwhelming feeling among the delta communities is that they have been duped by Nigeria. There is a feeling that they were used in the civil war as cannon fodder and then robbed and insulted. It is a feeling that will not be easily assuaged. Two things are responsible for this:

In the first place, the Nigerian Constitution does not protect minority ethnic groups. Human rights provisions in the Constitution protect individuals only; the organic communities which make up the Federation have no constitutional provision protecting and preserving them, their property and institutions. Consequently, the majority ethnic groups, even in democratic regimes, use or misuse their numerical superiority to trample upon these minorities.

Secondly, revenue allocation which lies at the heart of a Federal system of government. Oil is at the centre of Nigerian federalism at this time. Before oil became the main revenue earner, derivation was the central principle for allocating revenue. The Region of origin earned fifty per cent of all revenue derived therefrom. With the revenue earned from cocoa, for instance, the Yoruba under Chief

Awolowo, were able to free-educate all Yoruba children who have today become the captains of industry, commerce and politics.

But now that oil is the main revenue earner, and that oil lies pre-eminently in the minority areas, the derivation principle has been altered, Animal Farm-style, to benefit the majority ethnic groups.

The minority groups in the oil-bearing delta have been further disadvantaged by the simple expedient of splitting the majority ethnic groups into several states while corralling the minorities into polyethnic states and then basing revenue allocation on "equality of states," among other dubious criteria.

The Federal Government reserves for itself a huge chunk of oil revenue which it has expended on social projects and the mitigation of natural disasters in the non-oil-bearing areas. Federal Government appointments have eluded Rivers State citizens, for instance, and where they have been made at all, have been concentrated in one ethnic group or sub-ethnic group. In Bendel State, most of the appointments have gone to the non-oil-producing north of the State. Many people in the delta believe that the Federal Government has been acting out of spite, as no one can explain why, on the little matter of appointments, care cannot be taken to ensure equity and fairness.

The people of the delta cannot understand the precise reasoning behind the actions of the Federal Government. Is Nigeria a capitalist state, obeying the laws of the free market economy? If so, the resources in any area belong strictly to the people of that area. Is Nigeria a socialist state under which all property belongs to the Government? Why is it that Igbeti Marble is owned jointly by local communities, the Oyo State Government and the Federal Government in proportion? But not oil.

Based on what is happening now, the only conclusion that can be drawn is that the confusion of policies in which Nigeria wallows is sponsored so that the peoples of the delta can be fully exploited by whoever gains access in whatever way to Federal power.

Such exploitation can only lead eventually to dissension because the denial of rights is an invitation to fight for them. The danger of the nation is that oil is a very volatile product and most of the world is interested in it.

I should like to think that Nigerians are interested in averting a war in the delta. If so, more states must now be created in the oil-bearing areas of the delta and environs as a means of development and as a solution to ethnic tension.

Furthermore, the Federal Government must make new laws for the exploration of oil, laws which take into consideration the interest of those who live on oil-bearing land. It is also necessary to pay royalty to the landlords for oil mined from their land and the revenue allocation formula must be reviewed to emphasize derivation. Citizens from the oil-bearing areas must be represented on the

Boards of Directors of oil companies prospecting for oil in particular areas and communities in the oil-bearing areas should have equity participation in the oil companies operating therein. Finally, the delta people must be allowed to join in the lucrative sale of crude oil.

Only in this way can the cataclysm that is building up in the delta be avoided. Is anyone listening?

20

CARLOS CARDOSO

THE TIP OF THE ICEBERG: WHO WANTS TO KILL ALBANO SILVA AND WHY? (1999)

from *Metical*

INTRODUCED BY ERIKA RODRIGUES

Mozambique

Carlos Cardoso was a fearless and hardworking investigative journalist who dedicated his life to exposing injustice and corruption in Mozambique and in Africa. Originally a strong supporter of the Marxist-Leninist government that took office in 1975 after Mozambique's independence from Portugal, Cardoso became increasingly disillusioned with the rapacity of officials after the country transitioned to democracy in 1994.

In 2000, Cardoso, forty-nine, was murdered after uncovering a bank fraud involving prominent Mozambican businessmen protected by the police and the judiciary system. He is still remembered as a hero.

Born in 1951 in Beira in the center of Mozambique, Cardoso began his journalistic career in South Africa. While a student at Wits University in Johannesburg during the 1970s, he wrote extensively against the then-ruling apartheid government, which led to his deportation to Portugal on the eve of Mozambique's independence in 1975.

Cardoso was invited back to Mozambique soon after the Mozambique Liberation Front (FRELIMO) took power.[1] As a reporter at the state-run magazine *Tempo* in 1976, he became known for his meticulous investigative reporting and his emphasis on nation building and social justice. Cardoso "fought for a journalism of intervention, a journalism that was openly political and ideological," remembered his colleague Paul Fauvet.[2]

Excerpt from Carlos Cardoso, "The Tip of the Iceberg: Who Wants to Kill Albano Silva and Why?" *Metical*, January 21, 1999. Translated by Erika Rodrigues.

Cardoso also continued his campaign against the apartheid governments in Rhodesia and South Africa, which caused tension with South Africa and often made conservative members of FRELIMO uncomfortable. Cardoso's close intellectual relationship with the first Mozambican president, the charismatic Samora Moisés Machel, allowed him to continue with this work. He eventually became a close adviser of Machel's, even if the two didn't always agree.

When Machel died in 1986 in a bizarre aviation accident, which Carlos Cardoso investigated, socialism in Mozambique died too. Cardoso became deeply disillusioned with the rise of a neoliberal economy run by the International Monetary Fund and the World Bank. Cardoso ended up leaving AIM, the government's information agency, in 1989, which he had led since 1987, and dedicating himself to poetry and painting. After private media were legalized and censorship outlawed in 1991, he joined Mediacoop, the country's first independent cooperative of journalists, founded by some of the biggest names in Mozambican journalism.

Mediacoop conducted groundbreaking investigations of corruption and the country's economy. Cardoso focused especially on defending Mozambique's domestic industries against detrimental Bretton Woods policies backed by the new government.

The cooperative also drew attention to the decaying moral fabric of Mozambican society, where theft and bribery had become common practice. Cardoso's articles, published in *Mediafax*, Mediacoop's daily news sheet, quickly became famous for their quality and his dogged determination to follow stories wherever they led.

Despite the popularity of *Mediafax*, Cardoso eventually left due to an internal disagreement. He formed a similar daily fax sheet named after Mozambique's currency, *Metical*, dedicated mainly to economic issues. At *Metical*, Cardoso investigated land-grab allegations against the then–first lady, wife of former president Joaquim Chissano; the obscure business maneuvers of the president's son, Nyimpine Chissano; the local treatment of toxic waste;[3] and organized crime activities in Mozambique. He wrote fierce editorials against the "gangsterization of the economy" by political and business elites.[4]

Cardoso also began probing the largest bank fraud in Mozambique's history, the theft of $14 million from the Commercial Bank of Mozambique (BCM). Cardoso had investigated the privatization of the two public banks, BCM in 1996 and the People's Development Bank (BPD) in 1997. Focusing on BCM, Cardoso revealed that the buying consortium, headed by the Portuguese Mello Bank, had been put together by Portuguese businessman

António Simões, who owned two companies in Mozambique. Cardoso wrote articles questioning $17 million in loans, never repaid, that Simões's companies had received from BCM between 1992 and 1994. Cardoso speculated that Simões had used them to buy his share of the bank.

The BCM scandal had begun before its privatization. In 1996, private accounts opened by the Satar brothers, notorious loan sharks in Mozambique, were drained of $14 million. The bank transactions were made possible by a BCM branch manager, Vicente Ramaya. The fraud was detected in 1996, but the investigation was blocked. Cardoso dwelt relentlessly on this case and on May 9, 2000, he dedicated an entire issue of *Metical* to the illicit activities of the Satars. He was becoming a liability for the influential businessmen and state officials involved.

On November 22, 2000, Carlos Cardoso was shot dead on his way home from work. The trial that followed was the first ever conducted in open court and televised live. All six accused—the Satar brothers, Ramaya,[5] and three hit men—received the maximum penalty, but the president's son, Nyimpine Chissano, whose key involvement in the murder was revealed during the trial, escaped punishment.[6] Cardoso was posthumously awarded a number of journalism prizes, including the 2000 Index Courage in Journalism award, sponsored by *The Economist*, in 2001.

Today, Mozambique is enjoying a mining and natural gas boom. Concerns about the misuse of the revenues it is bringing have reached new heights. But, still struggling to fulfill its role as watchdog, the media are starting to show promising glimmers of hope. Thanks to new media technology, bloggers, citizen reporting, and dedicated newspapers like @Verdade[7] and SAVANA,[8] a new generation of investigative reporters is emerging, ready to take up Cardoso's vision. He remains an inspiration to all.

MAPUTO—The assassination attempt on the lawyer Albano Silva[9] on Monday seems to be only the tip of an iceberg, whose explosion will be felt by the judicial, police, and financial apparatus in the country. It is about the $14 million theft at BCM that the lawyer was investigating.

It happened around 8:30 p.m. on Monday. Albano Silva was driving on Mao Tse Tung, in the direction of Julius Nyerere. He was driving at around forty to fifty kilometers per hour with the window on his side open. As he passed the student residence between Amilcar Cabral[10] and the third police station, a small dark car approached from his right. Moments later, the passenger in front brandished a Makarov and fired at close range. Miraculously, the bullet missed the lawyer and smashed the back window on the opposite side.

Albano immediately pulled up by the sidewalk, where a group of students had witnessed the incident. Soon after, officers from the third police station showed up.

Yesterday, one of the students told *Metical*: "We were watching television when, suddenly, we heard a bang. Initially, it sounded like a tire explosion but when we looked outside the window we saw a man parking his car and he looked very worried. He left the car door open and ran to the residence asking for help. He was very worried and asked us to take him to the police station."

The same student added: "Before we went to call the police, Dr. Albano Silva asked us to go to his car and get his briefcase, which was open, and a cellphone. We did that and then called the police. After he went to the station, a team from the criminal investigation police (PIC) came by. We don't know what happened afterward."

Yesterday morning, a police official from the third police station stated that he was not authorized to talk, but he offered two facts: he confirmed the presence of the lawyer at the station around 8:45 p.m. and declared that the two policemen on duty that night were surprised how quickly two *SAVANA* reporters had made it to the area. "They appeared within three or five minutes and wanted to speak to Dr. Albano Silva himself, but he refused. Afterward they tried to photograph the car but we didn't allow it."

The two *SAVANA* reporters were journalist Paulo Machava and photographer José Mathlombe. The latter told *Metical* yesterday that "we were alerted by a witness. And what the commander is saying about us trying to take pictures is a lie because there is no way we can take photographs at night when the flash is not connected to the camera. I only showed Paulo Machava the car window of Dr. Albano Silva's car, which was broken by the bullet. This is more or less what happened."

According to another source, one of the eyewitnesses got into a car and took off in the direction of the *SAVANA* headquarters. In his opinion, this might explain the swift arrival of the reporters at the 3rd police station. [. . .]

A Little Bit of the Rest of the Iceberg

What could be behind this attempt, which took place barely three months after the lawyer suffered an odd armed robbery in Maputo? Could it be the Kapendra case, as suggested by a couple of his friends? The Mcbride case? A combination of all the difficult cases he has taken on?

The main suspicion falls on the BCM case, the famous $14 million fraud that remains unresolved. Yesterday, Albano Silva indicated to the police that he viewed the Satar brothers—Momade Assif, Ayob, and Asslam Abdul Satar (the latter currently not in the country)—owners of the currency exchange business "Unicâmbios," as the main suspects behind the attempt.

Yesterday we heard from Ayob Abdul Satar. He denied any kind of involvement. "Dr. Albano Silva is the bank's lawyer, as everybody knows. This does not mean he is our enemy. We have nothing against him. We are really sorry for what happened."

When probed about the lawyer's suspicions, Ayob retorted: "Dr. Albano Silva needs to substantiate his claims. It is not enough to say that he has suspicions. We deplore what happened. Like him, we want the truth to emerge." In response to one of our questions, he said that as of yesterday at 12:30 p.m., when the brief contact with *Metical* took place, the police hadn't contacted him.

The BCM case is explosive. In total, the investigation focuses on twenty people: the three Satar brothers, the manager of the BCM Sommerschield branch, Vicente Norotam, various Criminal Investigation Police agents, and five prosecutors (for withholding evidence and bribery), three of them from the Republic's Attorney General. Two of the investigations requested by BCM focus on the former attorney general, Sinai Nhatitima, and on the current one, António Namburete.

Last week, during the national judiciary meeting of the Public Administration, Albano Silva, who was attending as a guest, was able to talk after a brief debate on whether a guest should be able to voice his opinion. He spoke little. They cut him off, arguing that it was not in the tradition of these encounters to discuss specific cases. But he spoke enough to inform all the prosecutors that there was, in his opinion, enough evidence in the BCM case to incriminate leading figures of the Public Administration.

21
RAFAEL MARQUES

THE TALE OF A BRAVE WOMAN (2005)
from *A Capital*

INTRODUCED BY LISA MISOL
Angola

Rafael Marques de Morais of Angola considers himself both an investigative journalist and a human rights activist. His extensive body of work has helped shine an important spotlight on the problems of "blood diamonds" and oil-fueled corruption in Angola. This work has earned him international recognition and led to intense pressure and reprisals at home. Marques is also pursuing a bold legal campaign: he has filed a criminal complaint against several high-ranking Angolan generals, accusing them of crimes against humanity.

Marques has pushed boundaries since beginning his journalism career. He was forced out of his job at state-owned *Jornal de Angola* for his outspoken views and became a regular contributor to the country's new independent media. Following his July 1999 publication of an article titled "The Lipstick of Dictatorship," in which he held Angolan president José Eduardo dos Santos responsible "for the promotion of incompetence, embezzlement, and corruption as political and social values," Marques was arrested and prosecuted for criminal defamation of the president. His conviction and six-month suspended sentence in that case did not silence him.

Marques continued to publish articles criticizing the dos Santos government during and after Angola's long civil war that ended in 2002. He frequently denounced governmental corruption and mismanagement of

Rafael Marques, "The Tale of a Brave Woman," *A Capital*, July 25, 2005, 10. Translated by Rafael Marques.

Angola's vast oil revenues, which he claims have deprived the country's poor of funds to meet their urgent social needs. Marques also edited two reports, in 2002 and 2003, drawing attention to allegations of serious governmental abuses in the oil-rich enclave of Cabinda.

Marques has dedicated much of his career to work on Angola's diamond fields. In 2005 and 2006, he co-authored hard-hitting reports, based on scores of interviews, alleging that government security forces and private security companies carried out arbitrary detentions, beatings, torture, and killings in a campaign to dissuade local residents from mining illegally in private diamond concessions. Mixing journalism and activism, he used the media to draw attention to his findings domestically and internationally.

In the article featured here, Marques vividly described abuses by government and private security forces against "human beings with faces and names who get killed, tortured, maimed, or dispossessed on a daily basis in the diamond-rich region." The article names one of the security firms implicated. Importantly, Marques separately traced the ownership of several of the private security companies implicated in abuses back to senior generals in Angola's armed forces. The fact that Marques exposed and strongly criticized the generals' arrangements angered powerful players in Angola's government who had long chafed at his reporting. Over time, government pressure and surveillance became so intense that Marques was no longer able to reliably find local media outlets to feature his investigative work. In 2010, a leading weekly ceased publishing Marques's investigative reports and a company with close ties to the government purchased the newspaper. Marques switched to publishing primarily through an independent anticorruption website he founded, Maka Angola (www.makaangola.org).

In 2011, he published *Diamantes de Sangue: Corrupção e Tortura em Angola* ("Blood Diamonds: Corruption and Torture in Angola," not yet available in English) in Portugal. The book cataloged the results of more than two years of field research on brutality against informal diamond miners, including allegations of homicides, torture, and forced displacement, and exposed the web of companies allegedly implicated in the abuses.

He then filed a criminal complaint in Angola against two mining companies and a security company, as well as their representatives, including several top Angolan generals. The complaint alleges that those named have committed crimes against humanity in Angola's diamond areas. The attorney general's office refused to take the case. As before, Marques's daring was soon met with a reprisal: a 2012 criminal defamation lawsuit against him in Portugal by twelve generals. When the Portuguese court declined to pursue that case, the plaintiffs lodged a civil defamation lawsuit in Portugal against Marques and his Portuguese editor. Back in Angola, several generals and executives of the private companies named in Marques's book filed a further eleven criminal defamation lawsuits against him. Not to be outdone, the state-owned *Jornal de Angola* published a front-page article in March 2013, "Lies in Portugal," accusing Marques of supporting illegal mining and the theft of Angola's diamond wealth.

———————

LUANDA—On July 1, in the afternoon, I received an SOS from the Northeastern town of Cafunfo, in the diamond-rich Cuango Valley, via satellite. A contact person called for help claiming the police had gone on a shooting rampage against *garimpeiros* (diamond diggers). The caller said that two diggers had already been killed.

The contact person called me back after midnight in despair, but got the voice mail. A member of his own family, a woman, had been hit in the raid. Later in the day, July 2, he phoned again to request immediate assistance to evacuate Manasseja Lituaia, thirty-four, to the Angolan capital Luanda. She had also lost her child, who was strapped to her back when a bullet was fired at the child's head. The bullet passed through her son and into her own back. She was in urgent need of medical assistance.

In such a circumstance, I could only say "let's see what we can do" as I had no means to provide specific help. On July 6, as I lay the table for breakfast, Manasseja Lituaia stood by my doorstep, a slow-motion, lean, and bent frame with a wrap covering her head. She had a swollen face and a penetrating look. Wrapped around her waist, she carried all her travel possessions in a bundle.

"Before you take me to the hospital or whatever happens, I want to speak to the radio first so people may know how Vadinho [a police officer] shot me in the back and killed my son Amorzinho [Little Love]," she said before sitting down.

I felt rather strange and helpless to invite such a wounded person, who had not received proper medical care in five days, to have breakfast. As a matter of fact, she had not eaten properly for days as well. She had only a one-way ticket for the only plane that regularly flies to that area, a shabby Russian cargo. I had to buy time to figure out how best to help.

In the meantime, she explained how it happened. Several police officers, who filled up three Land Rovers, arrived at the informal mining area of Lucola, Cafunfo, besieged the area and went on confiscating dredging materials, diamonds, cash, et cetera.

By the mining area, there was an informal market where Manasseja Lituaia was selling meat and fish stocks. A police officer she identified as being an investigator at Cafunfo Police Command, named Vadinho, got out of the car with a pistol at the ready and went to question the market vendors.

"I told the police officer that we were on a survival scheme. If he wanted us out of the market, all he had to do was to tell us to leave and we would do so, but he could not threaten us, because we had done nothing wrong," said the vendor. She further explained that, in his reply, the officer "said he would kill us."

"I took my son Amorzinho from underneath my meat and fish stand, and I wrapped him in the back and walked three steps out of the place when I heard the gunshot and felt my arm go cold." As she looked back, she saw a stream of blood running from Amorzinho's head. Her son was dead.

The *garimpeiros*, as Manasseja Lituaia continued to explain, reacted immediately by throwing stones and bottles at the police officers. "Thus, the 'war' started. The police opened fire against the youth and I saw two of them falling dead. Then, the police retreated," informed the vendor.

In an act of solidarity, the *garimpeiros* immediately, according to an eyewitness, regrouped to provide a burial for the dead as the two men were not from the area and had no families around to call upon.

A Body Procession

Early in the evening, a man passing through with a vehicle transported Manasseja Lituaia along with the body of her son close to the Cafunfo Police Command. "I took my son to the police station and told them they were responsible for his fate and it was up to them to dispose of his body," she said.

In response, the police took her to the hospital to spend the night, where she did, next to her dead son. According to her account, the hospital staff refused her treatment or to take care of her dead child's body and forced her out of the hospital early in the morning.

After her release, she immediately walked back to the police station with her son's body in her arms. As she met with police resistance to address the matter, she laid down the cadaver in the station's veranda and decided to walk away. The local police commander, Caetano, then ordered his rank-and-file to prepare the body, and buy a casket for burial.

The child was buried without a single member of his close or extended family in attendance, but only police officers. He lay in a cemetery in Bairro Gika against the family's will, who wanted it to happen in their neighborhood cemetery of Bala-Bala, thus bringing up a long-standing ethnic issue. By Manasseja Lituaia's words, "the police commander said that they could not have the burial in Bala-Bala because it is 'a place full of bandits.' What he meant is that Bala-Bala is the Tchokwé predominant area while Gika is Bângala."

The local police command gave the family a total of US$500 for the wake's expenses (food and beverages).

A police officer, Machado, who at the time of the raid was also harvesting for diamonds, was locked up in jail, in case it was necessary to produce a suspect. Days later, I received the information that he had escaped jail.

By 10:30 a.m., I called Superintendent Carmo Neto, the spokesperson of the General Command of the Police (Comando Geral da Polícia Nacional—CMGPN), about the case and he promised to see me in a matter of two hours.

I explained to the victim that there was no other way but to report the case to the police, and that they would find a solution. She stressed that the police killed her son and that she would rather go to the radio to tell the story of Amorzinho.

In the Headquarters

At CMGPN, Superintendent Carmo Neto received copies of the case's briefing to ease the bureaucracy. In the following two hours, Manasseja Lituaia was on top of the police agenda. A meeting of the top brass was happening at that time, and they all came to know about her case. A number of them saw her, sitting like a bundle, next to the VIP elevator they use.

Finally, one of the top police commanders, Commissar Octávio Van-Dúnem, came personally. He gave his assurances that she would have the best care possible and her case would be handled accordingly. Immediately, a duty officer typed a formal report of the crime, upon hearing Manasseja Lituaia, and annexed the briefing.

By the time she entered the military hospital, the medical staff was readily awaiting for her. An X-ray demonstrated that the bullet had hit her and fallen. It was probably, according to the doctor, due to a loss of impact after piercing the child's head. She did not need to stay in the hospital.

Another top police officer who heads the police medical services, Dr. Dias, went to the military hospital to accompany the matter personally. Before she was released, he ordered for her to get a tetanus shot to prevent infections. He arranged for the accommodation of Manasseja Lituaia, at a police guest house, and reassured her that the high hierarchy of the police was on top of her case.

The grieving mother traveled back home, escorted by a police delegation, which now has the task to conduct an enquiry. She is waiting to be served with justice. There is no outcome to compensate her for the loss of her Amorzinho, but it might be a good starting point for the police to live up to the principle of serving and protecting the people.

Private Justice

João Baptista, thirty, a diamond digger, was tied up, thrown into the grass, and set on fire by guards of a private security company Alfa-5, on June 23, 2005, in Cajivunda, Xá-Muteba, Lunda-Norte. I could only get the pictures of his scarred body. He is still alive and one day he might be able to also tell his story, in person.

Alfa-5 could not respond on the matter as, according to the secretary, the directorship of the company is out of the country for a period of time.

Like this story, there are plenty more of human beings with faces and names who get killed, tortured, maimed, or dispossessed on a daily basis in the diamond-rich region of the Lundas. Who cares about human rights, where money, diamonds, and politicking buy or silence consciences, both in Angola and abroad?

Informal mining of diamonds is illegal. Yet the authorities, in fighting against it, must not ignore that they are dealing with human beings whose lives and dignity must be preserved.

The case of Manasseja Lituaia is a landmark because it has triggered the compassion of the police top brass, and it has motivated them to follow up the case directly.

Such compassion brought together for the first time the police and a human rights activist, usually labeled as "anti-patriot." There was a mutual understanding and gratitude for the way the issue was handled by both sides.

"After all, it is the people we all must serve, this is our duty," stated the police spokesperson, Superintendent Carmo Neto.

22

KEN SILVERSTEIN

OIL BOOM ENRICHES AFRICAN RULER (2003)

from the *Los Angeles Times*

INTRODUCED BY LISA MISOL

Equatorial Guinea

When Ken Silverstein reported in the *Los Angeles Times* in January 2003 that the oil wealth of Equatorial Guinea was stashed in a Washington, D.C., bank under the personal control of that country's president, Teodoro Obiang Nguema Mbasogo, it set off a chain reaction, leading to law enforcement investigations in at least five countries and a French arrest warrant against a sitting vice president.

It began with the mid-1990s discovery of oil in the tiny West African country of about six hundred thousand people. Huge sums began to flow from American oil companies to the Obiang government. As Silverstein noted in a 2002 piece in *The Nation* after visiting the country, the proceeds offered an opportunity to dramatically raise living standards. Instead, in a hallmark case of the "resource curse," they have entrenched and enriched an autocratic leader and the elite close to him while most of the population suffers under harsh repression and needless poverty.

Obiang, in power since 1979, is Africa's longest-serving ruler. He has claimed at least 95 percent of the vote in each of the presidential elections, all marred by serious fraud and intimidation. His ruling party and its allies control 98 percent of the country's legislative seats. There is virtually no free press. Security force abuses, including serious mistreatment of prisoners, remain a problem. Independent civil society activists and the political

Excerpt from Ken Silverstein, "Oil Boom Enriches African Ruler," *Los Angeles Times*, January 20, 2003. *Times* staff writer Warren Vieth contributed to this report.

opposition are severely constrained, frequently harassed, and vulnerable to arbitrary detention.

Obiang's record on economic and social rights is no better. More than three-quarters of Equatorial Guinea's population lived in poverty in 2006, according to an official study. While the government spends lavishly on high-profile projects, such as an $830 million resort complex built to host the June 2011 African Union summit, social needs have been a low priority. In 2013, the Obiang government revealed that about half of the population still lacked clean water or adequate sanitation facilities.

Against the backdrop of this stark discrepancy, Silverstein's *Los Angeles Times* story revealing that Obiang exercised personal control over national oil revenues exposed the risk of diversion of public funds. The U.S. investigative television program *60 Minutes* followed up in November 2003 with a story on the Riggs Bank accounts and the misuse of funds. Next, the U.S. Senate Permanent Subcommittee on Investigations launched an official inquiry, making full use of its subpoena power.

The resulting Senate report, issued in July 2004, was a blockbuster in the battle against kleptocracy. It detailed how the bank "turned a blind eye to evidence suggesting that [it] was handling the proceeds of corruption" in its dealings with President Obiang, his family, and other officials. In one example, millions of dollars of Equatorial Guinea's national oil revenues were transferred to a private offshore account in the name of a shell company that Senate investigators concluded was controlled by President Obiang. The affair led to one of the largest fines against a bank in U.S. history, for failing to report suspicious transactions involving senior officials from Equatorial Guinea (and, separately, funds controlled by Augusto Pinochet), and ultimately to the takeover of Riggs Bank.

Scrappy human rights lawyers followed the money trail to Europe, when they found indications that Equatorial Guinea's oil proceeds had paid for expensive real estate and luxury goods in France and Spain. NGOs filed legal complaints in 2007 and 2008, which in turn led to official judicial inquiries into suspected misappropriation of public funds in both countries that are ongoing at this writing. The French investigation, nicknamed the "*biens mal acquis*" (ill-gotten gains) case, encompasses the ruling families of Gabon and the Republic of Congo as well as the Obiangs.

Back in the United States, the Senate prepared a 2010 follow-up report featuring a detailed case study on Obiang's eldest son and presumed successor. Known as Teodorín, he was Equatorial Guinea's longtime forestry minister. The report described Teodorín's alleged laundering of more than $110 million in suspect funds through U.S. bank accounts between 2004 and 2008, to finance an opulent lifestyle that included a fleet of sports cars and motorcycles worth $9.5 million and a party featuring a live white tiger. The sheer ostentatiousness of Teodorín could hardly contrast more with the lives of his fellow citizens, many of them living in houses with dirt floors on unpaved roads in slums without running water or reliable electricity.

Ken Silverstein stayed on the Obiang story after moving from the *Los Angeles Times* to *Harper's Magazine*, publishing at least ten stories, including a long investigative piece in February 2011 on "the surreal playboy life of Teodorín Obiang" in *Foreign Policy* magazine. He also reported on a related issue: the global controversy over a UNESCO prize named after and sponsored by President Obiang. In September 2011, French police seized numerous high-end vehicles belonging to Teodorín from outside his Paris mansion near UNESCO's headquarters, valued at nearly $200 million. In a later raid, they also seized the eye-popping contents of the 101-room mansion itself, including King Louis XIV furnishings and works by Degas, Gauguin, Matisse, Renoir, and Rodin.

Writing in October 2011 on *Foreign Policy*'s blog, Silverstein was the first to report that the Department of Justice, which in 2007 had quietly launched a corruption and money-laundering investigation against Teodorín, was moving to seize his U.S. assets. The items sought, totaling over $70 million, include a mansion, jet, several luxury cars, and Michael Jackson memorabilia, most famously "one white crystal-covered 'Bad Tour' glove." The DOJ's legal filings in support of its case contain allegations of bribery and embezzlement on an astounding scale, some of attributed to President Obiang himself. Newly released documents indicate that Italian authorities investigated Teodorín and his father on suspicion of corruption and money-laundering. An inquiry was also opened in Brazil.

Teodorín has denied any wrongdoing through his lawyers. He has the full backing of his father, who in October 2011 named him deputy permanent delegate to UNESCO and in May 2012 appointed him second vice president (a position not envisioned in the country's constitution). Obiang's government then claimed the posts conferred diplomatic immunity from prosecution and tried to sue France for acting against Teodorín. The tactics failed. In July 2012, France issued an arrest warrant against him on money-laundering charges a few days before UNESCO awarded the prize, renamed to reduce the association with his father. A French court rejected the claim of immunity, upholding in June 2013 the arrest warrant and seizures. In July, the French authorities auctioned off Teodorín's cars, netting $3.6 million.

WASHINGTON—As vast offshore oil fields generate hundreds of millions of dollars for tiny Equatorial Guinea, there are few signs of the petroleum boom in the impoverished West African nation.

Most of the population lives on about a dollar a day, and a U.S. State Department report found "little evidence that the country's oil wealth is being devoted to the public good."

So where has the money gone?

That has been declared a "state secret" by Equatorial Guinea's ruler, Brig. Gen. Teodoro Obiang Nguema Mbasogo.

But the Guinean ambassador to the U.S. and other sources close to Obiang say the country's oil funds are held in an account at Riggs Bank in Washington.

According to several of those sources and others familiar with the account, more than $300 million of the country's energy earnings has been deposited in the account by international oil companies active in Equatorial Guinea, including ExxonMobil Corp. and Amerada Hess Corp. The money is under the direct control of Obiang, the sources say.

The arrangement has raised concerns at the International Monetary Fund, where officials have refused to provide assistance to Equatorial Guinea until Obiang accounts for his country's oil money and have urged him to transfer it to its home treasury. It has also complicated efforts by the Bush administration to improve ties with the country, which soon will become sub-Saharan Africa's third-largest oil producer after Nigeria and Angola. Critics say the administration should not embrace Obiang's regime until it improves its human rights record and implements anticorruption reforms.

Oil company payments into offshore government accounts are not illegal, and several other African energy-producing countries have similar arrangements. But they are sharply criticized by international financial institutions and anticorruption groups, because they increase the possibility for diversion of oil revenue into private bank accounts of well-placed officials.

Alejandro Evuna Owono, a top aide to Obiang, denied that the government was secretive about oil revenue. "The IMF and the World Bank know national production figures, but we can use the money as we see fit," he said. "We are an independent country and they cannot interfere with the management of those resources."

Owono would not say whether the government held its oil monies at Riggs. But Guinean Ambassador Teodoro Biyogo Nsue, who is Obiang's brother-in-law, mentioned that oil revenue was held at Riggs during a presentation on Equatorial

Guinea late last year at the Center for Strategic and International Studies in Washington, according to three people who attended.

Multiple sources, including another Guinean government official, have since told the Los Angeles Times about the Riggs account. Several sources familiar with the account said it was controlled exclusively by Obiang and its balance has ranged from $300 million to $500 million during the last two years.

An ExxonMobil spokeswoman declined to comment on payments it makes to Equatorial Guinea, citing a confidentiality agreement with the country. Amerada Hess and Riggs did not return phone calls.

The bank has provided mortgages on one of Obiang's two luxury homes in Maryland and on an official residence for Nsue in Virginia. A Riggs banker assisted Obiang's brother—accused in State Department reports of ordering the torture of political prisoners—in the purchase of a home in Virginia. The banker vouched for Obiang's brother as a "valued customer" in correspondence with the seller's agent.

Concerns about Equatorial Guinea are rooted in a history of petroleum-fueled corruption in its neighboring nations. [. . .]

"Without pressing forcefully for improvements in governance and human rights, the U.S. could end up coddling a number of oil-rich dictatorships," says Arvind Ganesan, director of the business and human rights program at Human Rights Watch.

Oil company officials have said they are obliged to accept the terms set by the governments in the countries where they operate in order to obtain exploration permits.

Obiang has ruled Equatorial Guinea since 1979, when he took power in a coup against his uncle. On Dec. 15, Obiang won 97.1% of the votes in a presidential election that was widely viewed as fraudulent.

Until the mid-1990s, Equatorial Guinea's economy seemed to be on the verge of collapse. Since then, foreign companies—led by American firms such as ExxonMobil, Marathon Oil Corp., Amerada Hess and ChevronTexaco Corp.—have discovered huge reserves in the country and invested about $5 billion in its oil sector.

Equatorial Guinea's oil production has jumped from just 17,000 barrels per day in 1996 to a current rate of more than 220,000 barrels per day.

As a result, the Bush administration has initiated a political thaw with the Obiang regime. In late 2001, President Bush authorized the reopening of the U.S. Embassy in Equatorial Guinea, which had been closed six years earlier, in large part due to the country's horrific human rights record.

There's been little if any improvement since then on that issue. A recent State

Department report said the country's security forces "committed numerous, serious human rights abuses," including torture and beatings, and that citizens "do not have the ability to change their government peacefully."

The World Bank has censured the regime for failing to account for oil revenue, which it says has had "no impact on Equatorial Guinea's dismal social indicators." [. . .]

Gavin Hayman, who tracks Equatorial Guinea for Global Witness, says Obiang "has taken advantage of a rash of secret deals with U.S. oil companies to privatize his country's oil wealth."

Oil and banking experts say Obiang's account with Riggs is uncommon, particularly if he exercises sole control over it. Standard practice for a national account would require dual control, typically exercised by the minister of finance and the head of the central bank. [. . .]

U.S. banking rules call for financial institutions to closely monitor accounts set up by foreign political leaders, which the Federal Reserve classifies as a "high-risk" activity that calls for "enhanced scrutiny." If the source of income or spending from the account raises concerns about corrupt practices, banks are required to file a Suspicious Activity Report with the Treasury Department.

The Treasury Department will not disclose whether it has received such reports on the Guinean account and Riggs is prevented by the Bank Secrecy Act from saying whether it has filed one.

Founded in 1936, Riggs has long specialized in offering discreet services to foreign governments and wealthy individuals. The Web site for the bank—which maintains offices in the Bahamas and the island of Jersey, two jurisdictions with strong bank secrecy protections—promises its wealthy clients "the utmost discretion." The site boasts that Riggs has "repeatedly demonstrated the ability to work as a financial confidant to heads of state, diplomats, business leaders and prominent individuals and families."

Riggs' reputation for discretion has attracted controversial clients in the past. They have included CIA agent turned Russian spy Aldrich H. Ames, who moved some of his payments from Moscow through a Riggs account in the early 1990s.

Equatorial Guinea's account is managed by Simon Kareri, a senior vice president and senior international banking manager at Riggs' Dupont Circle branch in Washington. Kareri handles embassy banking for Africa and the Caribbean region and also offers private banking services for wealthy individuals with a minimum of $1 million to invest.

Kareri did not return phone calls. [. . .]

Property records show that Kareri and Riggs helped with Obiang's local real estate purchases. In late 1999, the Guinean president paid $2.6 million in cash for a mansion in the Maryland suburbs that has 10 bathrooms, seven fireplaces and an indoor pool, according to the real estate listing.

Early the following year Obiang bought a second Maryland property for $1.15 million. He took out a $747,500 mortgage from Riggs on the property, and paid it off nine months later, real estate records show.

Kareri also is listed as the contact on a $349,000 Virginia townhouse purchased in 2000 by Obiang's brother, Armengol Ondo Nguema, who heads the country's security apparatus. Nguema is one of the most feared men in Equatorial Guinea.

A 1999 State Department report said that he directed security forces to urinate on prisoners, kick them in the ribs, slice their ears with knives and smear oil over their naked bodies to attract stinging ants. Five of the prisoners allegedly died. According to the State Department, one person who survived said the prisoners were beaten to death on Nguema's orders.

Kareri's signature appears on a letter vouching for Nguema's ability to pay cash for the Virginia townhouse. "We are please [sic] to confirm and certify that Mr. Armengol Ondo Nguema is a valued customer of Riggs Bank NA," says the letter to the seller's agent. "We verify that Mr. Nguema has the financial capacity and available funds with this bank to purchase the property."

A Guinean official said Obiang, who controls a private business group with large holdings in his country, used personal funds to pay for the Maryland properties. He said Guineans don't care whether Obiang leads a lavish lifestyle as long as they have food. "People don't mind if they're saying that the president's family is buying jets or something," he said. "It's a different culture."

23

LISA GIRION

PIPELINE TO JUSTICE? (2003)

from the *Los Angeles Times*

INTRODUCED BY KATIE REDFORD

Burma

In the early 1990s, two multinational oil companies—Total of France and Unocal (now Chevron) of the United States—formed a partnership with the notorious Burmese military regime. Their purpose was to exploit natural gas reserves in the Andaman Sea and build the Yadana gas pipeline across a narrow stretch of land in southern Burma (Myanmar). The pipeline contract provided that military units would act as security agents for the oil consortium's executives and foreign personnel. In carrying out its part of the deal, the Burmese army transformed a previously peaceful area into a highly militarized pipeline corridor, resulting in widespread forced labor, torture, rape, and summary executions of villagers who lived there.

Activists, shareholders, business lobbyists, and even the White House had something to say about this project, which became a lightning rod in growing debates around corporate globalization. In the legal world, Unocal and its executives became defendants in a groundbreaking legal case, *Doe v. Unocal*, which established the precedent that corporations could be held legally accountable in U.S. courts for complicity in human rights abuses. Unocal's actions in Burma were not unique. The *Doe v. Unocal* precedent was followed by other cases against companies like Shell and Chevron for their alleged complicity in killing environmentalists in Nigeria, and claims that Chiquita aided and abetted torture and killing in Colombia. But this landmark case in Burma put global corporations on notice that they could

Excerpt from Lisa Girion, "Pipeline to Justice?," *Los Angeles Times*, June 15, 2003.

be held accountable for their involvement in human rights abuses wherever they operate, sending a strong message of deterrence and forcing them to factor human rights risks into their bottom line.

I was one of the lawyers representing the John and Jane Doe plaintiffs, and I helped the journalists connect with our clients on the Burma border. Notably missing from these dramatic debates were the voices of the Burmese people themselves. Silenced in their own country, those who had the most at stake had no public forum to speak about what Unocal's pipeline meant to them. Retaliation against critics of the regime and its supporters was violent and well documented. The junta strictly controlled the press, and foreign journalists were prohibited from traveling to the pipeline region. Thus, while the oil company had a sophisticated public relations strategy and staff to ensure that their story was packaged and told, the villagers from Burma remained in hiding, out of sight and, to Unocal's benefit, out of mind.

The *Los Angeles Times*, in Unocal's hometown, stood out as the important exception. Other outlets argued that Burma was too far away, too risky, or too expensive, but *Times* staff repeatedly traveled to this remote region to bear witness and give voice to all sides.

After the case began in 1997, staff writer Evelyn Iritani visited the pipeline region, first with the companies and then to the Thai-Burma border with me. She was unable to include firsthand testimonies in her story due to a Burmese military offensive that made it too dangerous for our clients to travel to a secure meeting place. Undeterred by the risks that this experience highlighted, staff writer Lisa Girion returned to the Thai-Burma border in 2004, attempting once again to meet with the people at the center of the case, which was now heading to trial. The nature of this story required these journalists to commit significantly more time and resources than a "normal" story would require. Beginning with clandestine travel to refugee camps and war zones, the cumbersome security protocols that we demanded, and realities such as flooding or military offensives, this story required determination, patience, and time.

What Iritani began in 1997, Girion finished in 2004, finally allowing the victims and witnesses in this case—the survivors of the abuses—to have their say. Prior to Girion's two-part, front-page features, the *Doe v. Unocal* story was the story of a legal battle, a policy debate, or a case study on globalization. With the story that follows, these issues became human. By telling the stories of the individuals who were directly affected, the journalists brought the words of the Burmese victims directly to Unocal's hometown— and these words were the stories of abuse, survival, and justice.

THAILAND, NEAR THE MYANMAR BORDER—Carrying her gravely injured infant daughter, a woman emerged from the jungle and struggled to make her way to a refugee camp, where she told of their harrowing exodus from Myanmar.

They had been assaulted by soldiers searching for her husband after his escape from a crew of forced laborers. Unable to find him, the soldiers lashed out at her. An officer berated her, beat her and kicked her so hard that she and the newborn she was nursing fell into a cooking fire.

"My baby wasn't even crying anymore, she was so badly burned on her head," the woman said, recalling how she cradled the girl, just a month old, as she searched for help.

The woman blames the "project of the white people" for her misery. Her husband was among hundreds of villagers forced to work for Myanmar's Tatmawdaw, the People's Army. The army had been assigned to guard a $1.2-billion natural gas pipeline built by Unocal Corp. and a French partner through the wooded flatlands and mountain rain forests of the Tenasserim region.

Nine years later, the woman, identified in court documents only as Jane Doe 1, waits to be called as a witness in lawsuits accusing the El Segundo-based company of complicity in human rights abuses—including forced labor, murder, and rape—allegedly committed by Tatmawdaw soldiers in the country formerly known as Burma.

If Jane Doe 1 and 14 other plaintiffs succeed in forcing Unocal to defend itself in a courtroom thousands of miles from the scene of the alleged crimes, they will make history.

More than two dozen suits have been filed in U.S. courts over the last decade against U.S. corporations—including Exxon Mobil Corp., Ford Motor Co. and IBM Corp.—for alleged human rights abuses in countries from Colombia to South Africa. None has been tried.

Should the Unocal case be the first, a Los Angeles jury will face questions moral as well as legal: Can a corporation be held liable for human rights violations by a foreign government that is a business partner? How much of a hand in the abuses must the company have had to be found responsible? What if it simply turned a blind eye? [. . .]

Jane Doe 1 and other plaintiffs, living in hiding under a court-ordered cloak of anonymity, told their stories from safe houses here. The interviews were supplemented with court documents and declassified diplomatic cables. The plaintiffs' lawyers asked that the men and women not be identified by The Times for fear of retribution. [. . .]

As Jane Doe 1, a petite woman wearing a loose-fitting shirt over faded black pants, began her story in her native Karen, her big, dark eyes welled with tears. Though she and her husband were frightened, they ignored the soldiers' evacuation command. They moved instead to a nearby village, the one where she had grown up, hoping to continue to tend the cows, hens, rice paddies and cashew trees on their small farm.

They sold livestock to satisfy the soldiers' demands for money, she said, until they had nothing left. Then the soldiers took her husband, John Doe 1.

He testified that he worked on a pipeline road. The government was eager to build a line to tap an enormous natural gas field 150 feet below the surface of the Andaman Sea. The field is called Yadana, the Burmese word for treasure. [. . .]

Back at headquarters in California, at least one executive was concerned that Unocal would be relying on the Myanmar junta to provide protection for the pipeline and that the military would be "out of our control," as Stephen Lipman, then Unocal's vice president of international affairs, recounted in a deposition. [. . .]

Under U.S. and California law, participants in a business deal can be held responsible for one another's misconduct. As the plaintiffs' lawyers describe it, a bank that contracted with the Mafia to collect its debts could be held responsible should the mob get rough.

"When you enter into a partnership with the devil knowingly," said Dan Stormer, a Pasadena lawyer representing some of the plaintiffs, "there are going to be bad results." [. . .]

John Doe 8's job for the People's Army was to carry supplies—bullets, boots and rice—in a basket held in place against his back by a strap stretched across his forehead. The loaded basket weighed so much he couldn't sit or stand without help. Even during the most searing hours of the tropical afternoon, the soldiers never gave him water.

"The load was so heavy and I was so hot and thirsty that I just had to suck on my own sweat," he said from a safe house, recalling how he would stick his tongue out to catch the beads of perspiration as they dripped off his brow.

The porters cleared land and built barracks for the battalions the ruling generals sent to the Tenasserim, toiling for 10- or 15-day stretches several times a year. They had to abandon their crops, sometimes for so long that they couldn't feed their families.

One day, porter John Doe 5 remembered, a fellow laborer got sick and collapsed under the weight of the basket on his back, and a soldier kicked him and punched him "over and over," leaving him on the side of the road. John Doe 5 said he later found the man's body in the brush.

In the United States, some Unocal shareholders were growing uneasy.

The international community had long decried the brutality of the Myanmar regime and its widespread use of forced labor. At Unocal's annual meeting in the spring of 1994, there was a vote on a resolution to force Unocal to issue a report on operations in Myanmar. The resolution, opposed by management, was defeated. [. . .]

Unocal's [then-president John] Imle made no apologies for the military's conduct, especially in a country beset by ethnic insurgency.

"What I'm saying is that if you threaten the pipeline, there's gonna be more military," Imle told human rights advocates who met with him at company head-quarters in early 1995, according to a transcript of the session entered into evidence in the suits. "If forced labor goes hand in glove with the military, yes, there will be more forced labor. For every threat to the pipeline there will be a reaction."

Later, in a deposition, Imle sought to clarify his remarks. "I did not intend to agree that there was forced labor being used in connection with this project, because I'm not sure." [. . .]

Before the building of the pipeline began, according to court filings and interviews with plaintiffs, some of the forced laborers chopped trees and pulled out mus-cular roots to clear the jungle floor for infrastructure later used by Unocal and Total.

John Doe 9 testified that he was forced to lay roads leading to the pipeline construction area and help build a helipad that was used by Unocal and Total executives visiting the region. [. . .]

John Doe 7 said in an interview that one day, while he was clearing the ground for a helipad, a chopper touched down and dropped off three "Westerners," who he assumed were pipeline workers. He said he got a good look at the strangers, but they didn't see him. His overseers, he said, "knew the helicopter was coming and told us to stop work and hide in the bushes."

The companies say villagers who believe they were forced to work on pipeline-related projects must be confused. [. . .]

As Jane Doe 1 searched for medical assistance, she said, she, her baby and her older daughter were caught twice by soldiers, who robbed them and forced them to sleep outside in the cold. When they reached the border camp about two weeks after the assault, doctors told Jane Doe 1 that her baby had a broken back and had been bleeding internally for some time. "They said there was no hope."

She held Baby Doe in her arms for two days, comforting her until she died.

"The project of the white people turned our life upside down," Jane Doe 1 said. "We believe they are responsible for that." [. . .]

Executives from Unocal and Total take pride in their efforts to improve the lives of thousands of villagers in Myanmar.

The companies have spent about $1 million a year to help build schools, medical clinics, a pig farm and other facilities. They hired and trained teachers and midwives. And they brought the first doctors to the area to treat malaria victims, inoculate children and perform emergency caesarean sections.

Some of the companies' efforts to reach out to locals, however, are being used against them in court.

Total, for instance, paid porters engaged by the military. It also gave them food as well as physical exams, according to an embassy cable. John Doe 8, for one, said a doctor brought in by Total once handed him 600 kyat, the equivalent of about $10.

Though Unocal and Total paint such acts as gestures of goodwill, the plaintiffs portray them as evidence that the companies were in league with the Tatmawdaw.

In February 1996, Herve Chagnoux, then Total's regional coordinator, captured what he saw as the ambiguity. When it came to the military's use of conscripted labor, he wrote to Unocal, "let us admit between Unocal and Total that we might be in a gray zone."

Others believe that the situation was more black-and-white.

John Haseman, a former military attache at the U.S. Embassy in Yangon who worked as a consultant to Unocal, told the company in December 1995 that there was no doubt "egregious human rights violations have occurred and are occurring now" in the Tenasserim.

In a letter, Haseman said that Unocal's reputation had been harmed when one of its spokesmen was quoted as saying the company was satisfied with the Myanmar military's assurances that human rights weren't being abused in the pipeline region.

That, Haseman wrote, made Unocal appear "at best naive and at worst a willing partner in the situation."

The Unocal lawsuits were filed in 1996. Jane Doe 1 and her family live on the food her husband receives in exchange for odd jobs, often no more than a tin or two of rice a day.

Before fleeing to Thailand, "I had my own farm, my rice fields, my kettles, my house," she said, as she fed her youngest, a daughter born last year, a bottle of sugar water.

"We never had hunger. We had extra food. Now I live on nothing. We used to own our land, and they took it away. They made a big hole in our lives."

24

TATIANA ESCÁRRAGA

VILLAGES SWALLOWED BY COAL (2013)

from *El Tiempo*

INTRODUCED BY AVIVA CHOMSKY

Colombia

Journalism is a dangerous profession in Colombia. Over a hundred journalists have been murdered in the past several decades, and many more subjected to harassment and death threats. Their enemies are in the illegal armed groups and the drug cartels, but also among the political and economic sectors whose interests journalists might challenge with their reporting. In 2006 what came to be known as the "para-politics" scandal came to light, with over a hundred government officials, including many close to then-president Alvaro Uribe, being accused of ties to the right-wing paramilitaries. Dozens have been convicted. Despite—or because of—the danger, Colombian journalists play a crucial role in making society aware of both the abuses and the social movements protesting them.

Colombia's important mining and energy sector, with petroleum and coal among the country's top exports, has also been an epicenter of violence. Official and extralegal groups vie for their share of its lucrative profits. A study by a mining union leader found that the incidence of violence in the country correlated strongly with the discovery and exploitation of mining and energy resources.

To report on abuses carried out by the mining sector is to challenge both the country's entrenched economic and political interests, and also those of illegal armed groups. Still, courageous journalists like Tatiana

Excerpt from Tatiana Escárraga, "Villages Swallowed by Coal," *El Tiempo* (Colombia), June 22, 2013. Translated by Aviva Chomsky and Nicolo Gnecchi-Ruscone.

Escárraga are investigating the social and environmental impact of mining. Escárraga is a young Colombian journalist who has published on a variety of topics. For several years she lived in Spain writing for *El País*, the major Spanish daily.

This article was published in *El Tiempo*, one of Colombia's oldest and largest-circulation daily newspapers. Founded in 1911, the paper has passed through several different owners; from 2007 to 2012, the Spanish publisher Grupo Editorial Planeta took majority ownership. For many years it was affiliated with the mainstream Liberal Party, and with the powerful Santos family that includes a former vice president and the current (since 2010) president, Juan Manuel Santos. Like other mainstream papers, though, it occasionally publishes investigative reports that challenge even the interests of its owners.

Many of Colombia's mines are located in remote areas of the country, so their social and environmental effects remain out of sight to Colombia's growing urban middle class. Coal mining began in the 1980s in Colombia's two most northeastern departments, La Guajira and Cesar, on the Venezuelan border, an area sometimes referred to as Colombia's "wild west."

Until late in the nineteenth century, this region remained largely outside of state control. The population consisted mainly of autonomous indigenous groups—in particular the Wayuu, the largest indigenous grouping in Colombia—and free blacks and mixed-race peoples. The area became a haven for runaway slaves, who founded independent communities there. Even through the twentieth century the national state barely established a presence outside of some of the major cities. Left-wing guerrillas took advantage of the remoteness, while right-wing paramilitaries served the interests of ranchers and businesses and, increasingly, multinational mining companies.

For Latin America, the turn of the twenty-first century in many ways recapitulated the turn of the twentieth. As the nineteenth century drew to a close, governments known as "liberal dictatorships" eagerly sought foreign loans and investment to build new extractive and export economies in the wake of independence. Rural peoples lost their land to the spread of new plantation agriculture, as coffee, bananas, and rubber fed growing demand in the industrializing North, while new industrial minerals like copper and tin, and fossil fuels like oil and coal, fed the insatiable industries. The export model was later criticized as "dependent development"—a kind of economic development that made Latin America's economies dependent on the Global North, and distorted economies to serve the interests of the few and the privileged.

The neoliberal turn in the late twentieth century revived many of these free-trade ideas. Free markets and free trade would reign as governments cut back on social welfare programs and safety nets. State-run industries were privatized and the private sector deregulated as foreign investment was welcomed.

The tide shifted again as twenty-first-century socialist movements and governments challenged the neoliberal model and tried to create more activist, redistributive social welfare states. While still relying on extractivism to fund their socialist policies, they imposed greater controls on investors and increased the state role in the sector. Nevertheless, skyrocketing demand for agricultural products, minerals, and fossil fuels both in the Global North and in new manufacturing and consumption centers like China made it extremely difficult for Latin Americans to imagine a future beyond the export of these primary resources.

Colombia was probably the South American country most wedded to neoliberalism and most resistant to the tilt to the left that swept Latin America at the end of the 1990s. It was one of only three South American countries to pursue a free trade agreement with the United States (finally implemented in 2012). Presidents Álvaro Uribe Vélez (2002–10) and Juan Manuel Santos (2010–present) actively encouraged foreign investment in mining, with Santos calling the mining-energy sector the "locomotive" of Colombia's economy.

Many elite and middle-class Colombians, to say nothing of consumers in the United States and Europe who benefit from Colombia's coal and other mining and energy exports, would rather not know what's happening in the areas like La Guajira and Cesar that have been turned into sacrifice zones. The writing of Tatiana Escárraga brings the voices of the victims to the forefront and makes it clear that they will not be silenced.

Villagers went crazy with joy when they heard the news. It was 1995, remembers Flower Arias, a sturdy, dark-skinned man. People came out of their houses to celebrate the event: the U.S. mining multinational Drummond was coming. They thought that the huge mining company would bring development to their poverty-stricken region. The first settlers had been black slave rebels who had chosen this area to begin a new life far from the nightmare of the slave regime.

"We even had fireworks," recounts Flower on this hot May evening. Not a leaf stirs in Boquerón, a village of approximately one thousand inhabitants in the municipality of La Jagua de Ibirico, in the middle of the department of Cesar. [. . .]

"What we didn't expect was that it would end up expelling us from our land . . ."

Along with the villages of Plan Bonito and El Hatillo, Boquerón sits atop the thirty-kilometer coal belt between La Jagua and La Loma that is now home to five coal mines run by three companies: Calenturitas (Prodeco), Descanso Norte and Pribbenow (Drummond), and El Hatillo and La Francia (Colombian Natural Resources [CNR]).

Huge dumps line the road, mountains of refuse left by the coal operations. Particle emissions are so high that breathing the air has become dangerous to the health and survival of the surrounding communities. In 2010 the Ministry of Environment ordered the three companies to relocate the villages of Boquerón, El Hatillo, and Plan Bonito. Together, these towns are home to some two thousand people. This complex and traumatic process is without precedent in Colombia. This is the first time that a resettlement (actually, a forced displacement) has been ordered because of the critical environmental conditions created by mining. Coal has literally swallowed the towns.

Air quality studies in the region are sobering. In 2010 El Hatillo had PM10 (particles of 10 micrometers or less) levels of 60 micrograms per cubic meter, and up to 87 during the dry season. The situation was even worse in Plan Bonito: 177 micrograms per cubic meter.

These tiny particles, measuring less than a hairsbreadth, have dire consequences for human health. Long-term exposure to high concentrations of PM10 is associated with an increase in lung cancer, premature death, severe respiratory symptoms, and reduced lung function.

"In Colombia people don't realize the impact of mining. The situation here is apocalyptic," says Mauricio Cabrera Leal, a government geologist and environmental analyst.

For each ton of coal that is extracted, ten tons of waste are created. Between 1990 and 2011 the departments of La Guajira and Cesar exported at least 1 billion tons of coal. The result? Some 10 billion tons of potentially toxic waste rock and mine tailings.

"There is no legislation governing the management of mine wastes. There is no obligation to reclaim the affected areas," Cabrera explained. In the long run, betting on mining will have serious consequences for Colombia. [. . .]

Coal is not the only thing that hangs like a curse over these villages in Cesar. Residents there have also been cursed by the presence of guerrilla and paramilitary groups, as well as by successive administrations that have diverted the economic benefits brought by the mining activity.

When the topic of royalties comes up, residents of Boquerón, Plan Bonito, and El Hatillo look the other way. "Coal has only brought us misery," they say. [. . .] Last February, residents of El Hatillo declared a food emergency. A UN commission that visited the area found that 17 percent of the families in the three villages had no means of subsistence. The companies won't offer them work. Forty-six percent of households were receiving nutritional assistance; 15 percent depended on charity to survive. The median family income was $250.74 pesos [about US$130] and daily meals consist of flour, sugars, and oil, with little nutritional content.

Another study carried out by the Cesar Health Ministry found that 50 percent of El Hatillo's population suffered from respiratory problems, apparently due to pollution. The water was found to be unfit for human consumption. (Recently, the county government of El Paso provided a water treatment plant.)

"We never imagined this kind of outcome. The worst thing is that we don't know what's next. This displacement brings us infinite sadness," says Flower Arias, with heaviness in his voice. The only thing to be heard here is sadness. [. . .] "My soul aches, but I have to leave Plan Bonito to survive," explains Orphanor Imbré, forty two, who says he suffers from complications of a spinal hernia since working in the Calenturitas mine. Now he makes his living selling avocados.

The residents of Plan Bonito, where Imbré lives, got tired of waiting. A failed resettlement a few years ago has led them to give up. [. . .] The sense of defeat was such that every one of the eighty-six families identified in the census (363 people) decided to negotiate an individual settlement (the amount of which is still unknown), and will leave on their own, going wherever they can find a home.

The case of Plan Bonito (the name, "Beautiful Plan," sounds ironic now), "is not ideal," according to Renato Urresta and Mauricio Díaz, manager and project co-director for Replan, the Canadian company contracted by the multinationals to carry out the resettlements since the 2010 ruling. Normally, they explain, communities are relocated collectively, preserving their social fabric, so that they can grieve and receive psychological assistance after suffering this kind of trauma. "We know from experience that many families are not used to handling large sums of money and they can end up in worse conditions," they warn.

Logically, a resettlement should be carried out before the mines begin operating. Not after, when the damage has been done. [. . .] After the preliminary settlements are agreed upon comes the more difficult stage: the search for the promised land that, in theory, should be nearby and fertile, that is, not contaminated. Given the mining map of Cesar, this is a tall order. Once the resettlement is carried out, the company will offer accompaniment for no more than three years.

Meanwhile, uncertainty reigns in Boquerón. "We don't have the alternative of saying 'I'm not leaving.' Our only option is 'they are kicking me out.' How can we survive our uprooting? What will remain of our village? Our traditions? Our beliefs? What will happen to our cemetery?" Lesvi Rivera wonders, dismayed.

Of the three companies, only Drummond was willing to offer comments on the process. The company declared that none of the three communities was in its area of operations and that it was therefore challenging its legal responsibility, though it "would not interfere with the resettlement."

THE ENVIRONMENT AND
NATURAL DISASTERS

25

DESTRUCTION OF THE CITY OF SAN JUAN PROVOKES UNANIMOUS DISMAY (1944)

from *La Prensa*

INTRODUCED BY ERNESTO SEMÁN

Argentina

At eleven minutes to nine on the night of January 15, 1944, a 7.4 earthquake shattered the city of San Juan, the capital of the province of San Juan on the west side of Argentina. In less than a minute, the city was reduced to rubble. The earthquake left around ten thousand dead and half the province homeless. It was the worst natural disaster in national history, but it was also a watershed in Argentina's political history. It was in the immediate aftermath of the earthquake, while aftershocks continued to shatter the province, that an obscure member of the national military government, Colonel Juan Perón, came to the fore. Perón launched a campaign of solidarity with the victims, setting in motion one of the most powerful political movements in the Western Hemisphere.

The article published in *La Prensa* is a typical example of how journalism functioned in the 1940s. There is no byline to this piece. With communications totally destroyed, the article was most likely made up of direct reports gathered by journalists and then sent from the neighboring province of Mendoza. In Buenos Aires, editors mixed vivid testimonies from witnesses of the tragedy with official information from the government. With its almost absurd juxtapositions, the piece encapsulates the chasm between journalists reporting on the ground, aware of the magnitude of the tragedy,

Excerpt from "Destruction of the City of San Juan Provokes Unanimous Dismay," *La Prensa*, January 17, 1944. Translated by Nicolo Gnecchi-Ruscone.

and those mimicking the government's jargon of indifference, unaware of the changes ahead.

Perón traveled by train to the province and, unlike any other official or political leader, he mingled with the victims, spoke their language, felt their pain, offered them immediate solutions for their urgent needs and a vision of what had to change. It was the first time that the notion of a national government's political or moral obligation to the poor and to victims of a natural disaster became evident. It was at a festival organized in support of victims of the San Juan earthquake that the young actress Eva Duarte met the rising colonel, creating a synergy that changed the Argentine working class and continues to inspire it today.

From a contemporary perspective, it's almost uncanny to read the reports of Perón's actions in the immediate hours after the earthquake. These reports gave no sign of the importance that they would acquire. It was the last time that it happened: Perón's journey by train to San Juan was widely covered by the national media. A few weeks later, the news about the festival in which he met Evita already overshadowed the actions of President Ramirez. By the end of the year Perón was the undisputed leader of the emerging working classes in Argentina. As vice president, secretary of labor and welfare, and secretary of war, he was also the most powerful one, powerful enough to order the closing of *La Prensa* as it stressed its opposition to his political project.

Until the recent release of *The Ruins of the New Argentina* by historian Mark Healey, the connection between the San Juan earthquake and Perón's rise had been recognized but not analyzed. The city's destruction was not entirely caused by nature: the vast majority of the buildings destroyed were made of adobe, a material used by the poor population of this prosperous province. Perón's rapid reaction to the disaster not only set him apart from the rest of the regime, it was also an indictment of the old regime and the elites that had prospered immensely on the basis of a fragile economy and an unequal society. However, with time, the reconstruction of San Juan also revealed the limits of that indictment: the conflicts that tamed the dreams of modernization also converted the city into something notoriously less egalitarian than Perón had promised, though substantially better than before the earthquake. It is probably this contradictory legacy that turned the earthquake into an uncomfortable memory.

The reports of that day extensively chronicled the magnitude of the tragedy, the damage that it caused, and the precarious infrastructure unveiled by the devastation. With very different approaches, the national media (and that of Chile, the neighbor country across the Andes) offered wide coverage of the earthquake. Yet as time passed, the attention to the episode waned. And as important as it was for the foundation of Peronism, its leader's attention to the urban working classes and to the project of national industrialization he embraced left behind the centrality of that remote episode as well as the notorious limitation of the city's reconstruction.

Articles like this one act as a chronicle of things forgotten, stubbornly fixed in its time and space and characters and rubble, unmoved by the epic built upon the tragedy, or by later attempts to erase earthquake and epic from the face of the earth.

A sensation of spinning tragedy survives these moments in the capital of the province. Blocks of desolation and ruin can be observed everywhere and the collective pain is most felt in observing the spectacle of the shapeless mass of rubble accumulated where yesterday used to exist a progressive and highly developed city.

Nearly 90 percent of the houses and buildings were no more than sad ruins; the roads covered in rubble; the water supply dysfunctional; the squares filled with people; groups of neighbors running about attempting in vain to find their loved ones; others in pain and anguish, giving help to wounded family members or watching over their dead relatives. Uncertainty was everywhere.

The federal government and their secretaries, just like the military officials who are helping the authorities in emergency tasks for the victims, installed themselves last night in the plaza 25 of May, from where they deliver their orders.

One of the most dramatic aspects of this terrible tragedy consists of, without doubt, the wakes that appear on the streets and in the city's neighborhoods [. . .] the remains are put onto big tables or improvised coffins, in front of which lamps are lit as women, men, and children gather in circles to pray.

When the disaster occurred there was a wedding taking place in the church of the Merced. There were many invited to the ceremony, and when the priest was about to consecrate the wedding, the tremors began and the church collapsed in the midst of screams of horror, covering in rubble all the people in the aisles.

From the first moments of the morning they began setting up tents in the city's squares and parks to accommodate the hundreds of families who have been left without homes. It is believed that in one moment or another the authorities will order a total evacuation of the capital.

The morgue of the Rawson Hospital had soon run out of sufficient space and bodies began to be deposited in the hospital gardens, one next to the other, for the bereaved to reclaim their dead. As they sat all day under the sun, the majority had already begun to decompose. Even the cemetery had run out of space. The bodies accumulate in the gardens and to top it all off, many cracks have appeared as a consequence of the earthquake, the consequences you can imagine . . .

Late that night we made our way to the Rawson Hospital. Weaving between obstacles, rubble, and corpses, we reached the hospital as dawn began to break to witness the caravan of injured still arriving. All the rooms showed cracks on the walls and the garden had been converted into outdoor clinics, covered with the wounded. Doctors were performing all sorts of emergency operations and under the trees, lit by kerosene lamps, they had improvised an operation table. [. . .]

The plazas of 25 of May and Trinidad are packed to the brim with people who rest or sleep. In the City Hotel, we received the first of a series of lurid testimonies of the moment the seismic tragedy struck. A traveler told us:

"Yesterday, the hour the earthquake struck, I was in my hotel room. When it started to shake, I heard anguished screams from two ladies who occupied the opposite room, and when I came out into the corridor, I met one of them. She was so scared that she could not do nothing but cry, begging me to rescue her friend. In that moment, the force of the tremor was intensifying and you could only hear more screams . . . when the tremor subsided, I ran into the other room to look for the lady's friend. She was not there. A moment later we found out that in blind desperation she had run out onto the balcony, which is on the second floor. A little later we found her dead on the street."

Emptying the streets of corpses has been one of the more difficult problems for the authorities. In the early hours of the morning, they had resorted to burying remains in the municipal cemetery but they still needed proof of identity for each body. They had also predicted obtaining a considerable number of coffins for the same ends, but eventually procedures came to a halt due to the overwhelming mass of bodies. The authorities, with the accord of the local chief, resorted to cremation of the bodies, which was carried out in the very same cemetery. [. . .]

His Excellency the President of the Nation, General Don Pedro Pablo Ramirez, who since the very first news of the earthquake has kept permanently informed, has resolved before the gravity of the circumstances to appear in the affected areas to get a personal impression of the disaster and view the efficiency of the actions taken. The train in which the premier will travel will include two carriages of medicines, aid, and other necessary help for the rescue of the victims.

A collection has been organized for the victims of the earthquake. The secretary of labor and welfare, Colonel Juan D. Perón, in the name of the first magistrate, in a speech presented on air on the LRA state-owned radio, assured the success of the collection which has been officially requested to help the victims of the San Juan catastrophe.

26

QIAN GANG

ABOUT MYSELF AND MY TANGSHAN (1986)

from *The Great China Earthquake*

INTRODUCED BY YING CHAN

China

At 3:12 a.m. on July 28, 1976, a magnitude 7.8 earthquake leveled Tangshan, an industrial city of one million people in northeastern China. Among the People's Liberation Army soldiers dispatched to help in the rescue effort was Qian Gang, then a twenty-two-year-old based in Shanghai with the "cultural work team," an elite PLA propaganda unit.

For weeks, the team dug through mountains of debris, pulling the living and the dead from the ruins while struggling to attend to the survivors. With an instinctive interest in the men and women on the street, Qian talked to the survivors extensively. He also bonded with dozens of children orphaned by the earthquake as he escorted them to a neighboring province to meet their adopted families.

The earthquake came at the tail end of the Cultural Revolution, and the details of the tragedy were kept secret by Communist Party officials. But after China began to open up in 1978, facts and figures began to filter out, and Qian began collecting them. He made regular trips to Tangshan, then being rebuilt, to interview the survivors and eyewitnesses. He also began studying the science and the history of earthquakes, focusing on government policies on early warning systems.

The result, in 1986, was *The Great China Earthquake*, Qian's book that

Excerpt from Qian Gang, "About Myself and My Tangshan," *The Great China Earthquake*, trans. Nicola Ellis and Cathy Silber (Beijing: Foreign Languages Press, 1989), 6–14.

has since been hailed as a seminal work of nonfiction reportage and a modern classic in disaster reporting.

Qian was born in Hangzhou, in central China, and joined the People's Liberation Amy in 1969 at age fifteen. Communist Party control over the economy then was absolute, and military service was a career choice typical of teenagers from poor Chinese families. But Qian's real passion was words.

No one wrote about the devastation of the earthquake at the time it happened. In those days of absolute ideological purity, the party-run newspapers were filled with tales of heroism and praise for the party leaders for directing the rescue, but the number of casualties and the scale of the destruction were considered a state secret.

Mao Tse-tung died in September 1976, less than two months after the quake, bringing the ten-year chaos of the Cultural Revolution to a close. Three years later, the state news agency, Xinhua, reported for the first time that more than 240,000 people had perished in the quake and 160,000 had been injured. Xinhua made the revelation in an innocuous story on the occasion of the founding of the Chinese Earthquake Studies Organization, but the impact was profound: the Tangshan quake had been revealed as the deadliest of the century.

Still, most of the details of the disaster and its aftermath were kept from the public.

Qian, by this time an aspiring writer, had been quietly taking note of the dribs and drabs of information that were being released. He was also gaining confidence in his own reporting and writing skills after having served as an embedded reporter in the Sino-Vietnamese border war of 1979.

The year coincided with the launch of Deng Xiaoping's policy of "reform and open up," which ushered in market reforms that would lead to monumental changes in China. By the early 1980s, change had spread to the news media. At the PLA daily, master writers who had honed their skills in the pre-communist era were "rehabilitated" from the countryside, where they had been condemned during the Maoist years to hard labor. Studying under these veterans, Qian developed an appetite for the books trickling in from the West, in particular nonfiction writing and reportage by legendary reporters. One of his favorites was *Hiroshima* by John Hersey, who became his literary hero.

In 1984, Qian enrolled in the Literature Department of the PLA Arts College and began contemplating writing on the Tangshan earthquake. He began his visits to Tangshan to interview people who had lived through the quake, while continuing with his scientific studies.

In March 1986, he published a book-length article, "The Great Earthquake," in *PLA Literature*, the military's monthly magazine. The special issue became an instant sensation as the story of the devastation was told to the public for the first time. The article described the sudden deaths, the desperate search for loved ones, and the hardships of the rescue. It documented the heart-wrenching scenes in the mental hospitals, the jails, the shelters for the blind, and the hotels where expatriates congregated. Qian's poignant reporting brought readers back to that summer night ten years earlier and sparked emotional and heated discussions. A historic news event that had been buried by party dogma had finally been exposed to the light.

The Great China Earthquake, which was soon published as a separate book, is not only an intimate portrayal of how Tangshan's people coped with the monstrous destructive power of mother nature, it also serves as a window into the lives and times of Chinese society on the eve of China's opening up to the world.

The book won China's National Award for Literary Journalism, and has been translated into English, Japanese, and Korean. Excerpts have been translated into French. The book's introduction, "My Tangshan and I," from which the following excerpt was taken, became required reading for students in Hong Kong: from 1988 to 2011, all high school students in the city were required to write a book report on *The Great China Earthquake* before graduating.

Qian was forced to quit the PLA in 1989 for committing the crime of visiting the student protesters in Tiananmen Square. He went on to become a documentary filmmaker, an executive producer of an acclaimed investigative journalism program on China Central Television, and the managing editor of *Southern Weekend*, one of China's most respectable—and one of its most aggressive—market-oriented newspapers. After being pushed out of the paper for stepping on too many Communist Party toes, Qian joined the Journalism and Media Studies Centre at the University of Hong Kong in 2003 to conduct research on China's news media. He has continued to write while keeping up his study of the science of earthquakes. He divides his time between Shanghai and Hong Kong, and visits Tangshan and its people often.

The people of Tangshan will never forget. These years, every July 28 at dawn, human figures sway on the streets of Tangshan. In mournful, solitary silence tiny clusters of tongues of dull red flame flicker. Pair after pair of sad eyes shine in the firelight—eyes of the old, eyes of the middle-aged, and in their hands, the mock paper money burned to the dead—"to my son," "to my daughter," "to my parents."

In the first rays of the morning sun, the pale yellow paper becomes smoke whose wisps gradually form a layer like a white fog, floating among the new buildings. The ashes drifting in the fog are magical black butterflies in the eyes of children, soaring so high, slowly sifting down. [. . .]

I have walked those streets of floating ash many times. I know that those who died in the Tangshan earthquake don't have graves; the intersections below tall buildings, the old, narrow alleys, the hills newly formed after the earthquake, even sites of new factories just mapped out, are all unmarked graves. Ten years ago, in these very places, people were felled by house beams, crushed by floorslabs, smothered alive by rubble and falling earth. Ten years later, the ruins are gone. But I can make everything out. [. . .]

The Tangshan earthquake is the most tragic page in the over-four-hundred-year history of world earthquakes. The book *Tremors of the Earth*, published by the China Earthquake Publishing House, presents this dire fact to all mankind:

Killed 242,769
Seriously Injured 164,851

[. . .] What do these figures signify? Simply that the number of people killed in the Tangshan earthquake is 2.4 times that of the Tokyo earthquake that stunned the world, 3.5 times that of the earthquake in Chile, and over 1,300 times that of the Alaska earthquake.

But even more important are the tragic fates of the people behind the figures. [. . .]

Not long ago, I interviewed a Tangshan woman in her home. She brought out fruit and candy, and, to be polite, I asked her to join me. She shook her head repeatedly. "No," she said. "No. Ever since that earthquake I haven't eaten anything sweet." She told me that she had been buried in the ruins for two days and two nights. The first thing she was given to eat upon her rescue was a jar of glucose. Ever since, anything sweet provokes a violent conditioned response in her. Apples, oranges, Lantern Festival dumplings, New Year's cake, even a child's chocolate—they all bring back the feelings of a thirst that nearly drove her mad in the wreckage ten years ago. "I can't touch sweet things. I can't stand them!" It's been ten years, but the bitterness has never left her, never.

[. . .] [A] middle-aged teacher, in a voice perfectly calm, though through the calm seeps an inexpressible grief, says, "I haven't thought about those painful things for years. I've forgotten. I've forgotten them all." Has he really forgotten? That year, he dug through the rubble for a whole day trying to save his wife. Finally a huge fire forced him to give up. He told me that his wife had burned alive in the ruins, and he had passed out on the spot. How could he forget it? It was a terrible fire. While gathering material for this story, I had someone roll up his sleeve and show me a scar on his arm. He said that his relatives burned in the fire, and that the scar was branded on by the boiling-hot oils of human flesh. [. . .]

One by one, 240,000 people have felt like this.

This trip to Tangshan I stayed at the No. 255 Army Hospital; 400 of the 1,200 people there were killed in the earthquake. There's a small mourning chapel at the hospital where the ashes of some of them are kept. My chest tightens whenever I enter that dimly lit room. Pair after pair of living eyes look out at me from the photographs of the cinerary boxes. [. . .]

There is a small mountain outside the mourning hall. It's the pile they made, when clearing out the rubble after the earthquake, of the broken walls and bricks and tiles of the whole hospital. On this "mountain" there are stone steps, a pavilion, and playing children—those born after the earthquake. Reinforcing rods bent ten years ago and corroded with rust, twisted pipers, and heating ducts stick out in spots through cracks in the rock. [. . .]

It seems this is the first time I've looked at my people, my nation, my planet from the disaster angle. It's cruel; it's also completely new. A disaster so shocking, so grievous—such massive death and suffering—I can't begin to think about it in normal terms. Those things so beautiful they hurt, those things so tender they break your heart, those things so hard they make you tremble, those things so small and feeble you cannot help stepping forward to the rescue—they're all part of being human.

This is my Tangshan.

In 1985, I spent the Spring Festival in Tangshan. On New Year's Eve, the firecrackers began first thing in the morning. In the afternoon they grew ever louder until, by dusk, there were so many you couldn't tell one from another—the whole sky shone red. [. . .]

Lu Guilan, a woman who had been buried in the wreckage for thirteen days, and whom I had interviewed ten years ago, invited me to her home to wrap dumplings. Old and all alone after having lost both husband and daughter in the earthquake, she practically considers me her only relative. It hurt to hear her call me "my child." When I stood up to go, I found my handbag suddenly heavier. She had filled it with jujubes.

I walked along the streets of Tangshan with my heavy bag. Broken firecrackers littered the ground; the air was filled with the smell of gun powder. [. . .]

27

LIU JIANQIANG AND CHENG GONG

TIGER LEAPING GORGE UNDER THREAT (2004)

from *Southern Weekend*

INTRODUCED BY ROBERT BARNETT

China

One day in early September 2004, the journalist Liu Jianqiang received a phone call from a colleague: would he be willing to go to Yunnan in southwest China to investigate a plan to build a hydroelectric dam across Tiger Leaping Gorge, one of China's most famous scenic spots? Liu, already well established as an investigative reporter, had just finished his first environmental story, an exposé of sedimentation at China's largest hydropower project, the Three Gorges Dam. During his research, he had seen other cases where hydropower companies had concealed or manipulated information to get dams built, often with tragic consequences for local people.

Liu set out with a colleague, Cheng Gong, to investigate the story and three weeks later their paper, *Southern Weekend*, published their report. A copy reached the office of China's premier, Wen Jiabao, and a few days later Wen ordered the dam building to be halted. It was an important milestone for environmentalists in China.

Like most journalists in China, Liu had begun his career writing articles saying that a party leader "went to a place" and "had a very important speech," as he put it in a 2006 interview with the *Wall Street Journal*. He changed his career path by taking a graduate course in journalism at Tsinghua, one of China's top universities, which included four months of study in

---

Excerpt from Liu Jianqiang and Cheng Gong, "Tiger Leaping Gorge Under Threat," *Southern Weekend*, September 29, 2004. Translated by Dong Han.

Hong Kong. By the time he graduated in 2003, "my whole world changed: I learned what real news was."

Liu secured a full-time job at *Southern Weekend*, which ten years earlier had become one of the first papers in China to rely on its sales revenue, generated mainly by its investigative stories. These had to focus on issues that the government considered appropriate for what it called "supervision by public opinion," and had to limit its targets to local-level officials and companies in areas remote from the newspaper's offices. Liu's initial reports covered the spread of AIDS through blood sales, the social problems forcing women into prostitution, the cover-up of a fatal accident by a wealthy BMW driver, and the murder by a provincial-level official of his wife. The last one, written by Liu in the summer of 2005, was banned from publication by the central authorities: by that time, restrictions on cross-regional investigations were again increasing.

Liu had focused till then on cases of corruption, which he saw as doing little to improve society. "Maybe the official was fired," he wrote, "but it didn't change anything because you'd just find another." But environmental issues were "another story because I thought, 'I can change something.' " Preventing environmental damage was part of the government's agenda, and carefully worded exposés of environmental abuse were less likely to be censored.

By this time, environmentalists in China were increasingly concerned about hydropower construction. China had by then some 45,000 large dams—half the world's total—and 22.9 million people were relocated in China from 1949 to 2007 to make way for water projects, often leading to impoverishment. But one year earlier a coalition of environmentalists, NGOs, and journalists in China had scored a major victory by persuading the government to suspend a hydropower project on the Nu river (the Salween). In the nearby Tiger Leaping Gorge project, Liu and Cheng quickly discovered a legal flaw: construction work had begun before formal permission had been granted by Beijing. It was this that led the premier to halt the project. But such achievements are short-lived—the hydropower sector, which stands to make huge profits from these dams, was able to get the Nu River project restarted in 2013, and Liu expects the same to happen with Tiger Leaping Gorge.

He regards the Tiger Leaping Gorge campaign as important for a different reason: it was one of the first instances where "China's newly emerging social forces—commercial media, NGOs, and the Internet"—were able to mobilize the local community in the affected area. While researching their article and in follow-up visits afterward, Liu and Cheng had worked closely with local environmentalists in discussions with local villagers, most of whom had no idea they were due to lose their homes. One of them, a retired village teacher called Ge Quanxiao, became a de facto leader in the movement. Two years after the article came out, when rumors spread that work on the dam was about to be restarted, ten thousand villagers staged a two-day siege of the local government headquarters. Ge was able to negotiate a promise from the government not to build the dam and to persuade protestors to avoid violence, ensuring that government officials had to take note of local opinion.

Liu regards the Tiger Leaping Gorge campaign as having demonstrated the journalist's primary role: "to give local people information, to tell them what is going on, what kind of danger they are in, that they have rights." The campaigns to stop the other twenty-four dams on the Jinsha River failed, he argues, because the media and NGOs lacked depth—they "didn't have the force of local people power." A social movement, he wrote, "is like a tree root, reaching deep into the soil. The deeper it goes, the taller and stronger the tree grows." Liu's approach proved too strong even for *Southern Weekend*, which sacked him in 2006, officially because of his interview with the *Wall Street Journal*. He now works as the editor of chinadialogue .net, a leading environmental NGO in Beijing, where he continues the kind of engaged journalism that he pioneered in the effort to help China's environmental movement develop stronger roots.

The Fate of a Natural Wonder

The Tiger Leaping Gorge, one of the most spectacular natural wonders in the world, is today becoming a place to mourn for, since a water conservancy project is going to be constructed there and, as a result, the gorge will disappear forever. [. . .]

According to the design plan report, the Tiger Leaping Gorge hydropower station will consist of one reservoir and eight dams. The whole project will stretch 564 kilometers along the middle reaches of the Jinsha (the upper reaches of the Yangtse in Yunnan) where the river has a total drop of 838 meters. The dam across the Tiger Leaping Gorge will be as high as 2,018 to 2,030 meters. It is reported that, besides generating electricity, the project would also alleviate the shortage of drinking water locally and provide clean water for Dianchi Lake, which is now heavily polluted. Tiger Leaping Gorge is in the northwest of Yunnan Province on the edge of the Three Parallel Rivers of the Yunnan Protected Area, an item on the World Heritage List. [. . .]

When the water conservancy project is completed, the water level will rise two hundred kilometers upstream from the Tiger Leaping Gorge. Thirteen towns and townships in four counties, including Lijiang and Shangri-La, will be flooded, and a population of one hundred thousand will be forced to relocate. Two hundred thousand mu (13,300 hectares) of prime farmland will be flooded. All this will add to the current troubles that the Three Parallel Rivers of the Yunnan Protected Areas are experiencing. [. . .]

Construction Without Approval

According to an official at the NDRC (the National Development and Reform Commission), the Report on the Design Plan for the Hydropower Development on the Middle Reaches of the Jinsha River was passed back in 2002. "That doesn't mean that construction can begin right now," he added. [. . .]

Yet, to everyone's astonishment, the construction of one of the eight dams is under way without having gone through the above-mentioned procedures. On September 13, 2004, reporters from *Southern Weekend* found that work was already going ahead busily at the construction site of the Jin'anqiao hydropower station which is downstream of the Tiger Leaping Gorge. The dam here will be 156 meters high with a total installed generating capacity of 2.5 million KW.

According to the plan, the damming of the river will begin in 2005. Construction work related to the plan has already begun, even though the central government has yet to approve the feasibility report. Concrete is being poured for the foundations of the dam. [. . .]

As a general procedure, any construction project with an investment of over RMB 100 million (about US$12 million) would be under the direct administration of the NDRC, not the local department. An official at the NDRC told reporters that the construction has not been approved by the central government.

Yet the local Lijiang authorities are happy to see the Jin'anqiao dam get under way, given that the project will bring about US$50 million a year in tax revenue once power generation starts. The city government regards the dam as its number one priority since its current annual revenue is just US$25 million. Wang Hui, professor at Tsinghua University's School of Humanities and Social Sciences, said, "The GDP-oriented development mode has been deeply rooted at all levels of governmental departments."

Tiger Leaping Gorge, Part of a World Heritage Site?

The Three Parallel Rivers of the Yunnan Protected Areas are the Nu (the Salween), the Lancang (the Mekong) and the Jinsha Rivers. In July 2003, UNESCO listed the Three Parallel Rivers National Park as a World Heritage Site on account of its special importance for geological research, extraordinary natural beauty, and wealth of biological and cultural diversity. It is the only site that fulfills all four requirements of the UNESCO World Heritage Program. A UNESCO report called the area "an epicenter of Chinese biodiversity" and a place "of outstanding universal value." [. . .]

Officials at the State Environmental Protection Administration (SEPA) expressed shock on hearing about the proposed dams in the Tiger Leaping Gorge. An official in charge of environmental assessment claimed that he knew nothing about the plans, saying: "How can big dams be allowed in the Tiger Leaping Gorge? The site is one of the most dazzling and precious natural wonders in all of China. SEPA will not approve any plan for building a big dam in that area." [. . .]

Problems Concerning Relocation

The local people are not at all keen on the dam projects. Reporters have traveled 250 kilometers along the valley, visiting six towns and townships that would be affected and interviewing two dozen people who would be among those forced to resettle. None of those interviewed expressed any willingness to move. Residents were particularly concerned that the project would flood the area's best farmland in the valley, which currently supports three hundred thousand people.

Rising waters would uproot prosperous farmers from the fertile riversides, where they now grow high-yielding rice and corn. Moreover, the project will force an estimated one hundred thousand people to move and live on higher land where they will have to adapt to cold weather, poor soil, and high altitude and grow less-profitable barley and potatoes. The Report on the Design Plan claims that the water conservancy project will alleviate poverty in the affected areas. Unfortunately, the opposite will be true. Mr. Tian in Jin'an Village complained that his family would have to give up their five mu of rice fields and would be given only one mu of farmland after resettlement. He was afraid that that would not be enough to feed his family.

According to a report in the China Youth Daily of July 28, 2004, since the founding of the People's Republic, large-scale water conservancy projects have caused 16 million people to be relocated. Of them, 11 million now live in poverty. Many of the people who would be affected by the project belong to ethnic minority groups, including the Naxi, the Tibetans, the Bai, the Yi, and the Miao nationalities.

The flooding would deal a devastating blow to local cultures, destroying many ancient villages with their distinctive architectural styles, ancient frescoes, stone coffins, and other relics.

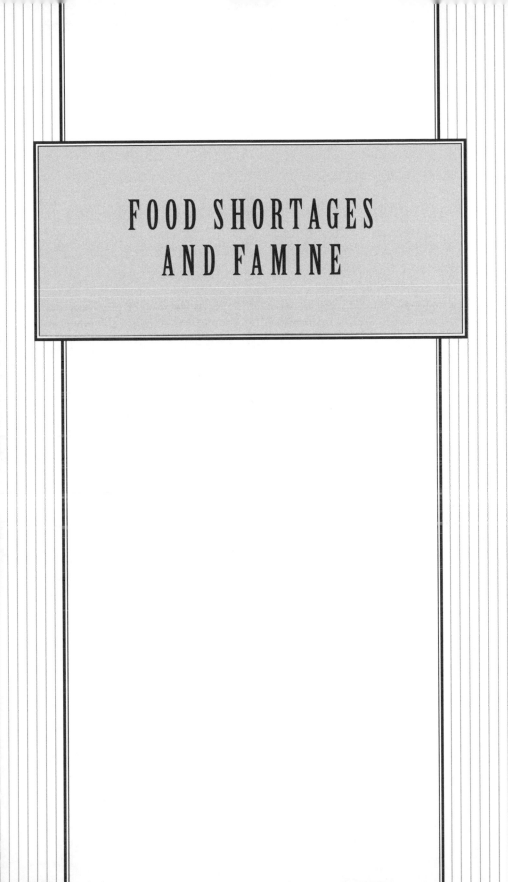

FOOD SHORTAGES
AND FAMINE

28

GARETH JONES

THE REAL TRUTH ABOUT RUSSIA AT LAST (1933)

from *Daily Express*

INTRODUCED BY RAY GAMACHE

USSR

Gareth Jones's reporting of the famine that ravaged the Soviet Union in 1932–33 constitutes one of the most important examples of investigative journalism produced in the twentieth century. As Jones travelled to the USSR in early March 1933, he was in the final weeks of employment as foreign affairs adviser to David Lloyd George, the former prime minister of Great Britain and a fellow Welshman, though Jones paid for the trip himself.

Fluent in Russian, German, French, Welsh, and English, Jones had graduated from Cambridge University in 1929 where he achieved First-Class Honors in Medieval and Modern Languages. Against the wishes of his parents who wanted him to pursue an academic career, Jones wanted a life of adventure, either in foreign affairs or journalism. In February 1930, he wrote to his parents: "I have come to the conclusion that the only life I can live with interest and [in] which I can really be of use is one connected with foreign affairs and with men and women of today; not with the writers of two centuries ago." Following in the footsteps of his mother, who served as a tutor to the granddaughters of Welsh engineer Arthur Hughes from 1889 to 1892, Jones travelled through the USSR in August 1930 and again in 1931 when he accompanied H.J. "Jack" Heinz II, heir to the Heinz fortune and a recent graduate from Yale University, as a favor to Ivy Ledbetter Lee,

Excerpt from Gareth Jones, "The Real Truth About Russia at Last," *Daily Express*, April 4, 6, and 7, 1933.

the most important practitioner of public relations in the United States for whom Jones worked in 1931–32 to assist Lee in writing a book about the USSR.

As a result of those two trips, Jones began his career as a journalist by publishing more than a dozen articles in the *Women's Liberal News, The Times*, the *News Chronicle*, the *Western Mail*, and *The Star*, detailing the impact of forced collectivization on agriculture and the campaign of dekulakization on the peasants, who were facing starvation conditions because of repressive grain requisitions imposed to satisfy Soviet exports of grain. Using Jones's reporter's notebooks/diaries, Heinz self-published an account of their journey in 1932, titled *Experiences in Russia 1931—A Diary*.

By March 1933, conditions in the USSR had deteriorated considerably. An internal passport system had been instituted in December 1932, meaning those facing famine were unable to travel to find food; additionally, a ban on travel outside of the major cities had been imposed on Western correspondents in February 1933, preventing them from reporting on conditions in the countryside. Despite this ban, Jones managed to secure permission to travel unescorted from Moscow to Kharkov, ostensibly to visit a tractor factory.

Having secured permission to travel unescorted from Konstantin Umansky, head of the Press and Information Department of the Soviet People's Commissariat of Foreign Affairs, Jones used the confidence entrusted to him to confirm what he had suspected since the previous fall when reports from people like Jules Menken of the London School of Economics and Bruce Hopper of Harvard University suggested that the harvest had been a failure and people were facing starvation. There is no question that the Soviet authorities would not have granted him this opportunity had they known he intended on getting off the train and walking forty miles through districts in Ukraine where famine was ravaging the population. At one point during his journey, Jones was accosted at a railway station by a militiaman and a member of the OGPU (Soviet secret police) as he was talking with peasants. Jones escaped arrest but was taken to the German consul in Kharkov (the British had no consulate there in 1933).

Upon his return from the USSR, Jones alerted the world to the famine when he gave a press conference in Berlin on March 29, 1933, resulting in articles by Pulitzer Prize winners W.H. Knickerbocker of the *New York Evening Post* and Edgar Ansel Mowrer of the *Chicago Daily News*. Jones's own account of the famine began with an article in the *Evening Standard* on March 31. Beholden to the Soviets and perhaps miffed at being scooped by Jones, Walter Duranty, the best known and highest paid journalist in the world, published an article in the *New York Times* on the very same day denying the famine and denigrating Jones by name. Several days later, Louis Fischer of *The Nation* also denied the famine, as he too was blinded by leftist ideology. Undaunted, Jones went on to write twenty more articles over the next three weeks: a series of seven for the *Daily Express*, a series of ten for the *Western Mail*, and a three-part series for the *Financial News*.

Published under the umbrella headline THE REAL TRUTH ABOUT RUSSIA AT LAST, the series of articles in the *Daily Express* document in stunning detail the famine conditions Jones witnessed on his journey, especially the little tragedies visited upon the peasants and workers he encountered in Moscow and the countryside. Jones uses more than forty vignettes to document the famine conditions, creating a sense of immediacy and giving voice to people who in all likelihood were destined to starve to death.

Despite his efforts, the journalism didn't make any difference. The United States and Britain did not send food aid, neither government willing to challenge the Soviets at a time when the National Socialist Party under Adolph Hitler had only recently come to power in Germany and Japanese militarism posed a challenge in the Far East. So intent were the Soviets in denying the famine that Stalin ordered that a million tons of grain be exported in 1933 from the USSR, a sadistic order which resulted in needless deaths. Stalin also ordered the borders closed so that millions of people, primarily in Ukraine, were left to starve. Ukrainians to this day remember this event as the *Holodomor*, meaning death by hunger, and accuse the USSR of genocide.

Even so, it is thanks in large part to Gareth Jones that the historical record was established and preserved in newspaper articles that documented direct, eyewitness accounts. Eyewitnessing has special significance in journalism mythology, for to have been there, to preserve for posterity something of the individual human experience within historical events and conditions, gives journalists an authority that no training can impart. Only by bearing witness and keeping their experiences alive through the discursive act of writing his newspaper articles did Gareth Jones keep alive the truth and authenticity about one of the most catastrophic events in human history.

" 'Bread! We Are Dying' "

One cry haunts the Russian of today and that is *"Hleba Nietu"* ("There is no bread.")

As you walk through the Tverskaya-street in Moscow, a rough-bearded peasant in a sheepskin coat will lumber up to you and say: "Give for the sake of God. I am from the Ukraine, and there '*hleba nietu*' ('there is no bread'). In my village they are dying off. I have come to Moscow for bread, which I shall send to my home by post. We are doomed in the Ukraine. In my village we had eighty horses. Now we have only eighteen. We had a hundred and fifty cows. Now there are only six. We are dying. Give us bread."

Further on, a little girl, about eight years of age, with dark brown eyes, her little face wrapped in a shawl, sells you scented white spring flowers for a rouble a bunch.

"Where do you come from?" I ask.

"I am from the Crimea," she replies, "where there is warm sunshine. Here it is cold, and I am freezing."

"Then why have you come up north to Moscow?"

"Because there is no bread in the Crimea and people are dying. There will be plenty of fruit there of all kinds, but that will not be until the summer. So my mother and I have brought flowers to Moscow and have come to find bread."

Ask that pox-pitted youth who sells wooden bowls with burnt-in designs on a street corner where he comes from and what he is doing in the great city, and he will say:

"I come from the Nijni-Novgorod region, and there we have no bread. So we carve these wooden bowls by hand and come to Moscow to seek something to eat."

Ask that peasant woman who stands in a side street and sells milk at three roubles (nominally six shillings) a litre why she is in Moscow, and she will reply: "I live fifty versts (thirty miles) from Moscow, and there we have no bread. We come to Moscow and bring bread back. Moscow is feeding us. If it were not for Moscow we should die."

"Nine to a Room in Slums of Russia"

My tramp through the villages was about to begin. My feet crunched through the snow as I made my way to a group of huts. A white expanse stretched for many miles. My first encounter was ominous, for the words I heard in the countryside were the same as those I had heard from peasant-beggars. A woman with bowed head walking along the railway track turned to me and said: "There is no bread. We have not had bread for over two months and many are dying here."

I was to hear these same words in the same tone from hundreds of peasants in that region, the Central Black Earth district, which was once one of the most fertile of all Russia. There was another sentence which was repeated to me time and time again: "*Vse pukhli.*" ("All are swollen.")

"What then do you eat, if you have no bread?" I asked one raw lad.

"Up to now we have had some potatoes, but our store has run out, and we only have cattle fodder left." He showed me what he had to eat. It was a kind of coarse beet which is given to cows.

"How long will this last?"

"Only a month. But many families have neither potatoes nor beet, and they are dying."

In every village the bread had run out about two months earlier. Finally, sunset came, and I talked to two men. One said, "You had better not go further, for hooligans will rob you of your coat and your food and all." The other added: "Yes, it is dangerous. They might jump out at you when it is dark. Come and stay with us in our village."

They took me to the village soviet, a hut which was full of peasants. There were two children there, one of which had a large swollen stomach. [. . .]

They all laid their griefs before me openly. They had no fear in telling me that never had it been so bad and that it was much worse than in 1921.

The cattle decrease, they told me, was disastrous. "We used to have two hundred oxen but now, alas, there are only six," they said. "Our horses and our cows have perished and we only have about one-tenth left." The horses looked scraggy and diseased, as do all the horses in the countryside. Many peasants in the village had died of hunger. [. . .]

In one of the peasant's cottages in which I stayed we slept nine in the room. It was pitiful to see that two out of the three children had swollen stomachs. All there was to eat in the hut was a very dirty watery soup, with a slice or two of potato, which all the family—and in the family I included myself—ate from a common bowl with wooden spoons.

Fear of death loomed over the cottage, for they had not enough potatoes to last until the next crop. When I shared my white bread and butter and cheese one of the peasant women said, "Now I have eaten such wonderful things I can die happy." I set forth again further towards the south and heard the villagers say, "We are waiting for death."

"15 Hours to Wait for the Shops to Open"

As I walk through the market I notice one group of people in the open, who sell home-made towels and clothes, some of which are decorated with artistic designs. A drunken peasant reels and totters, laughing loudly—an example of the dangers of vodka upon an empty stomach.

Nearby a little gipsy girl, about eight years of age, is singing a *tzigane* song with all the dramatic emotion of an operatic contralto. After each song she bows.

"Uncles, give me a rouble." I see another long queue, with its incessant bickering. At least a thousand people stand for bread, which is being sold at a high price. A highly-strung woman seeing that I am a foreigner snarls at me: "You see how fine it is here."

But the feature of the market which strikes me most is the number of ragged, homeless boys, the so-called "*bezprizorny.*" With the foulest of rags and the most depraved of faces, they hover about. In 1930 I saw few of these homeless boys. The Soviet Government had made a gallant fight to remove the swarms of ruffians who were the legacy of the civil war. In 1931 I saw still fewer, although they would sometimes shout in stations to passengers: "Give us cigarettes."

In 1933 I have seen the resurgence of the homeless boys. They wander about the streets of the towns. I have seen some being captured by the police and taken away. When I left Kharkoff it was the homeless boys who remained as the last and deepest impression.

In the station waiting-room three hundred of them were herded to be taken away. I peeped through the window. One of them near the window lay on the floor, his face red with fever and breathing heavily, with his mouth open. "Typhus," said another man, who was looking at them. Another lay in rags stretched on the ground, with part of his body uncovered, revealing dried up flesh and thin arms.

I turned away and entered the train for Moscow. In the corridor stood a little girl. She was well dressed. Her cheeks were rosy. She held a toy in one hand and a piece of cake in the other. She was probably the daughter of a Communist Party member or of an engineer.

In 1930 there were class differences. In 1931 they were as great as ever. In 1933 they are one of the most striking features of the Soviet Union. These children are not the relics of the civil war. They are the homeless children of hunger, most of them turned out from their homes to fend for themselves because the peasants have no bread.

The train rolled on to Moscow.

29

IAN STEPHENS

EDITORIAL (1943)
from *The Statesman*

INTRODUCED BY ANYA SCHIFFRIN
India

The role of *The Statesman* in exposing the terrible 1943 famine in Bengal is credited with inspiring Nobel laureate Amartya Sen's famous theory that democracy and a strong media prevent famines because the press serves as an early warning system that forces governments to act. Journalists around the world are familiar with this argument but few remember the details of what actually happened.

The Statesman was an English-language broadsheet founded in Calcutta in 1875, and incorporated the nineteenth-century newspapers *The English-man* and *Friend of India*. In the 1940s, its editor was Ian Stephens. In his memoir, *Monsoon Morning*, Stephens describes how as a young civil servant he became indoctrinated with the view that the Famine Codes laid down by the British in the late nineteenth century had effectively prevented famines in India. He also writes that he and his editorial team didn't have much background in economics or agriculture and so weren't prepared for what was to come.

"Looking back, I see myself as stumbling into doing the right thing about the famine at the right time vigorously and indeed soon with passionate humanitarian zeal almost by accident. That we emerged not merely with credit but with the editor in the Bengali public's eyes somewhat haloed is somewhat surprising."[1]

However, as conditions worsened in Bengal, Stephens and his colleagues

Excerpt from Ian Stephens, editorial, *The Statesman*, August 8, 1943.

realized that the government of India was not going to help the people of Bengal[2] and *The Statesman* needed to act. At the time, India was under wartime censorship restrictions imposed by the government of India. Reporting on the famine was strictly forbidden as information about food supplies was considered valuable intelligence that could aid the enemy. Local newspapers in vernacular languages covered the food shortages and these were mentioned in Communist Party pamphlets and in paintings and drawings. But mainstream newspapers such as *Amrita Bazar Patrika* and *The Statesman*, while covering the parliamentary debates and discussion about food supplies, held back on their reporting for most of 1943. *The Statesman* published a series of editorials criticizing the government but these were largely ignored.

Finally, in August 1943, Stephens and his colleagues could take it no longer. They ratcheted up the tone of *The Statesman*'s editorials, blasting the government of India for not doing enough. More powerfully, *The Statesman* published shocking photos of the families and children who had streamed into Calcutta looking for food.

As a foreigner editing a newspaper targeted to the elite colonizer, Stephens and his colleagues knew they would be able to publish what their local colleagues could not. Once the mainstream English-language newspaper had broken the government's wall of silence, others followed. The control over the famine news was gone. Although it still tried to downplay the numbers, the government was forced to admit what was happening. The story went international and was covered in the U.S. papers as well as the wire services, prompting inquiries in parliament. It was, however, too late for the millions who had died.

"We'd not merely smashed the censorship; by our sustained two months' harassment of the authorities we'd we believed forced them—we and the awful facts themselves—into decisive forms of practical action that ought to have been taken long before," Stephens wrote.[3]

Longer term, the case of the 1943 Bengal famine inspired scholarship about the role of the media, much of which was written by economists. In his famous Coromandel lecture of 1982, Sen compared the role of the press in India to that in China, crediting the press with preventing famine in India.[4] Timothy Besley and Robin Burgess looked at local-language media in India and found that in areas where there were more newspapers, government response to natural disasters (including famine and floods) was much faster and stronger than in other parts of India were there were fewer newspapers.[5] And so a school of thought about the importance of the media was born.

Blame for this extremely grave situation rests heavily on the Government of India. We find ourselves amazed by their lack of vision or consistency in this vital matter. From the knowledge in their possession, risk of a food shortage or rocketing prices should have been discernible to an alert eye within their organization from the moment of Japan's belligerence. Burma was weakly defended; loss of it, and its rice exports, must inevitably distort the fundamentals of trade in foodstuffs throughout the harassed Eastern provinces threatened with invasion. Yet a full year was allowed to elapse before a Food Department at the Centre was even set up. This time-lag over an elementary administrative obligation is beyond understanding. Long before the Department was inaugurated the Press and nonofficial publicists, exercising more commonsense, were demanding its creation. As over the subsequent problem of inflation, so over food, Government during a critical initial period evidently pinned faith on recitation of mantrams. By mumbling that food shortages did not exist, they willed themselves into belief that the dread spectacle would vanish.

Nor during the Department's first seven months, has it possessed anything describable as a well-considered policy. There has on the contrary been every sign of muddle-headed improvisation. Estimates of the amounts of food-grains which the Centre could make available to the deficit Eastern zone have fluctuated wildly. At the outset of the Department's career, the public was invited to admire the not very efficient controls in interprovincial foodstuffs. Suddenly these controls in Eastern India were cast away, and Government sought applause for its wisdom in that negative stroke. It is too much to expect that, once more, there should be applause in August when, as is now happening, the controls are clamped on again. . . . A populace three-parts starved is in no state to support armies or resist dangerous rumors. It may be a seedbed for devastating epidemics of disease which spread to the troops. For some weeks emaciated human beings migrant from foodless areas in the mofussil have been dying in the streets of Bengal's capital. This week the Central Assembly will discuss India's food problem. The condition of Bengal is so conspicuously bad as to call for heroic remedies. New Delhi must think less in terms of N.W. India's easier conditions and take due cognizance of bitter realities in the war-threatened Eastern areas, where what may fairly now be called famine prevails.

30

MIKE MULLER

MILKING THE POOR (1975)

from *The Guardian*

INTRODUCED BY MIKE MULLER

Africa

The Nestlé boycott that started in 1977 was one of the defining consumer boycotts of the last century, certainly one of the longest—even today, many people still think twice about buying that particular brand of chocolate or coffee. It was a new kind of campaign, personal in its politics and global in its scope—what could be more personal than feeding babies, more global than the formal engagement of the United Nations system in regulating multinational business? The campaign built links between diverse health, consumer, and development constituencies, joining health and development activists in the south together with their counterparts in the north.

Mother's milk is almost always better for babies than manufactured substitutes. In communities with poor sanitary conditions where people cannot afford adequate quantities of food, any action that discourages breast-feeding is dangerous, its consequences measured in sick and dead children. For the food industry, however, more sales mean bigger profits, and in the absence of regulation profits determine policy.

The Nestlé boycott and the wider baby milk campaign were driven by a powerful combination of activism and information. This was initially sparked by a 1973 article in *New Internationalist*, a magazine that had been started in the 1970s by British NGOs Oxfam and Christian Aid to promote a more critical "development journalism." *New Internationalist* reported long-standing concerns among health professionals about the damage that

Excerpt from Mike Muller, "Milking the Poor," *The Guardian*, February 7, 1975.

the marketing of baby milk products was doing in poor communities, causing what pediatrician and professor Derrick Jelliffe called "commerciogenic malnutrition."

What was the role of journalism in promoting the campaign? The initial *New Internationalist* report alerted other media and development agencies. The *Guardian* piece excerpted here, which is still widely read, was part of the ensuing coverage.

In November 1973, the editor of the (still very young) *Time Out* magazine asked me to follow up on the story. Local development NGO War on Want was keen to take up the issue and paid for a month's research, including a trip to talk to Nestlé in Switzerland.

Confident of its probity, the company made an elementary PR mistake and allowed me to talk directly to their technical and operational managers. I returned with six hours of taped interviews showing glaring gaps between the benevolent view from Head Office and the reality on the ground. The resulting report, "The Baby Killer," published in March 1974, was widely covered in mainstream British news and technical press and encouraged War on Want to work with other organizations to develop a campaign. Nestlé did itself no favors when they took our Swiss partners, *Arbeitsgruppe Dritte Welt*, to court for libel. The judge found that the title of their translation of "The Baby Killer" as *Nestlé Totet Babies* (Nestlé Kills Babies) was indeed libelous but he upheld the allegations that the company dressed salesgirls in nurses' uniforms and was promoting its products in communities that could not use them properly. If the company did not like those accusations, it should change its marketing practices, said the judge, as *Time* magazine reported.

That widely publicized decision gave new impetus to a growing global campaign, which proved that networked social action was possible, even in snail mail days. It was timely because United Nations agencies were grappling with the challenges posed by global business, whose activities national governments struggled to regulate. The baby milk issue, with its intimate personal focus, transcended the divide between international bureaucrats, anti-imperialist activists, and broader communities. It illustrated the need for, and gave legitimacy to, the UN's efforts to regulate the multinationals.

Activists such as Malaysia-based Anwar Fazal of the International Organisation of Consumer Unions, who was working with WHO and UNICEF, saw the opportunity and worked to broaden the coalition. Nestlé boycotts spread from Switzerland and Britain to the United States, where shareholder activism and court challenges against other milk companies, led by the Sisters of the Precious Blood, a religious order working under the umbrella of the Interfaith Centre for Corporate Responsibility, achieved a fine balance between grassroots organizing, legal process, and catchy communication.

The campaigns attracted widespread support from medical professionals, health authorities, and civil society in developing countries. So in 1981, the UN World Health Assembly (the governing body of WHO) recommended the adoption of an international code of conduct to govern the promotion and sale of breast milk substitutes. Global regulation of consumer industries was—and remains—a threat to business. UN resolutions are "soft law" that have little direct effect, yet often lead to hard national enforcement. And, indeed, the WHO resolution was strongly supported by Third World health authorities whose domestic attempts to control their local corporations had often been unsuccessful; now they had a UN resolution to refer to!

Back then, Nestlé's response was that their critics should do something to improve unsafe water supplies, which contributed to the health problems associated with bottle feeding. I spent thirty years doing just that in Mozambique, South Africa, and elsewhere but challenges remain, not least the affordability of food in poor communities. Meanwhile, health authorities in both rich and poor countries battle to maintain the profile of breast-feeding as the preferred way of feeding babies, not least because the subject is often not regarded as newsworthy by mainstream media. Their challenge is to find ways to promote often complex health information in a culture in which it must compete for space and time with commercial promotions that usually have a single, simple sales message.

In this respect, the baby milk campaigns have helped to keep breast-feeding on the public agenda. It is more newsworthy to report that corporations have broken the rules set out in the 1981 Code of Conduct than simply to report (again) that "breast is best." So citizen action is supported by the existence of a code which can—and is—used to hold Nestlé and other companies to account. For example, 2013 saw complaints by UNICEF about code violations in Laos, civil society groups making similar allegations in the Philippines, and controversy in India and Ireland about the involvement of health workers with milk companies.

Meanwhile, for Nestlé and the rest of the global food industry, the baby milk scandal has grown up rather than gone away. "Commerciogenic malnutrition" is now mainstream news, under many other names. The industry stands accused of harming the health of whole nations, not just their babies. What started as a skirmish in the nursery is turning into full-scale war on many fronts.

While the health issues are now obesity, diabetes, and heart disease rather than gastroenteritis and marasmus, the issues about the food industry's responsibility remain the same: its huge marketing budgets influence people's behavior, even if direct causality can't be demonstrated. Children and young adults may get fat because they do not get enough exercise. But if they are also offered and encouraged to "choose" supersaturated fat diets, dosed with excessive salt, and drinks laced with multiple sugars, can the industries that produce and promote those products absolve themselves from the ugly outcomes? Back in the 1970s, the Swiss judge ruled to the contrary. Today public and political opinion is again swinging in that direction. And solid, well-researched journalism—think *Super Size Me*—is in the forefront, informing and trying to balance the debate between people and profit.

A year after warnings about the danger of bottle feeding African babies, milk companies are still promoting their products to communities which cannot use them safely. As a result there has been an increase in infant malnutrition and death.

Dr D. J. O. Robbin-Coker, consultant paediatrician to the Sierra Leone Government, called for an end to the promotion of baby milks in his country more than a year ago. His concern has since been echoed by the World Health Organisation and other United Nations agencies, aid organisations and medical authorities in other Third World countries with similar problems. But the hard sell continues. Earlier this month in hospital wards in Sierra Leone I saw babies near death as a result.

Bottle-fed British babies tend to obesity according to last year's DHSS report, Present Day Practice in Infant Feeding. In poor communities in the Third World, the bottle-fed baby is more often thin, ill or dead. The problem is not that baby milks are inadequate foods. But the Third World mother who lacks kitchen facilities, even running water, is not easily able to prepare a bottle feed hygienically.

If she succeeds, she often overdilutes milk to save money. In Sierra Leone, it costs about £8 a month to bottle feed a baby adequately and a manual worker is lucky to earn £25 a month.

In these conditions, bottle feeding often results in "marasmus" (wasting malnutrition) precipitated either by gastroenteritis or just underfeeding.

This relation has been found in many developing countries. In 1968 Dr Derrick Jelliffe, a British paediatric nutritionist with wide experience in the developing world, described "commerciogenic malnutrition"—the malnutrition resulting when baby milks are promoted to communities unable to use them safely.

In a mission hospital in Segbwema, a small town 250 miles from Freetown, I saw the impact of today's promotion. Four-month-old Momoh was being treated for gastroenteritis and severe dehydration. His mother had developed an abscess on one breast. So she stopped breast feeding and bought a tin of Nestle's Lactogen: "We heard it would make baby strong and well" she told me, repeating a familiar radio commercial.

Dr Roger Coles, paediatrician at the hospital, was in no doubt about the cause of Momoh's illness: "We call this combination of marasmus, gastroenteritis and thrush Lactogen syndrome," he told me. If his mother had sought treatment for herself instead of relying on a bottle for her baby, there would have been no problem.

The impact of bottle feeding on the predominantly rural Segbwema community is just beginning. In Freetown, the swing from breast to bottle has progressed alarmingly according to Dr Robbin-Coker. It was the resultant upsurge in admissions of infants with gastroenteritis or marasmus which prompted his warning about milk promotion. Both conditions are rare in the early months of a child's life if it is exclusively breast fed according to authorities like Dr Derrick Jelliffe.

There has been mounting criticism in the past 12 months of milk companies which continue to promote their products in spite of these dangers. The Baby Killer, a report by the British aid agency War on Want, generated public concern in Britain and the Third World. The German translation retitled Nestle Kills Babies has provoked an action for libel. Experts will confront each other in a Swiss court later this year.

At last summer's WHO assembly, the British delegation's motion calling for a review of milk sales and promotion and the consideration of advertisement codes and restrictive legislation in countries where bottle feeding presents public health problems was unanimously accepted.

In Nigeria, Tanzania, Jamaica, and other countries, public concern combined with health authorities' representatives to curtail the promotional activities of the milk companies.

In Nigeria, executives from the British firm Unigate had consultations last year with leading paediatricians: the company has agreed to abide by whatever recommendations the Paediatric Association of Nigeria care to make.

A number of other companies have acknowledged the problems and pledged themselves to responsible conduct. According to Mr A. Keller, a senior executive of Nestle, his company's policies always take into account the "advice and recommendations of the responsible international organizations and, obviously, national health authorities."

But a year after Dr Robbin-Coker made his plea for restraint, Nestle was still crackling in Krio over Sierra Leone Radio: "Now Lactogen a better food cos it don get more protein and iron, all de important things that go make pikin strong and well."

Abbott Laboratories, a major American baby food producer, has published an impressive international Code of Marketing Ethics which states: "We wish to co-operate in every way with local health authorities in preventing the misuse of our products because of poverty, ignorance, or lack of proper hygienic conditions. And we do not encourage the use of our products where private purchase would impose a financial hardship on the family or inadequate facilities for preparation constitute a hazard to infant health."

This sentiment is hard to relate to Abbott's current promotion for its Similac, which appears to play down the danger of bottle feeding: "E milk good for my pikin when e sick-sick so?" asks a mother in a Sierra Leone radio spot.

"Yes" replies an authoritative sounding lady, "this milk not make pikin vomit so."

Many health workers whom I met believe that multinational giants such as Abbott and Nestle—which has an annual turnover 10 times greater than Sierra Leone's £200 millions GNF—should exercise more rigorous self-control. Where children's lives conflict with maximum profits they suggest that the companies can afford restraint.

MILITARY AND POLICE

31

EUCLIDES DA CUNHA

FROM *OS SERTÕES*, OR
REBELLION IN THE BACKLANDS (1902)

INTRODUCED BY LEOPOLDO M. BERNUCCI

Brazil

Euclides da Cunha occupies a distinguished place in Brazilian culture. An engineer by training, he was an intrepid reporter, an exquisite writer, and above all an acute interpreter of Brazil's history and society. More than one hundred years after the publication of the monumental *Os sertões* (1902; *Rebellion in the Backlands*), this book is still viewed as the "Bible of the Brazilian nationality." Originally envisioned as a reportage of the Canudos War in northeastern Brazil in 1897, da Cunha instead wrote a sweeping, lyrical, and splendid history of Brazil and its people's identity.

The war of Canudos, and the book that came out of da Cunha's reportage on the final campaign, became a defining moment in Brazilian history. The war was part of the brutal expansion of the Brazilian army into a hinterland populated by mixed-race people. In the battles that da Cunha describes, the impoverished and poorly armed inland northeastern people supported the messianic and fanatical leader Antonio Vicente Mendes Maciel, simply known as the "Conselheiro" (Counselor). Resembling a civil war, the Canudos military campaign was unique in its breadth and scope in the history of Brazil, resulting in more than 25,000 casualties in just one year of fighting.

Equipped with a sense of civic duty, da Cunha wrote *Rebellion in the Backlands* not only as a mea culpa on behalf of coastal Brazilians who had

Excerpt from Euclides da Cunha, "Chapter IX: New Phase of the Struggle," in *Rebellion in the Backlands*, trans. Samuel Putnam (Chicago: University of Chicago Press, 1944), 404–7.

spent years neglecting the backlanders, but also as an eloquent denunciation of the carnage executed by the Brazilian army during the war. Although the book was an immediate success, da Cunha never became wealthy. He was known as a sincere patriot who never abandoned his moral compass, and that contributed to his stature and made him one of Brazil's greatest writers.

Due to the lack of communication between the coast and the interior of the country, it was not at first clear that the Conselheiro and his supporters would be able to hold out for as long as they did or that the war would be as bloody as it was. By the time the prestigious *O Estado de S. Paulo* newspaper had hired da Cunha to accompany the fourth military expedition to Canudos, the war had worsened; three military expeditions had been shamefully defeated and the national army was completely demoralized. Da Cunha spent approximately twenty-one days in the war zone and the experience changed him forever. What he and many Brazilians had thought of as a war aimed at civilizing the Counselor's followers turned out to be a bloody atrocity. Da Cunha had planned to denounce the ineptitude of politicians and the army, and the role that the latter had as "mercenaries," but as he continued writing it became clear that he had to deal with matters even more grotesque: the atrocious method of decapitation of prisoners of war by the army as described in the final pages of his book.

Da Cunha was one of the pioneers in Latin America in combining text and image, in a similar manner to what would be called photojournalism today. He perceptively discovered the power of images in conveying the sense of reality and emotion to his audience. To that end, besides the maps and lithographic landscapes, he inserted in the book three photos by the army's official photographer, Flávio de Barros. Two showed the deplorable conditions of war prisoners and foot troops, and the third one a false impression of order among artillery soldiers. As well as images, da Cunha drew on a wide range of sources, including reportage done by other people and books on history, botany, geology, psychology, and religion. By the time *Rebellion in the Backlands* was published in 1902, the original journalism had evolved into a three-part volume that included a geographic treatise of the backlands, a history of the formation of Brazilian people, a cultural survey of the backlanders, and a short history of religious fanaticism in Brazil. The piece excerpted here gives a flavor of some of the differences of life in the hinterland and describes Queimadas, a village ninety miles from Canudos, used by the Republican army to support its troops.

As well as his powerful writing on human rights, da Cunha had, since the early 1900s, been denouncing the dreadful conditions that enslaved whites and indigenous people lived under in the rubber-producing areas of the Amazon. His statements on this topic include two powerful interviews printed after he returned from western Amazonia, in *Jornal do Commercio* (Manaus, October 29, 1905; and Rio de Janeiro, January 14, 1906), and an article, "Among the Rubber Stations," published in a 1906 issue of *Kosmos* magazine (Rio de Janeiro). In these three pieces, da Cunha deepened his analysis of human exploitation and abuse, and provided a convincing account more than one year before the exposés in the Iquitos newspapers of Benjamin Saldaña Rocca, *La Sanción* and *La Felpa*.

Tragically, da Cunha died in August 1909, after being shot by his wife's lover. Published posthumously in *À margem da história* (On the margin of history), da Cunha's essays attacked the greedy latex industry for what is known today as one of the greatest genocides in the area. In a major chapter of this book, da Cunha called it "the most heinous organization of labor ever conjured up by human egotism unbound."

Queimadas, a settlement dating from the beginning of the century but now in full decline, had become a noisy armed camp. A collection of poverty-stricken huts awkwardly clustered about an irregular-shaped *praça*, deeply furrowed by torrential rains, it was in reality a clearing in the wilds, and the monotony of the surrounding plains and barren hills gave it a mournful air, the appearance of a deserted village fast falling in ruins and overrun by wilderness.

There were, moreover, painful memories associated with the place. Here it was that all the previous expeditions had been assembled, on the bit of ground extending from the village square to the caatinga, whose parched, grayish-white leaves had given the place its name. Repugnant heaps of rags and tatters, filthy multicolored shreds of old uniforms, old shoes and military boots, kepis and soldiers' bonnets, smashed canteens—all the odds and ends of a barracks were scattered over this extensive area, along with the remains of bonfires left by those who had pitched their tents here ever since the start of the Febronio expedition. On this bit of offal-strewn ground ten thousand brawling men had bivouacked, with passions, anxieties, hopes, and discouragements beyond the power of description.

[. . .] One alights from the train, walks a few hundred yards between rows of squat houses, and forthwith finds himself on the edge of the village square—in the backlands.

For this is in reality the point where two societies meet, each one wholly alien to the other. The leather-clad vaqueiro will emerge from the caatinga, make his way into the ugly-looking settlement, and halt his nag beside the rails where natives of the seaboard pass, unaware of his existence.

[. . .] The new expeditionaries, upon reaching Queimadas, were aware of this violent transition. Here was an absolute and radical break between the coastal cities and the clay huts of the interior, one that so disturbed the rhythm of our evolutionary development and which was so deplorable a stumbling-block to national unity. They were in a strange country now, with other customs, other scenes, a different kind of people. Another language even, spoken with an original and picturesque drawl. They had, precisely, the feeling of going to war in another land. [. . .] The mission which had brought them here merely served to deepen the antagonism. There was the enemy, out there to the east and to the north, hidden away in those endless highland plains; and far, far away, beyond the plains, a terrible drama was being unfolded.

[. . .] What they were being called upon to do now was what other troops had done—to stage an invasion of foreign territory. [. . .] Here were those unknown woodsmen sending back to them, day by day, mutilated and defeated, their comrades who, a few months previously, had gone down that same road, strong of body and proud of spirit. As a result, there was no heart left in them; they had not the courage to strike out, unconcerned with what might happen, into the depths of those mysterious and formidable backlands.

[. . .] Happily, upon their arrival at Queimadas, the effect of all this was counteracted to a degree by the receipt of encouraging news from the front. [. . .] The rumour then began going the rounds that the Counselor was being held prisoner by his own followers, who had revolted when he announced his intention of surrendering and giving himself up to martyrdom. Other details were cited, all of them pointing to a rapid dying-down of the conflagration.

[. . .] The first prisoners were at last being brought back, after all these months of fighting; and our men could not help noticing, without attempting to explain the fact, that there was not a full-grown man to be found among them. These captives, escorted under heavy guard, were pitiful ones indeed: half-a-dozen women with infants wizened as fetuses at their bosoms, followed by older children, from six to ten years of age.

[. . .] It was a sorry spectacle as these ragged creatures, under the gaze of all those eyes—insatiable eyes that seemed to look straight through the tatters—came into the square, dragging their young ones by the hand. They were like animals at the fair, an amusing sight.

[. . .] One of the children—a thin little mite, barely able to stand—wore on its head an old kepi which it had picked up along the road and which came down over its shoulder, covering a third or more of its emaciated bosom. This big, broad hat kept swaying grotesquely at every step the child took, and some of the spectators were so unfeeling as to laugh at the sight. Then the child raised its face and looked them in the eye. Their laughter died on their lips; for the little one's mouth was a gaping bullet wound, from side to side!

32

BENJAMIN POGRUND

FROM *RAND DAILY MAIL* (1965)

INTRODUCED BY ANTON HARBER

South Africa

In the wake of the Sharpeville massacre of 1960, the apartheid government declared a state of emergency and arrested thousands of political activists. The resistance movement, such as Nelson Mandela's African National Congress (ANC) and its rival, the Pan-Africanist Congress (PAC), turned to armed struggle. Many were detained without trial for months; others who had joined the military resistance—like Mandela—were caught and jailed for life. So when the pioneering editor of the liberal *Rand Daily Mail* (*RDM*), Laurence Gandar, appointed young reporter Benjamin Pogrund to head a new investigations team in 1965, it was no surprise that one of the stories on their list was the country's prison conditions. Gandar had steered the conservative *RDM* into being the most outspoken critique of the apartheid government. It was a white paper, with no black reporters at that time, but it was a bastion of liberal values in a repressive state.

Pogrund was a young "Native Affairs Reporter" who had made his name earlier by being one of the few to stay in contact with Mandela while he was on the run. Pogrund also covered black and trade union politics at a time when few were doing this.

The Prisons Act—promulgated after *Drum* magazine's exposé of prison conditions in the 1950s—had made it a serious offence "to publish false information . . . without taking reasonable steps to verify such information."

Excerpt from Benjamin Pogrund, *Rand Daily Mail*, June 30, 1965, and July 2, 1965.

The result, Pogrund wrote in his memoir, *War of Words*, was that "a great silence descended over the country's prisons." Information about abuse and torture leaked out to reporters like Pogrund, but was unreported.

Pogrund got his lead while on holiday in the coastal town of Durban, where he met Harold Strachan, a maverick political prisoner released just a few weeks before after serving three years for sabotage. Pogrund wrote twelve thousand words based on taped interviews with Strachan, and planned a three-part series of Strachan describing his experience in great detail in his own words. "If what he [Strachan] said was true," Pogrund quotes the newspaper's lawyer saying, "then our jails are nothing better than concentration camps." There was a rush to print because it was known that security police were preparing a banning order for Strachan, which would prevent him being quoted.

Part one appeared on June 30, 1965, under the headline BEHIND THE BARS. "What happens behind the high walls of South African jails? Few people know because of the restrictions." It told of prisoners who had to wash and brush their teeth in a toilet, of a pristine cell which could not be used because it was only on show for outsiders, and of listening to the all-night singing of death row prisoners and the sound of the trapdoors as they were hanged.

The second part ended with the teaser "Tomorrow I want to talk about assaults," and that was when police struck with a raid on the newspaper offices to try and prevent further publication. The team hid away the type and rushed through publication.

Strachan was immediately served with a banning and house arrest order, and the public reaction was one of shock. Government-supporting media called it "an abominable smear campaign." The newspaper promised more: "We have opened a chink in the curtain of secrecy surrounding our prisons," a front-page editorial proclaimed. "We are now going ahead to bust it wide open." Pogrund continued to collect first-person accounts.

A second series of articles cast the net wider, based on the testimony of two prisoners and two warders, including the former head of a prison, Johannes Theron. They told of the electric shock torture of twenty to twenty-five convicts in Boksburg Prison, not far from Johannesburg. The *RDM* was raided again and the warders arrested. "That was the day our innocence ended," Pogrund wrote.

The next three years saw a relentless wave of state persecution of Strachan, Gandar, Pogrund, the *Rand Daily Mail*, and all their witnesses. Scores of prisoners and warders were paraded in front of sympathetic judges to contradict the newspaper's evidence. Defense witnesses were threatened, forced to either recant or face jail. Advocate Sydney Kentridge spoke of the "sorry procession of plainly untruthful warders and officers who gave evidence."

Strachan was sent back to prison for another thirty months (released after twelve), and Pogrund, Gandar, and the paper were handed fines and suspended sentences after painfully long and expensive trials. "We also discovered," Pogrund wrote, "the impossible odds in taking on the might of the state."

Pogrund had barely touched the surface of prison abuse and conditions in the repressive period of the 1960s, but the state reaction had devastating effects on press coverage for two decades thereafter. The authorities had shown the legal and extralegal lengths they would go to protect themselves from exposure; along the way, they radically increased the burden of verification. The price of investigative work had been raised to unbearable heights, and this led to a period of induced self-censorship that shut off from scrutiny key areas of apartheid life, such as prisons, the police, and the military. It is no coincidence that these were areas where the worst abuses occurred over the next two decades, sheltered as they were from public scrutiny.

I was sent first to the Port Elizabeth North End Prison and was there for about five weeks. The European, generally known among prisoners as a "hobo" jail, was occupied mainly by short term prisoners. [. . .]

We had a flush toilet in the cell which is quite unusual as far as prisons I have been in. But an interesting thing about this toilet was that you didn't only defecate in it, but you also washed in it; you brushed your teeth in it.

They had sufficient bathroom facilities. They had a very spick and span shower room with hot water and everything laid on, but we weren't allowed to use this because it had been beautifully polished—floor, taps and so forth—and mats were laid on the floor to keep it nice and tidy, and prisoners were seldom allowed to go in there. It was kept clean for inspection.

We were obliged to shower twice a week in cold water in another shower house around the back of the corridor where we were. The section warder would not allow us to go even to this little bathroom in the morning, and hard as it is to believe, one would stand up with one's toothbrush while a man was actually sitting on the pan, wait for him to finish and say; "Come on, get up, I want to brush my teeth."

And he would get up amidst all this bloody stink, and he would flush the thing.

Then a man would flush it again and then dip his toothbrush in the water and brush his teeth. Or wash his hands and face in it. [. . .]

I saw constant assaults on African prisoners. [. . .] Once I saw a young warder hitting each man—non-White—as he came through the door with a hefty blow on the back of the head. I said to him; "What the devil do you think you are doing?" He looked quite surprised and a bit abashed and said; "I am counting them." [. . .]

[. . .] At Pretoria Central Prison, I was first placed in the Observation Section. The theory of the observation of prisoners is an admirable concept. According to the theory, every long term prisoner is placed on his own in a reasonably comfortable cell, and is given time to think about his past life, his crime, his trial, his sentence and his future.

He is befriended by a qualified psychologist who remains his friend throughout his sentence and even afterwards. Now on paper this is what the Observation Section at Pretoria is. But in fact, the time you spend there is called the "penal period" by prisoners. The cells are seven feet square. That is very small.

I was lucky because I was alone. A warder told me this was because I was a political prisoner. But other prisoners were three to a cell. [. . .]

It was bitterly cold. [. . .] It's like a small dingy cave. In the middle of the day it was lit by an electric light, a very dull one, which somehow gave a feeling of even greater cold. We did nothing all day. You just sit. You are not allowed to lie down. No. That is an offence. You just sit. I used to wake up at half past five in the morning when the gong rang and just sit and hope and wait and shiver and pray for half past four in the afternoon, which was lock-up time when you were allowed to go to bed. [. . .]

This Observation Centre was called the "madhouse" by all the prisoners. I thought when I first went into it that it was called this because psychiatry was practised there.

But in fact it turned out that it was called this, not because you were mad when you went in but because you were mad when you came out. [. . .]

But they have also in Pretoria Central a Segregation Section for escapers, assaulters, dagga smokers and those who are generally ill-behaved. This is an ultra-maximum security section. [. . .]

[T]his segregation was also used, from what I saw, as a form of punishment for which there was no trial and no sentence. Prisoners find Segregation even harder to bear, I think, than solitary confinement. I have heard a man in Segregation when the Officer Commanding comes round on inspection, standing up and saying; "Sir, what am I here for?" And the officer says; "Ah, you tell me," and then he says; "Please tell me what I am here for then I will be able to face it." Then the officer says; "No, no, no. I will give you a piece of paper and a pencil and you just make a statement," and I have heard blokes in that situation going absolutely dilly, saying; "Please, Sir, just tell me what the matter is and then I can write a report on it."

Apart from people who are chucked into Segregation on suspicion there are, as I say, prisoners who are put there for attempting escape or other reasons.

These days prisoners don't stay in Segregation, as far as I know, for much more than about 18 months. You really go mad in there. [. . .]

Men used to go off their heads in jail and go rushing at the walls and door of their cell, screaming and weeping, banging with their fists and kicking. Some also mutilated themselves.

There was one man, for example, whom I questioned about his speech impediment. He showed me that the front part of his tongue had been cut off. He said he had done this while in Segregation. There were other prisoners with their wrists scarred from being slashed with razor blades and so on.

They Laughed and Crouched Naked—Waiting

[. . .] I want to talk about assaults. I did not see any serious assaults at Pretoria Central. The worst assaults I have seen were on non-European prisoners at Pretoria Local Prison.

[. . .] Orders were often accompanied by a blow. We saw Africans being driven into their section—we peeked through our windows—they were driven in like animals by *poyisas* (black warders) with sticks and with leather straps.

They used the long double strap of their truncheons or keys as a whip. Each man as he came past running would get a blow with the whip. Our windows at one time over looked the yard and the non-European reception office at the Pretoria Local and we could see these men being driven across the yard for showering or other purposes by these *poyisas* with these straps.

We could see these men also being hit with fists and open hands. [. . .]

This was general. But the worst assaults I saw anywhere in jail were those on Africans at the hospital and sometimes non-European patients in the hospital at Pretoria Local. For most of my time there, the hospital yard was straight under my window.

All prisoners when they came into prison went to the hospital to get examined and so forth. Non-European prisoners who had to see the doctors were brought out at about 6:15 in the morning, and it could be freezing cold in Pretoria.

They stood naked: 60, 70, 80 of them at a time. Huddled up like birds trying to keep warm. Like poultry. Stark naked. They had to stand with frost thick on the ground, barefoot, clutching each other to try to keep warm. Shivering.

And they would stand there until the doctor came at nine o' clock, sometimes later. [. . .]

I saw occasional assaults on the patients themselves. I saw one man, who was apparently suspected of smuggling dagga, dragged out of the hospital by a warder—Kruger—whom we called "Florence Nightingale."

This warder was a burly man with a deformed face. He dragged out this prisoner who was wearing the hospital grey robe and forced him to kneel down on all fours, stripped naked in front of all the other patients who were allowed to sit around in the sun during the day.

They were laughing at this man and other African prisoners standing around were also laughing at him. [. . .]

Forced him to kneel while the African prisoner who acted as hospital orderly stood with an enema can of soap and water. The enema was administered.

The prisoner was stood up; blood was dripping down his legs; he was not allowed to get rid of this soapy water. It was blue soap. I saw them making it. He had to stand with his buttocks clenched together with his hands.

He was then forced to jump around from leg to leg, doing a sort of quick march, a sort of knees up to horizontal position but still clutching his buttocks so the stuff couldn't come out.

The burly warder kicked him as he jumped in this way, kicked him on his arms, his back, his hips and his belly. Until finally a pot was brought out by one of the African prisoners.

The man then sat on the pot and got rid of all this water in the presence of the warder and everyone else. And while he was doing it he was being beaten over the head. Where the man had been standing and jumping there was a puddle of blood. When he got up from the pot Kruger went and poked around in it with a stick. I did not see him pull anything out. [. . .]

One thing I learnt in jail was to fall asleep, and I used to sleep up to 15 hours a day. I used to just put myself to sleep rather than face the realities of being awake.

33

JACQUES PAUW

BLOODY TRAIL OF THE SOUTH AFRICAN POLICE (1989)

from *Vrye Weekblad*

INTRODUCED BY ANTON HARBER

South Africa

In the late 1980s, apartheid was in its death throes, violent and unstable. State security forces were going all out to suppress a growing popular uprising, and this included mass detentions, torture, and killings, overt and covert, legal and extralegal. At the same time, elements of the ruling party were toying with the idea of negotiations, and cabinet ministers were secretly meeting with Nelson Mandela in prison. It was this confluence of forces that allowed for one of the most sensational stories—which had been bubbling under the surface for some years—to burst into the open.

On October 20, 1989, the *Weekly Mail*, a small, "alternative," antiapartheid newspaper where I was co-editor, ran the contents of a sworn affidavit from a former policeman on death row, Albert Nofemela. He had been sentenced to death for ordinary criminal murders, but said he had been part of a police hit squad that had targeted antiapartheid activists.

Nofemela's life was saved by human rights lawyers who normally acted for his victims, but wanted him to tell his story and rushed to court to get a last-minute stay of execution. Over the next few weeks, he gave the first explanations of various assassinations and disappearances that had taken place over a number of years.

Few took much notice, probably because he was a lowly black and criminal policeman and it was such a risky story. Except for one crucial person:

Excerpt from Jacques Pauw, "Bloody Trail of the South African Police," *Vrye Weekblad*, November 19, 1989. Translated by Mia Swart.

Nofemela's commander, Captain Dirk Coetzee. Coetzee saw that the game was up, fled into exile, and talked to a journalist he had known for years, Jacques Pauw, of a spunky Afrikaans "alternative" newspaper, *Die Vrye Weekblad* (Free Weekly).

On November 17, Coetzee's story was splashed over four pages in *Vrye Weekblad*. "Meet Captain Dirk Johannes Coetzee," it said, "commander of a South African Police death squad. He tells exclusively of the full gruesome details of political assassination, poisoning, bomb attacks in foreign countries and letter bombs."

"I was at the heart of the whore," he said, referring to a farm called Vlakplaas, headquarters of the killer squad.

The story spread around the world, though the mainstream local media mainly carried the official denials, leaving the "alternatives" to pursue the story. A few months earlier, these papers would likely have been confiscated or closed down (as had happened a year earlier), but there was enough political uncertainty in the air for the security forces to be constrained.

Mandela was released from prison within a few months and negotiations began. This—and related stories which emerged over the next few months—were to be crucial in exposing, and constraining, the source of much of the violence of the transitional period and its origins in security-force elements who wanted to disrupt negotiations.

On September 21, 1990, Eddie Koch of the *Weekly Mail* published details of the Caprivi 200, a paramilitary unit trained by military intelligence at a secret base in Namibia, and which became central to the violence of that period. On July 19, 1991, the *Weekly Mail* broke what became known as Inkathagate—secret police funding for the ANC's rival, Inkatha. In August came a story of how the Caprivi 200 were training Inkatha squads. In January 1992, an Inkatha youth leader defected and gave an insider's details of collaboration between military intelligence and Inkatha to counter the ANC. In the same month, there was a story of vigilante units trained by the Caprivi 200 at work in other parts of the country. In May 1992, journalist Drew Forrest exposed a network of front companies and safe houses being used in covert anti-ANC activities. In September 1992, Louise Flanagan wrote about secret and illegal military operations in the Eastern Cape area. In the same month, Paul Stober and Eddie Koch exposed the Directorate of Covert Collections, another dirty tricks operation in the military.

The newspapers were largely free from state interference during this period of negotiations. But the scientist and doctor who had been named as the source of poison used against activists, Dr. Lothan Neethling, sued *Vrye Weekblad* and the *Weekly Mail*. He lost, but won on appeal at the end of a lengthy case that drained the resources of *Vrye Weekblad*. Since then, more evidence has emerged against Neethling. *Vrye Weeklbad*, however, closed in February 1994 shortly before the country's first democratic elections of 1994 went off relatively peacefully.

Hit Squad's Register of Terror

Captain Dirk Coetzee admits that he had, until and including 1982, actively participated and helped plan various murders and terror attacks that were committed by the South African Police's special unit at Vlakplaas.

Then he still kept in touch with several members of the hit squad and is aware of other acts of terror in the following years.

Here is his register of death:

The murder of the anti-apartheid activist and Durban lawyer Griffiths Mxenge:

"In November 1981 I was called from Vlakplaas to Durban by Brigadier Van der Hoven, the then head of Security in Natal, where I was instructed to kill Mxenge.

"The police knew that money for the ANC was channelled through him, but could not prove it. I was told to ensure that the murder looked like a robbery, because Van der Hoven said the police were not in the mood for another Biko case.

"The security police in Durban pointed out his home to us and informed us about his movements. Captain Koos Vermeulen, Warrant Officer (now Lieutenant) Paul van Dyk and I laced four pieces of meat with strychnine to poison his dogs with and gave it to my Askaris, Almond Nofomela, David Tshikalange, Brian Ngulungwa and one Joe.

"I instructed them clearly that he should be killed with knives and not be shot. I was then informed of all their movements: how they followed him, the poisoning of his three dogs and the trap they had set for him on the side of the road.

"They told me how they had stopped, kidnapped and taken him to the Umlazi Stadium where they stabbed him to death with knives. They also cut his throat and cut his ears off.

"After the incident I met them late at night at a pre-arranged meeting place where they had Mxenge's jacket, watch, wallet and car keys. They assured me that it looks like a robbery.

"I've since reported back to Van der Hoven, who instructed that the team must return to Pretoria.

"There I was called to Brigadier Marius Schoon, who very anxiously wanted to know if we had left any traces. He ordered that Mxenge's car should be burned immediately. It was done close to the Swaziland border.

"I later heard that General Johan Coetzee, then Head of the Security Police, after my report back, had been called out of a meeting to hear the news of the successful operation.

"The Askaris each received R 1000 for their good work."

The murder of two ANC members near Komatipoort:

"After the army's raid into Maputo in 1980, two suspected ANC members, Vusi and Ghost, were kidnapped and brought into South Africa. Ghost was taken to Vlakplaas where he later willingly started to work with the police. Vusi was held in the police cells in Brits, where he had the attitude of 'Charge me or shoot me.'

"Schoon gave the instruction that Vusi and another captive ANC member that was held at Vlakplaas, Peter, had to be gotten rid of. I collected Vusi (his MK name) from the police cells and took him to an abandoned farm near the Kopfontein border post where Captain Koos Vermeulen and Peter were already waiting for us.

"I first let Vusi sign three different, predated invoices with three different pens so it would seem as if he was still alive and in our service three months later.

"Vermeulen and I poured poison, that had been prepared by the forensics laboratory, into their cold drink and beer. Everyone talked about Lothar's poison (General Lothar Neethling is head of the forensics laboratory). We were assured that 60 grams would be enough to let them die of a 'heart attack.' The poison would not work. We increased the dosage to 360 grams each, but nothing happened.

"We later took the two to Komatipoort where Paul van Dyk waited for us. From there we went to a farm nearby where major Archie Flemington of Security at Komatipoort met us.

"We gave Vusi and Peter sleep medication that had also been prepared by the forensics laboratory. We had been asked beforehand to keep notes of the effects of the sleep medication. When the two 'terros/terries' were sufficiently confused, Vermeulen shot them through the head with a Makarov pistol with a silencer.

"The two bodies were then burned along with wood and tyres that we found on a rubbish dump. It took seven hours before the bodies were burned out. The ash and the remains were dumped into the Komati River.

"During the burning of the two 'terries' (terrorists) security men of Komatipoort told me how they had distributed strong alcohol, laced with poison, among

ANC members in Maputo. The poison is injected through the lids of the bottles with a micro needle."

The burning of a "second Biko" [. . .]
>   The murder of activist Patrick Makau and a young child [. . .]
>   The bomb attack on Chris Hani, military leader of Umkhonto We'Sizwe [. . .]
>   The murder of (exiled journalist, researcher and activist) Ruth First [. . .]
>   Hit on Marius Schoon [. . .]
>   A diamond trader is killed by the hit squad [. . .]
>   An ANC member is blown up in Swaziland [. . .]
>   A Kidnapping from Swaziland [. . .]
>   The blow-up of ANC offices in London [. . .]

Coetzee speaks of several other days of terror that he personally was involved in or that he knew of. He speaks of other incidents, especially in Swaziland where ANC members were murdered and kidnapped.

34

HORACIO VERBITSKY

THE CONFESSION (1995)
from *Página/12*

INTRODUCED BY ERNESTO SEMÁN

Argentina

In November 1994, a man approached journalist Horacio Verbitsky on the subway. Verbitsky was on his daily commute to the office from which he had produced the most insightful investigative reporting in Argentina for more than a decade. The man was Adolfo Scilingo, a naval officer who had spent the 1976–1983 military dictatorship stationed at the Navy Petty-Officers School of Mechanics (ESMA), the largest concentration camp of the regime.

"We did terrible things there, worse than the Nazis," he told Verbitsky. Scilingo then revealed the most gruesome episode in Argentine history: the armed forces had disposed of political detainees, *the disappeared*, by throwing them naked, drugged, and alive from military airplanes into the ocean. He admitted to having personally participated in the deaths of at least thirty detainees.

Verbitsky's interview with Scilingo appeared on March 3, 1995, a few months after their first encounter on the subway. Though there had been evidence of the armed forces' procedures, "The Confession" provided tragic detail about the so-called "Death Flights" that made that evidence intelligible. Until then, nobody had confessed to how it had been done—the victims had died, and the perpetrators had remained in a pact of silence. Moreover, the repressor's confession made it clear that those, and many other human

Excerpt from Horacio Verbitsky, "The Confession," *Página/12*, March 3, 1995. Translated by Nicolo Gnecchi-Ruscone.

rights violations, were not random acts committed by isolated members of repressive forces but part of a systematic plan approved and ordered by the military junta.

The words of Scilingo opened a window into the recent past, but also set in motion spectacular events that reached into the future. Only a few months later, under pressure from the public outcry generated by the interview, the army chief of staff, General Martín Balza, arrived on one of the most-viewed political programs on Argentine TV. There, to the surprise of most viewers, he became the first head of the army to publicly acknowledge (and to apologize for) the role of the armed forces in the massive violations of human rights committed during the military dictatorship.

The importance of these events can hardly be overstated. They are at the center of the redefinition of human rights that occurred in democratic Argentina. In 1983, determined to tackle impunity, the first democratic president, Raúl Alfonsín, made the decision to send the military juntos to jail and opened massive investigations into violations of human rights, a singular step among the many countries labeled under "democratic transition." But he faced fierce opposition from the armed forces. In 1987, after a mutiny staged by members of the army, Congress passed a law promoted by Alfonsín that dramatically narrowed the scope of the prosecutions. In 1990, President Carlos Menem reversed what the country had achieved, declaring a general amnesty that set the juntos free and precluded further action from Argentine justice.

Verbitsky's interview turned the tide in the battle for justice. Human rights organizations demanded that cases against members of the military forces and the chiefs who had given the orders be opened. The revelations led to new ones about other crimes against humanity, including the theft of babies born in prisons. Toward the late 1990s, judges from Spain, France, and other countries took some of these cases into their own hands, claiming that Argentina's amnesty laws precluded it from fulfilling justice, adding pressure for the laws to be revised. It was only in 2003, under the administration of President Néstor Kirchner, that the amnesty laws and other restrictions were declared unconstitutional, restarting the trials for violations of human rights. At press time, over fifteen hundred members of the armed and security forces are standing trial and more than half of them have already been convicted, including all the members of the military junta. Many of those convicted, including dictator Jorge Rafael Videla, have died in jail.

At the center of these political changes was the explosion of investigative journalism in democratic Argentina, a rise symbolized by the publication of the newspaper *Página/12* in 1987. Aligned to the left of the political spectrum, *Página/12* became the first paper to center its coverage in investigative reporting, and the most persistent in following cases rather than press releases, bringing to an end the more passive kind of journalism shaped during the dictatorship. While Verbitsky and others brought the baggage and debates from the 1970s, a new generation of young journalists joined the paper attracted to the mystical aura of the old guard as well as to the fresh air the paper brought to the public sphere. From then on, some of the most relevant political investigations were revealed by *Página/12*, from political deals to corruption cases to crucial decisions in foreign policy. Over the following years, the major and more traditional newspapers incorporated these contributions. Journalism in Argentina had changed. Yet the *Página/12* coverage of human rights, the crimes committed during the dictatorship, and their prosecution in democracy were its trademark. Verbitsky's interview with Scilingo was, in fundamental ways, a culmination of that evolution.

In 2005, a Spanish court found Scilingo responsible for crimes against humanity, including extrajudicial executions. He received a sentence of 640 years and must serve the legal limit of thirty. He is currently in a Spanish prison.

The year after the interview appeared in *Página/12*, Verbitsky published an extended version of his conversation with Scilingo. The book, called *The Flight*, was translated into four languages and was an immediate bestseller in Argentina. It is clear why the former member of the navy approached Verbitsky: besides having denounced several scandals that occurred in democratic Argentina, he had investigated the most atrocious human rights violations committed during the dictatorship and published his findings. In his dual role of journalist and activist, he became president of CELS, one of the largest human rights organizations in Latin America. He is a journalist who explicitly takes sides in the fractious politics of contemporary Argentina. In the tradition of Rodolfo Walsh, Verbitsky embodies the essence of "periodismo comprometido" in these times, committed journalism in the form of a nonnegotiable search for the truth: a form of the profession that yields fruit for readers as much as it does for citizens.

[. . .] Up to now no protagonists [of the repression] have revealed what had happened to the victims of the interrogations. According to [the captain of Corbeta and ex-chief of the the Navy Petty-Officers School of Mechanics, Adolfo] Francisco Scilingo, up to fifteen hundred and two thousand detainees at the the Navy Petty-Officers School of Mechanics were thrown to their deaths in the Atlantic Ocean from aeroplanes [. . .] between the years 1976 and 1977, with orders that came down the navy's chain of command. Human rights groups have estimated between four and five thousand. [. . .] Scilingo was never mentioned by survivors or taken to court. Before the criminal trial against Molina Pico, he had written a letter to the ex-director Jorge Videla, to the ex-chief of the admiralty of the navy, Admiral Jorge Ferrer, and to President Carlos Menem, requesting that they inform the country of the situation. None of them replied. In his letter to Ferrer, Scilingo said that in the the the Navy Petty-Officers School of Mechanics "they have ordered me to act on the margin of the law and have turned me into a delinquent." [. . .]

A Christian Death

According to his account, the elimination of prisoners by a method not mentioned in military regulations was due to a direct order, communicated to all the officials assigned to the naval area Puerto Belgrano after the coup of 1976, from the commander of naval operations, vice-admiral Luis María Mendía.

"Mendía said, in the base's cinema, that subversives who were condemned to death or who were ordered to be eliminated would fly, and as there are persons who have problems, some would not reach their destination. He also said that they had consulted with the religious authorities to find a way that was Christian and non-violent," explained Scilingo, the author of that account.

Returning from their flights, the chaplains would comfort the officials with quotes from the Gospels over the necessary separation of the husk from the seed, he added. He participated in two of these flights under orders from the chief of defense of ESMA, frigate captain Adolfo Mario Arduino, who was later promoted to vice-admiral and commander of navy operations.

—In conversation among yourselves, how did you refer to this?

—It was called flight. It was normal, even though in this moment it is considered an abnormality. Just as Pernías or Rolón said to the senators, the question of torture to get information from the enemy had been adopted as regulation, well, this as well. When I received the order, I went to the basement where we kept those who would fly. Below there was nobody left. They were informed that they would be transferred to the south and for that reason they would be administered a vaccine. The "vaccine" consisted of a dose of sedative to render them dumb. That was how we put them to sleep.

—Who applied it?

—A naval doctor. Then they were loaded onto a green navy truck with a canvas cover. We drove to the Aerodrome, entering from the back gate. The subversives were loaded onto the plane like zombies. [. . .]

—Who participated?

—The majority of the officers of the navy did a flight, people were on rotation, a sort of communion.

—What does that communion consist of?

—It was something that had to be done. I don't know what the executioner's experience is when they have to kill, whether by the knife or the electric chair. No one liked to do it, it wasn't something we enjoyed. But it was done and it was understood that it was the best way, it wasn't discussed. It was something supreme that we were doing for the country. A supreme act. When the order was received the topic was never mentioned. It was obeyed automatically. They came on rotation from all over the country. One person might have been excused as only an exception. If only it was a small group, but it wasn't. It was the whole navy.

—What was the reaction of the detained when you informed them of the vaccine and transfer?

—They were happy.

—No one suspected what was going on?

—No way. No one was aware that they were about to die. Once the plane took off, the doctor who was on board gave them a second dose, a strong sedative. They were totally asleep.

—When the prisoners were asleep, what would you guys do?

—This is very morbid.

—What you did is morbid.

—There are four things that still pain me. The two flights that I did, the person who I saw get tortured and the memory of the sound of the chains and of the screams. I saw them only a couple of times, but I cannot forget that sound. [. . .]

—How would you take the sleeping people to the doors?

—Two of us. We would lift them up to the door.

—How many people do you calculate were assassinated this way?

—Between fifteen to twenty every Wednesday.

—For how long?

—Two years.

—Two years, a hundred Wednesdays, between fifteen hundred to two thousand people.

—Yes [. . .]

—Which naval personnel went on each flight?

—In the cabin there was the normal flight crew.

—And with the prisoners?

—Two officers, a sub-officer, a corporal, and the doctor. On my first flight, the corporal of the Prefecture totally didn't know the mission. When he became

aware of what he was supposed to do onboard he had a nervous attack. He began to cry. He didn't understand anything and began mumbling. I didn't know how
to deal with a man from the Prefecture in such a critical situation. At the end he
was sent to the captain's cabin. We finished undressing the subversives.

—You, the other officer, and the doctor?

—No, no. The doctor only gave the second injection, that was all. Then he
would go to the cabin.

—Why?

—They said because of the Hippocratic Oath. [. . .]

—So you would go and throw thirty people alive into the sea, return, and not
speak between yourselves about the subject?

—No.

—You would return to routine as if it never existed?

—Yes. Everyone wanted to erase it. I cannot.

35

PATRICIA VERDUGO

FROM *CHILE, PINOCHET, AND THE CARAVAN OF DEATH* (1989)

INTRODUCED BY FRANCISCA SKOKNIC

Chile

This excerpt is from one of the first bestsellers published in Chile that exposed some of the human rights abuses committed by the military during the brutal regime of Augusto Pinochet.[1] Originally published in 1989, *The Claws of the Puma*, as it was titled in Spanish, electrified the public. In this classic of the genre, investigative reporter Patricia Verdugo exposed the macabre "Caravan of Death" that resulted when, in October 1973, a military commission traveled from South to North Chile in a Puma helicopter landing in different cities. Most of the victims were supporters of Salvador Allende's government who handed themselves in voluntarily after the September 11 coup d'état, when the new military authorities made a public call to detain them. Despite their compliance with the new regime, seventy-five people were savagely murdered without trial.

The military commission was led by General Sergio Arellano Stark, one of the conspirators who turned against President Allende. It was Arellano who involved Augusto Pinochet in the coup. Once in power, Pinochet asked him to lead what would come to be known as "The Caravan of Death."

It took sixteen years for the truth about General Sergio Arellano Stark's commission to be unveiled. Patricia Verdugo published the first edition of

Excerpt from Patricia Verdugo, *Chile, Pinochet, and the Caravan of Death* (Miami: North-South Center Press at the University of Miami, 1989), 89–90.

Chile, Pinochet, and the Caravan of Death after the 1988 referendum that defeated Pinochet, but when the country was still under his dictatorship. The book was widely read and, most important, it set the record straight about crimes that had remained largely unnoticed.

Chile, Pinochet, and the Caravan of Death is probably Verdugo's most important journalistic legacy. Verdugo painstakingly collected testimonies from a wide range of sources, from local military officials to the families of victims, to connect the events of October 1973 and link them directly to Pinochet. She also describes how in many cases the local media was used to print the official line on the killings. After Pinochet was arrested in London in 1998, the judge who prosecuted him for the first time in Chile, Juan Guzmán, used the book as a guide to investigate the crimes and admitted it as evidence during the trials. Although forty years have now passed since the murders, some of the trials remain open. Arellano Stark was sentenced to six years of prison for the four murders that took place in the city of Cauquenes but the case was later dismissed because he suffers from Alzheimer's. The other crimes, connected to the remaining seventy-one deaths, are still being investigated.

Patricia Verdugo was part of a group of brave journalists that took great risks to report and publish exposés during the dictatorship. Curiously, it was during those years of danger and restrictions on freedom of expression that Chilean investigative journalism flourished and later declined after the return to democracy in 1990. Patricia Verdugo wrote ten books about Pinochet's dictatorship and human rights violations, one of them investigating the murder of her own father following his arrest. She was the co-founder of *Hoy* (*Today*), which "soon became established as Chile's premiere magazine, and an important voice for counter-official truth. Verdugo remained one of its leading writers until 1990."[2] She was awarded the Maria Moors Cabot Prize from Columbia University and the Chilean National Journalism Prize, among many other awards. She died in 2008.

––––––––––

Everything indicates that the Puma Helicopter that carried General Sergio Arellano and his entourage landed in Copiapó at approximately 7 p.m. on October 16, 1973. Commander Lapostol bid goodbye to the general in the La Serena airport at around 6:00 p.m., and he was certain about the next destination: Copiapó. "I witnessed the arrangements made with the control tower for the flight plan. He went straight to Copiapó," Colonel Lapostol told me.

General Arellano was received by the Commander of the Number 1 Motorized

Engineers Regiment of Copiapó, Lieutenant Colonel Oscar Haag Blaschke, who was responsible for holding dozens of political prisoners at the military base. One of the former political prisoners, Lincoyán Zepeda recalled that all were "members or leaders of parties [branches] of Popular Unity, with the exception of four imprisoned priests. Our relationships with the soldiers and noncommissioned officers were good. However, that was not the case with the officers. They treated us very harshly."

There were also many prisoners in the Copiapó jail. Both the ones from the base and from the jail went through interrogations in the main office, where the court-martial, from what has been found out, was made up of Major Carlos Enriotti Bley (military prosecutor), Major Carlos Brito Guttierrez, and Police Major Rene Peri. There is no further information on the operations of this court-martial.

Former prisoner Zepeda stated that on the morning of October 16th, the prisoners were told that a general from Santiago was coming. "We were made to get up very early, leave everything neatly arranged, and clean up. I remember that we were even told that this general could have some good news for us. The noncommissioned officers thought that he was coming to review the cases of the political prisoners and give them a quick solution.

"At approximately 2:00 in the afternoon, we had the first indication that nothing good could come from this visit. In a break from routine, we were forced to go back into our cells at approximately 2:30pm. The soldiers' treatment was harsh, and the atmosphere was very tense. At approximately 9:00 in the evening, the door suddenly opened, and a group of soldiers that we had never seen before on the base entered the area where we were. They looked us over, and they made the following comment, 'here are the little pigeons,' and they left. My impression is that they were officers. Two hours later, the group returned, a list was read and they made the people on that list leave. It was the last time we saw them alive."[3]

Another Former prisoner, Juan Lafferte, age 66, said "I still don't understand why they didn't take me that day. I remember that the soldiers came that night, asking if anyone knew Mansilla or Palleras. The political prisoners were held in tents and in one of the barracks. I was in the tents with a French priest. There was an atmosphere of great anxiety. The soldiers, who were not from the base, began to call the prisoners. Guardia was in the tent next to mine, and they took him away. They looked at me but didn't say anything. They left later, and we heard noises that sounded like people were being hit with gun butts and groaning. It seemed that one of the prisoners got cocky. After that I heard screaming. Just imagine, I was about 10 meters away, and I heard it. Afterward there was a noise that sounded like heavy bales being thrown into a truck. Then the sound of an engine and silence."[4]

What had happened that night was communicated to the people of Copiapó on Thursday, October 18, 1973, through a military proclamation, published on the front page of the town's local daily newspaper, *Atacama*.

36

OGEN KEVIN ALIRO

UGANDA: HEROES TURNING IN THEIR GRAVES? (1998)

from *The Monitor*

INTRODUCED BY GEORGE W. LUGALAMBI

Uganda

Until Ugandans voted to restore multiparty politics in a constitutional referendum in 2005 after a twenty-year suspension of political parties, the media shouldered the burden of providing the only meaningful checks and balances on government. Uganda was for all intents and purposes a one-party state for as long as formal party activities were broadly restricted. Without an institutionalized opposition to challenge the party in power—the National Resistance Movement—and to hold public officials and the government to account, the media inevitably filled a void that in a functional democracy would be the space for robust competitive political contestation.

By playing the role typically performed by opposition and independent civil society actors, the media naturally rubbed the government the wrong way at every turn. In a dominant-party system such as Uganda's, the media asked all the questions that a pliant legislature was incapable of asking. In return, the media took all the heat that would have been directed at opposition politicians and other government critics in civil society.

Citizens with grievances against the state, including human rights violations, had no other recourse but to bring their issues to the media in the hope that exposure in the public domain would help them get redress. Back in the 1990s, there were very few political restraints on government, and only bold journalists had the guts to call it out for its excesses and to demand

Excerpt from Ogen Kevin Aliro, "Uganda: Heroes Turning in Their Graves?," *The Monitor*, June 9, 1998, allafrica.com.ezproxy.cul.columbia.edu/stories/199806090099.html.

answers. It is in this context that journalists like the late Ogen Kevin Aliro of *The Monitor* mustered the courage to take on the government and to ask it to account for its actions.

Aliro was arguably the most intrepid journalist of his time. *The Monitor*, Uganda's foremost independent newspaper then and now, single-handedly fought to expand the realm of public discussion on issues that were deemed sensitive or which the state had an interest in covering up. For its unwavering commitment to shining a light on issues the government wanted to keep out of public view, *The Monitor* paid a high price. For several years in the 1990s, for instance, the government withheld all its advertising from the paper. With government being the single biggest source of advertising revenue for the media at the time—the private sector was in its infancy—the advertising ban was clearly intended to ruin *The Monitor* as a business and to get it to toe the government line if it wanted to remain a viable commercial operation. Its circulation at the time was only about 25,000.

In November 1996, insurgents of the Allied Democratic Forces (ADF) launched an attack on the western Uganda town of Kasese from their base in the Democratic Republic of Congo (DRC). This came on the heels of a similar invasion in February 1995 on Buseruka, also in the west of the country. The Kasese attack was quickly snuffed out by the military—the Uganda People's Defense Forces (UPDF)—but then mutated into a bombing campaign aimed at targets in the capital city Kampala. There were at least five bombing incidents in different areas of Kampala in 1998, which claimed about a dozen lives. The carnage plunged the country into a feeling of being under siege, and predictably provoked a gritty response from the government.

The city bombings, which the government blamed on the ADF, sparked a wave of arrests of young Muslims whom the government suspected of treason by virtue of their alleged participation in rebel activities. Various organizations protested the way these suspects were treated, including the Uganda Muslim Youth Assembly, the Uganda Muslim Supreme Council, and the government's own Uganda Human Rights Commission, which confirmed on June 2, 1998, that security agencies were holding the missing suspects in "ungazetted places." These places were known in security circles as "safe houses."

With mounting pressure from the media, victims' families, the Islamic community, and human rights watchdogs, the government eventually owned up to this troubling trend of young Muslims being arrested and put away in undisclosed locations without trial. The internal affairs minister reported that about half of the estimated sixty-two detainees had been charged with treason, a claim that the suspects' relatives did not buy as they insisted that they remained in detention without due process.

The Monitor's dogged pursuit of this story, its relentless efforts to get to the bottom of the issue, and its skepticism of official explanations brought the plight of these suspects to the attention of the nation. In his article "Uganda: Heroes turning in their graves," whose timing in *The Monitor* was the nationally commemorated Heroes Day on June 9, 1998, Aliro reflectively summed up the situation of the Tabliq youth. "Many of them have been held incommunicado for ages and have never appeared in court (within 48 hours) as required by law," he said. "There is also no official police record of why they were arrested, or where they are being held—and by whom."

The 1990s were an edgy period in Uganda's politics. The country had been through the first multiparty election in 1996, a year after promulgating a new constitution. Political parties had been freed to organize and contest for power after a decade-long suspension of all but a highly circumscribed fraction of their activities.

Meantime, the Lord's Resistance Army insurgency was raging in northern Uganda. The government accused its nemesis, the Sudanese regime, of fomenting trouble for it as well as funding and giving the rebels sanctuary. Moreover, there were several other rebel groups fighting the government. The ADF, a motley collection of groups, was particularly active in western Uganda and eastern DRC. And it appealed to some of the young Muslims of the Tabliq sect, while the larger Islamic community went the extra mile to distance itself from the sect's ideology and actions. The government was accused of profiling people on religious grounds given its reaction to the ADF attacks.

The political sensitivities of the day notwithstanding, *The Monitor* as the main independent newspaper never shirked its responsibility of speaking truth to power. The paper groomed a breed of hard-nosed investigative reporters like Aliro who asked tough questions of the government. Whether the so-called safe houses were real or imaginary, the term itself came to symbolize a throwback to the dark days of Uganda's vicious politics and, for many people, evoked memories of state-inspired brutality against citizens. Aliro and *The Monitor* played no mean role in exposing the state's behavior and compelling it to explain itself.

KAMPALA—When rumours that mainly Tabliq youths and other citizens were being arrested, and some had even "disappeared" after being picked in the middle of the night by "security agents" first surfaced, most of us dismissed them.

It sounded like the ravings of an extremist Islamist group. And, it was not like the Museveni government to start picking people, detaining and torturing them in secret, ungazetted jails.

But the rumours kept coming and coming, until recently when even such respected Muslims as Makerere's Hajji Abbas Kiyimba also added their voices to those already condemning the unexplained arrests and alleged "disappearance" of some citizens.

Then, June 2, our worst fears were confirmed. Uganda Human Rights Commission (UHRC) chairperson, Margaret Sekagya, spoke out—challenging police and other security agencies to set free Muslims being held in ungazetted places.

Many of them have been held incommunicado for ages, and have never appeared in court (within 48 hours) as required by law. There is also no official police record of why they were arrested, or where they are being held—and by whom.

The army (UPDF) has denied it is the one arresting or holding any people in ungazetted places. UPDF spokesman at the general headquarters in Bombo, Capt. Shaban Bantariza, was quoted denying UPDF's involvement. Acting Chief of Staff, Brigadier James Kazini, also denies the army is holding Tabliq youths or causing citizens to "disappear."

"It cannot be us . . . the UPDF is not involved," he intimated to me recently.

The Police too are not involved. If they were, the suspects would be in police cells or remand prisons, and there would be official records of who is being held where, and why.

So which is this "faceless" security agency that comes like a thief in the night to cause citizens to "disappear"?

The possibility of a return to the state terror that haunted us under Idi Amin and Obote II hit me two weeks ago when a businessman friend called me to tell me "some security people" had come and picked one of his managers—a Muslim—and taken him away, claiming he was a rebel.

Another friend told me of a girl and boy who were dumped in Luzira prison for almost two years, without any fair trial, simply because they had angered the wife of some "big man."

Before I had digested that, came the sad story of Hassan Nyanzi which is featured elsewhere in today's issue of The Monitor. The youth speaks of "hell" in the secret cells used by the faceless government security agency for which neither the police nor the army shall accept responsibility.

Nyanzi, said he was blind-folded, tied kandoya,[1] kicked and hanged upside down in the various secret places where he was detained—including a garage and toilet! He was once locked up in a toilet without food or water for two nights.

At another detention centre, the youth speaks of other inmates—detainees who have been maimed by torture. Some can hardly walk, they were either being helped to walk by their colleagues or simply crawled.

"A man came close to me and thrashed me with a big stick on my head and this is how I joined the rest in the wailing. They again tied me kandoya and I was kicked by more than five people before they hanged me upside down," he narrated.

Under torture, Nyanzi cried out the names of some of his workplace friends who, according to him, were later also picked up and have not been seen to date. Nyanzi now claims they were not "rebels" or "terrorists"—he only mentioned their names to save himself from further torture.

Nyanzi's testimony is sad. And no right-thinking Ugandan can continue to keep quiet when citizens, even suspected criminals, are arrested, tortured and jailed in "secret cells" without trial—and by a nameless security network.

The government too must come out to explain. First, it's strange that a government—which though at the bottom of its popularity rating ever   is still generally acceptable to many Ugandans, should resort to such crude torture methods.

It's not enough for the army and police to deny responsibility. The fact is that these arrests have been going on, and the secret torture chambers exist somewhere around this town. Nyanzi, if he is telling only the whole truth, is living testimony of it all.

The government must tell us why it seems to be targeting mainly a section of Muslims. There is no defence for criminals, even if they are a religious sect. But if government has unearthed a sinister plot by Tabliq youths or other Islamist groups, they should tell the nation—and justify the arrests and alleged disappearances.

In any case, let those arrested be taken to court and charged with treason, terrorism or whatever crimes they are supposed to have committed. They must be held in gazetted places, and allowed access to food, medical care and their relatives.

Otherwise, as we celebrate Heroes Day, today, the true heroes who went to the bush and shed their blood so that we could have real freedom, must be turning in their graves.

A true patriot and hero couldn't have gone to the bush so that a citizen of Uganda is once again blindfolded, suspended upside down, tortured and detained in dark, private toilets.

The heroes we remember today couldn't have gone to the bush so that citizens "disappear" without trace like was the case under Idi Amin and Obote II.

Neither can government continue hiding under that escapist defence that such horror stories of arrests, torture and killings are "just isolated incidents."

There are too many of those "isolated incidents" now—and if we are not careful, or dare speak out in time, next time it'll be you or me in one of those blood stained secret cells that almost swallowed Nyanzi.

37

MEHMET BARANSU

FIRST HE PULLED THE PIN, THEN HE HANDED OVER THE GRENADE (2009)

from *Taraf*

INTRODUCED BY ANDREW FINKEL

Turkey

The news item presented here from a Turkish newspaper might not seem an astounding man-bites-dog revelation, although the incident it describes is one of astonishing cruelty. An officer punishes a private asleep on duty by making him clutch a primed hand grenade. The soldier blows himself up, along with three other colleagues, and the army tries to hush up the incident as an accident. *Taraf*, a small independent daily, gets the story and (to reveal the sequel) the officer is eventually sentenced by a military court for nine years, two months on a charge tantamount to manslaughter.

In the Turkish context, where the military had been a closed book, more used to manipulating headlines than being held accountable by them, it was the very "ordinariness" of the story that that caused so huge a sensation. In 2009, it earned reporter Mehmet Baransu that year's top prize by the Turkish Journalists Association. He was responsible for even more substantial stories that undermined the authority of the military, including controversial revelations of an attempted coup. For this, he was forced to take on a bodyguard. Yet in a curious way, this simple story was the more striking. Everyone knew (or assumed) that the Turkish army plotted against its government. But in a country with universal conscription, in which all young men must serve, the revelation that it was so wanting in pastoral care for its

Excerpt from Mehmet Baransu, "First He Pulled the Pin, Then He Handed Over the Grenade," *Taraf*, August 28, 2009. Translated by Isobel Finkel.

charges that it would cover up the deaths of four young recruits was arguably more shocking.

It's no surprise that it appeared in *Taraf*, a newspaper that from its earliest days printed the stories no one else would touch, and that tried to hold accountable an establishment that basked in impunity.

Taraf was born in 2007 as an informal alliance of antiestablishment forces that had been repressed under the old Turkey and hoped to shape the new. It adopted a leftish, liberal take and spoke up for Kurdish cultural rights and Turkey's non-Muslim minorities. It defended those excluded from public life, be it for wearing an Islamic headscarf or having an LGBT lifestyle. Its stubborn questioning of authority set it apart from most Turkish newspapers, which still tiptoe around the news, putting the financial interests of their corporate proprietors above that of their readers' right to know. While others kowtowed, *Taraf* had attitude—best summed up as insolent.

It would be nice to be able to report that this studied disrespect helped break the mold of the Turkish press, but if anything the paper became a lesson in just how difficult it is to swim against the current. In the years after *Taraf* was founded, the media's tendency toward self-censorship gained momentum with even mainstream commentators afraid to raise their voices. An Amnesty International report published in 2013 continued to identify a raft of legislation, including a broad definition of abetting terrorism, used to penalize individuals not for acts they committed but for the opinions they express. The report condemned the court's wide powers of pretrial arrest and the continuing practice of meting out punishment out at the commencement of lengthy prosecutions rather than after sentencing. The New York–based Committee to Protect Journalism in 2012 and 2013 awarded Turkey the dubious distinction as the world's largest jailor of journalists. When Turkey sat down to negotiate European Union membership in 2005, the consensus was that the government had embarked on what appeared to be an unstoppable program of democratic reform. But as that changed, many questioned the government's commitment to freedom of expression as a basic right. For many the crunch came in 2013 when newspapers and television stations were so intimidated, many hardly bothered to report the wave of major demonstrations in Turkish cities against government high-handedness.

Yet however well-directed such criticism toward officialdom, it does not address a culture of complicity whereby the Turkish press has itself knowingly limited the range and depth of public debate. Media organizations, hamstrung by the economics of their industry and by the financial dependence of their non-press parent organizations on government grace and favor, are willing accomplices in the restrictions of their own freedoms.

If the press seemed more independent in the 1990s, this was because press barons had more freedom of action. They acted as king makers exercising power behind the scenes as Turkey went through a series of unstable coalition governments. For the last decade, and the era in which *Taraf* was born, the Justice and Development (AK) Party has maneuvered to consolidate its rule, and in so doing created a press far more subservient to its own cause. The press either supported the government or went into a lonely and expensive exile.

In this farrago, *Taraf* was an important experiment. Its proprietor, Başar Arslan, the owner of a chain of successful bookstores, made the unheard-of decision to leave the paper's editorial content to the editor, Ahmet Altan. Altan was a best-selling novelist and an outspoken columnist with a flare for irritating Turkey's old guard. He was also the scion of an influential press family who managed to assemble around him a team drawn from the journalistic mainstream. These included deputies Alev Er, himself a former editor-in-chief, and Yasemin Çongar, a long-serving Washington correspondent. This professional core meant it could not be dismissed as fringe or (despite a name that translates as "Partisan") ideologically driven.

"We didn't plan to fight the military," said Çongar.

It is a David aiming its slingshot at Turkey's powerful chiefs of staff is how *Taraf* will be best remembered. The confrontation built gradually. In October 2007, the Kurdistan Workers Party (or PKK—the Kurdish militants who had been waging a separatist campaign since 1984) mounted a sophisticated attack on a military post near the Iraq-Iran border, killing twelve, wounding seventeen, and taking another eight soldiers prisoner. The incident at Dağlıca prompted Turkey to mount a cross-border raid. It also occurred just days before a constitutional referendum on the office of the presidency. *Taraf* reported the incident along with the rest of the Turkish media but uniquely asked a series of questions about how the PPK was able to launch an assault that would have required weeks of preparation at a place under constant surveillance.

In a country where "causing an institution of the state to be held in disrepute" is a criminal offense, accusing the generals of incompetence took courage. In October 2008, after another PKK attack that left seventeen soldiers dead, the paper got its hands on defense satellite photos with time stamps, which revealed that Turkish military intelligence had more than ample warning that a large PKK contingent was moving into position. This prompted the military to roundly condemn the paper, announcing that a critical media would be responsible for "blood that has and will be shed." *Taraf*'s editors were expecting a raid on their Istanbul offices and Alev Er was sent into hiding so that the paper could continue to publish come what may.

As the whistle-blowers' paper of choice, it was viewed with suspicion by the authorities. In 2008, the national intelligence services—which report to the prime minister—ordered wiretaps on Altan, Çongar, and Baransu's phones. That same year, the AK Party was fighting a battle for its very survival in the Constitutional Court against a charge that it had undermined the secular nature of the Turkish state. It was convicted in July 2008, but with the warning of a fine and well short of the full penalty of being shut down altogether. On the principle that the enemy of my enemy is my friend, *Taraf* became the government's unlikely ally.

Taraf and Baransu published an entire suitcase full of leaked documents and computer discs, which led to the notorious Sledgehammer and Ergenekon trials in which the armed forces were accused of actively plotting to overthrow the AK Party government. The proceedings led to the sentencing or pretrial detention of almost 30 percent of the senior officer corps. They also led to accusations that the paper was an accomplice in a miscarriage of justice.

The defense team argued that much of the evidence had been fabricated—and not very well. The paper maintained that the weight and detail of the material it received and the seriousness of the proposed plot was so compelling that it had no option than publish. It was up to the courts, not the press, to decide on the admissibility of the evidence. It declined responsibility for the lengthy detention of suspects or the decision of the prosecutor to go after junior officers with the full severity of the law.

If I use the past tense it is because in December 2012, the paper under Altan's editorship ceased to exist (Alev Er had resigned much earlier). The paper had always struggled to pay its bills, and at a certain point its fight with the government became a luxury its proprietor could not afford and for a period at least the paper began to adopt a softer critical line. It still continues to publish. To declare my own hand, for over year I contributed, unpaid, a weekly column on current events, motivated by the paper's ideals. I watched *Taraf*'s battle against the odds and though I still wish it well, I no longer have the same sense of loyalty.

In a peculiar sense, *Taraf* was part author of its own demise. It fought against an establishment that tried to preserve antidemocratic prerogatives. It successfully took on the Turkish military. Yet while it helped to clear the battlefield of the government's traditional foes, it stood friendless in trying to fight the autocratic tendencies within government itself.

As time went on, the paper became increasingly outraged at what it saw as the readiness of Prime Minister Tayyip Erdoğan's government to sacrifice reform on the altar of political expediency. In his well-honed daily columns, Altan attacked Erdoğan as a "hollow bully," ready to adopt ultranationalist policies to further his own ambitions. The prime minister won a libel suit against Altan for calling him "arrogant, uninformed, and uninterested."

Taraf did make mistakes. In 2009, it was forced to retract a story suggesting that a television station had caused a fatal helicopter crash by persistently dialing a right-wing politician's mobile phone. It turned out the calls were made after the accident.

Yet while *Taraf* may not have been a great newspaper, it managed to do some great things. It changed the face of Turkey on a shoestring simply by trying to do the right thing. What would Turkey be like today if its better-heeled cousins in the media had done the same?

A unit commander in Elazığ province punished a soldier for being asleep on duty by pulling the pin of a grenade and ordering the private to hold the live munitions. The grenade exploded and four soldiers lost their lives.

The incident occurred ten days ago at the Koçyiğitler Battalion and was originally reported as an accident. It now transpires that it was direct result of a military punishment. Lieutenant Mehmet Tümer lost his temper with İbrahim Öztürk, whom he discovered asleep at his sentry post. He pulled the pin of a grenade and handed it to Private Öztürk. The private spent forty-five minutes pleading for help, the grenade clutched in his hand. However, at a certain point, his strength failed him.

The date was August 17, 2009. News agencies reported that four people had died in Karakoçan district of Elazığ following the accidental detonation of an explosive being handled by a soldier. According to the reports, the Private İbrahim Öztürk was killed by the blast along with İbrahim Yaman, Ali Osman Altın, and Mesut Bulut, companions who had been standing close at hand.

However, written statements seen by Taraf confirm that the incident happened not as the result of an accident but as a result of Lieutenant Mehmet Tümer's intention to punish Private İbrahim Öztürk for falling asleep on duty.

The lieutenant is reported to have removed the pin from the grenade and handed it to Private Öztürk. "If you let go of the thumb latch you will die, if you don't you will live," he said. Öztürk died along with three friends while trying to locate a replacement pin.

On the morning of the incident, master sergeant Şakir Akçan, who was on patrol duty from 5:00 to 7:00, came across the guard post at 6:00, according to witness statements obtained by Taraf. He encountered Öztürk and his fellow soldier Ahmet Şensoy fast asleep and removed Öztürk's grenade and Şensoy's gun's flash suppressor attachment, which later that morning he handed to Lieutenant Mehmet Tümer as evidence of dereliction of duty.

He Pulled the Pin and Handed Over the Grenade

Tümer immediately went to the sentry post where İbrahim Öztürk was on watch. He asked Öztürk for his grenade, which Private Öztürk was unable to locate. Mehmet Tümer showed Öztürk the grenade and said, "It was taken from you because you fell asleep." He then pulled the pin out of the device and handed it over.

"If you let go of the thumb latch you will die, if you hold on to it, you will survive," he said explicitly before himself leaving the sentry post.

The Commander Would Not Return the Pin

With the detonated device in his hand, Private Öztürk approached Lieutenant Tümer's position asking for the pin, saying, "I'm twenty-five. I've got seventy-five days of military service left. You're going to kill me."

"Return to your station. I'll come and replace it when the time is right," Lieutenant Tümer replied.

Öztürk then went to get help from another sentry post to find another pin. He then went back to the lieutenant but met with the same negative response.

He began to walk around the sentry posts again. At some point the soldier's friends Mesut Bulut, İbrahim Yaman, and Ali Osman gathered around him. By this point Öztürk's hands were sweaty, and the grenade exploded with an enormous bang. Öztürk and his three friends lost their lives.

Not in the Training

In a statement to the ensuing inquiry, Lieutenant Mehmet Tümer explained that he had removed the pin from a grenade as part of on-the-spot training, in order to demonstrate to the (now deceased) Private İbrahim Öztürk that the device would not explode as long as held the latch. However eight witnesses statements denied that there had been any attempt at training.

Eyewitnesses Describe the Moment of the Event

Infantry Sergeant Yiğit Acar:

Special Sergeant Şakir removed a grenade and a flash suppressor from his bag and said that he'd taken them from the sleeping soldiers. I gave the grenade and flash suppressor to Lieutenant Mehmet. He went to find İbrahim Öztürk and returned fifteen to twenty minutes later. He took a grenade pin out of his cartridge belt. When he realized where it came from, NCO officer Soner and Master Sergeant Şakir said to him "What have you done?" "Let it be a lesson to him," Lieutenant Mehmet replied.

Sergeant Şakir Akçan:

I worked out that İbrahim Öztürk was asleep at his post when he was meant to be on lookout. I took the grenade that was beside him. My intention was to make sure he could not deny the charge. I also saw Emrah Göz asleep, and took his flash suppressor. When Lieutenant Mehmet woke at 9:30, we made the situation known to him. Lieutenant Mehmet took the equipment and left us. Fifteen to twenty minutes later he returned, with İbrahim Öztürk following. The lieutenant then ordered İbrahim to return to his post. He said that he would join him in a bit to replace the pin. We understood that the pin of the grenade had been removed. Fifteen to twenty minutes later there was an explosion.

Infantryman Recep Koyuncu:

Mehmet Teğmen came to İbrahim's sentry post. They were there for ten minutes. There was a hand grenade in the lieutenant's hand, which he handed to İbrahim, removing the pin. "If you let go of the catch you'll die, if you don't you'll live," he said, and then left for the munitions station. İbrahim asked the lieutenant to give him the pin. "I'm twenty-five. I've got seventy-five days of military service left. You're going to kill me," he said. Lieutenant Mehmet told him to return to his post and that when the time came he would replace the pin. Later İbrahim went to where the lieutenant was again. He asked for the pin. The lieutenant again refused him. Five or ten minutes later there was an explosion.

I Gave Him the Grenade and I Told Him to Stay There

The 8th Corps Commands began an inquiry into four soldiers' deaths. Lieutenant Mehmet Tümer's statement read as follows: "On the seventeenth of June I was temporarily assigned to the battalion's Elazığ-Karakoçan Nohuttepe base camp. Up until sixteenth August 2009, I carried out duties as Team Commander. The battalion had been posted to the Elazığ district Gendarmerie Command's operations and command. On the sixteenth of August 2009, I left the Nohuttepe base camp with my team at around 20:30. We marched to the Düztepe location.

At about 23:00 we erected a temporary shelter and posted a lookout until the morning. When I awoke at 9:30, Special Sergeant Şakir Akçan informed me that he had discovered İbrahim Öztürk asleep at the Bixi sentry post and had taken his grenade.

I Asked İbrahim About His Grenade

At about 10:30 I saw İbrahim Öztürk standing at his post, and went to ask him for his grenade. At this point Ahmet Şensoy was sleeping as part of his allocated rest. İbrahim looked for his hand grenade inside his sentry post, and was unable to locate it. He still hadn't worked out that his hand grenade had been taken from him. Standard practice at a post is to put the grenade somewhere close at hand. When he couldn't find the grenade I produced it. "It's here. It was taken from you in the night because you fell asleep in the night," I told him.

As impromptu training to teach him the importance of the grenade I pulled the pin and placed the grenade in his hand. I ordered him not to move from his post and returned to mine. There is roughly a fifteen-meter distance between the two posts.

When I was at my station I saw İbrahim Öztürk leave his own post for the rocket station to the west. There is almost twenty meters between these two posts. I warned him to stay at his post. He came over to me. He asked for the pin. Ordering him back to his post, I told him I would come and replace it.

He returned to his post, but then a few minutes later I realized that he had gone over to the rocket station again.

This time I called him over, and telling him that I would come and replace the pin I told him to return to man his post. At this point I was at my own post.

I Turned and Heard an Explosion

Next to me was Yiğit Acer; five meters away was NCO Soner Süvarı and Master Sergeant Şakir Akçan.

And I went to their location. İbrahim returned to his post. Perhaps fifteen minutes later, there was an explosion. I can't remember the time, it might have been eleven, eleven thirty. From what I heard afterward, İbrahim had snuck to a third post with the grenade in his hand making sure I couldn't see him leave. It was there the explosion took place. I ran straight to where the source of the explosion and saw Ibrahim slumped facedown . . .

38

ALMA GUILLERMOPRIETO

SALVADORAN PEASANTS DESCRIBE MASS KILLING (1982)

from *The Washington Post*

INTRODUCED BY MICA ROSENBERG

El Salvador

Alma Guillermoprieto came to journalism on an unconventional path. Born in Mexico City, she was a young modern dancer in New York until she traveled to Cuba in 1970 to teach dance at the height of the Communist revolution. The experience was a political awakening. Soon after returning to New York from the island, she left the dance world behind. In her memoir *Dancing with Cuba*, she describes stumbling "more or less by accident" into reporting when she found herself in Nicaragua during the leftist Sandinista revolt against dictator Anastasio Somoza.[1] From there she went on to cover some of the most harrowing moments of the Central American civil wars in the late 1970s and '80s, including one of the largest and most devastating massacres of the twentieth century in the tiny country of El Salvador.

More than 75,000 people were killed and countless more "disappeared" during the 1979 to 1992 conflict between El Salvador's military government and the Farabundo Martí National Liberation Front (FMLN) guerrilla movement. After the revolutions in Cuba and Nicaragua, the United States saw El Salvador as the next battleground where guerrilla forces were threatening to overthrow the government and install a Communist regime in its backyard. The Reagan administration trained and equipped the Salvadoran army despite reports of soldiers committing human rights violations against the civilian population.

Alma Guillermoprieto, "Salvadoran Peasants Describe Mass Killing," *Washington Post*, January 27, 1982.

In January 1982, the guerrillas invited *New York Times* correspondent Ray Bonner and photographer Susan Meiselas to a remote province near the border with Honduras. Bonner told Guillermoprieto, then working as a stringer for the *Washington Post*, of their plans and she made a round of frantic calls to arrange her own trip. After trekking for days deep into the conflict zone escorted by guerrilla contacts, Bonner and Meiselas found first, and Guillermoprieto saw soon after, in the small hamlet of El Mozote, a scene of gruesome carnage.[2] Rufina Amaya, the massacre's sole survivor, told the reporters she had hid while soldiers corralled the villagers into the center of town and systematically executed them, raping the young women before they were killed.

Journalist Stanley Meisler, in a book about news decision making, tells the story of what happened to the two reports after that. Guillermoprieto, eager to get the story out as quickly as possible, handwrote her account on seven notebook pages, rolled them into a plastic film canister, and persuaded a rebel courier to take them to Honduras where a local reporter dictated the pages over the phone to her editors at the *Post*. Bonner's editors at the *Times* had started publishing a series of his stories on the war but had not yet reported on the massacre when Guillermoprieto's piece ran on the *Post*'s front page on January 27, 1982. They rushed to put out Bonner's version later that same day.[3]

The reaction—or non-reaction—was almost immediate. The stories appeared the day before the Reagan administration sent Congress a certification that El Salvador was making a significant effort to comply with international human rights standards as a condition for continued U.S. aid. The reports made that assertion look ridiculous. U.S. officials said they had no reason to believe the massacre actually took place and conducted a fly-over of the province to investigate without ever setting foot in the rebel territory. An ambiguously worded State Department cable said no evidence could be found to confirm or deny that Salvadoran government forces had massacred civilians.[4] A *Wall Street Journal* editorial accused Bonner of peddling Communist propaganda. Guillermoprieto suspects she only avoided the same fate because of her paper's "well-meaning, and tortured" editing of her original story.[5] It would take a United Nations Truth Commission, an investigation by Argentine forensic scientists, and more than a decade for the world to accept without a doubt the truth about what happened at El Mozote and surrounding villages. The list of victims killed by Salvadoran soldiers was eight hundred names long.

Guillermoprieto, now an accomplished author of several books of essays about Latin America and a regular contributor to the *New Yorker* and the *New York Review of Books*, has said her writing relies on careful observation. "By being extremely specific in what I report, I don't just bring readers into a world of exotica and the grotesque, but into a world where human beings survive with dignity."[6] In her story from El Mozote, the reader is taken up the winding dirt tracks, past the overturned beehives and looted houses and the corpse of an infant with a bullet hole in the head. The details speak louder than the denials. The details speak for themselves.

Several hundred civilians, including women and children, were taken from their homes in and around this village and killed by Salvadoran Army troops during a December offensive against leftist guerrillas, according to three survivors who say they witnessed the alleged massacres.

Reporters taken to tour the region and speak to the survivors by guerrilla soldiers, who control large areas of Morazan Province, were shown the rubble of scores of adobe houses they and the survivors said were destroyed by the troops in the now deserted village community. Dozens of decomposing bodies still were seen beneath the rubble and lying in nearby fields, despite the month that has passed since the incident. In Washington, Salvadoran Ambassador Ernesto Rivas Gallont said, "I reject emphatically that the Army of El Salvador" was engaged in "killing women and children.

"It is not within the armed institutions' philosophy to act like that." He acknowledged that the "armed forces have been active in that part of the country," particularly during a December offensive against the guerrillas, but said that their actions had "definitely not been against the civilian populations."

The survivors, including a woman who said her husband and four of her six children were killed, maintained that no battle was under way during the second week in December when the alleged massacre took place.

The woman, Rufina Amaya, a 38-year-old housewife, said that the troops entered the village one morning and, after herding the residents into two separate groups—men divided from women and children—took them off and shot them. Amaya said she had hidden during the shooting and later escaped to the guerrilla-protected camp where she was interviewed.

At the same time, troops allegedly spread into the nearby countryside and smaller surrounding villages. Jose Marcial Martinez, 14, from nearby La Joya, said he had hidden in a cornfield and watched his parents, brothers and sisters killed. Jose Santos, 15, said he had witnessed the similar slaying of his parents, three younger brothers and two grandparents. A dozen other persons from the area interviewed by this correspondent said they had fled their homes during the December offensive and claimed to have lost family members in the military assault.

To reach the heart of Morazan Province from the north, it is necessary to walk for several days, passing through villages and guerrilla camps. After several months of requests, the Farabundo Marti Liberation Front agreed to take this correspondent into the province in early January, two weeks after the guerrillas' clandestine radio station first reported the alleged massacres in Morazan. It was clear that the guerrillas' purpose was not only to demonstrate to journalists their control of the region, but also to provide what they said was evidence of the alleged massacre in December.

As we neared Mozote, the group of young guerrillas who were my guides and I passed on foot through the village of Arambala, whose pretty, whitewashed adobe houses appeared to have been looted of all contents. The village was deserted.

About 45 minutes farther down the road, we entered another small town. Here the houses also were gutted and looted, but the overwhelming initial impression was of the sickly sweet smell of decomposing bodies. This was Mozote.

The muchachos (boys), as the guerrillas are called, walked us toward the central square where the ruins of what had been a small, whitewashed church stood. The walls of the smaller sacristy beside it also appeared to have had its adobe walls pushed in. Inside, the stench was overpowering, and countless bits of bones—skulls, rib cages, femurs, a spinal column—poked out of the rubble.

The 15 houses on the main village street had been smashed. In two of them, as in the sacristy, the rubble was filled with bones. All of the buildings, including the three in which body parts could be seen, appeared to have been set on fire, and the remains of the people were as charred as the remaining beams.

Several small rural roads led away from the village to other groups of houses that collectively are known as the Mozote community. We walked down one, an idyllic path where every house had a grove of fruit trees, a small chicken pen and at least one beehive. Only the fruit trees were intact; the hives were overturned, the bees buzzing everywhere. The houses were destroyed and looted.

The road was littered with animal corpses, cows and horses. In the cornfields behind the houses were more bodies, these unburned by fire but baked by the sun. In one grouping in a clearing in a field were 10 bodies: two elderly people, two children, one infant—a bullet hole in the head—in the arms of a woman, and the rest adults.

Although local peasants later said they had buried some of the bodies in the area, the guerrilla youths acknowledged they had asked that the corpses be left until someone from the outside could be brought to see them.

It was getting dark, and we traveled to a guerrilla military encampment.

The camp was populated by about 20 young guerrillas, all armed and obviously under military discipline. Farther down the road was a civilian camp, like the other a collection of small adobe houses, with about 80 peasants, refugees and guerrilla sympathizers. It was from this camp the next morning that the guerrillas sent for Amaya, who said she was the only survivor she knew of from Mozote.

The guerrillas left me alone to talk to her. She said that it was on the evening of Dec. 11, although she spoke more of days of the week than dates, that troops of the Atlacatl Brigade had come to Mozote. The brigade is an elite, 1,000-man unit of the Salvadoran Army, well known at least by name to most Salvadorans, that has been trained for rapid deployment and antiguerrilla offensives by U.S. military advisers here.

"The Army people had warned Marcos Diaz, a friend of theirs from our village, that an offensive was coming and that there would be no more traffic allowed from San Francisco Gotera [the provincial capital] in December and that we should all stay in Mozote where no one would harm us. So we did. There were about 500 of us in all living in the village."

The soldiers, she said, took those villagers who were in their homes and made them stand outside "in the road for about 1½ hours. They took our money, searched the houses, ate our food, asked us where the guns were and went away. We were happy then. 'The repression is over,' we said. They didn't kill anybody."

Amaya spoke with what appeared to be controlled hysteria. During our conversation, she broke down only when speaking of what she said were the deaths of her children. She said that while her two surviving sons have joined the guerrillas since the December incident, Mozote was not predominantly proguerrilla, although it is in the heart of a rebel zone.

She said the guerrillas had gone around the villages in early December warning the population of an impending government offensive and instructing civilians to head for towns and refugee camps outside the area.

"But because we knew the Army people, we felt safe," she said. Her husband, who Amaya said was on very good terms with the local military, "had a military safe conduct."

At around 5:30 the morning after their initial visit, she said, the troops, headed by the same officer she called Lt. Ortega, returned to Mozote. She said they herded the people into the tiny village square in front of the church, men in one line and women and children in another.

"Marcos Diaz, who had been told by the Army we would be safe, and my husband were in the men's line. I counted about 80 men and 90 women not including the children."

She said the women were herded with their children into a house on the square. From there they saw the men being blindfolded and bound, kicked and thrown against each other, then taken away in groups of four and shot.

"The soldiers had no fury," she said. "They just observed the lieutenant's orders. They were cold. It wasn't a battle.

"Around noon they began with the women. First they picked out the young girls and took them away to the hills. Then they picked out the old women and took them to Israel Marquez's house on the square. We heard the shots there. Then they started with us in groups. When my turn came and I was being led away to Israel Marquez's house I slipped behind a tree and climbed up. I saw the lieutenant then. He was personally machine-gunning people."

"I heard the soldiers talking," she continued tonelessly. "An order arrived from a Lt. Caceres to Lt. Ortega to go ahead and kill the children too. A soldier said, 'Lieutenant, somebody here says he won't kill children.' 'Who's the sonofabitch who said that?' the lieutenant answered. 'I am going to kill him.' I could hear them shouting from where I was crouching in the tree.

"I could hear the children crying. I heard my own children. When it was all over late at night the lieutenant ordered the soldiers to put a torch to the corpses. There was a great fire in the night."

Amaya said she escaped while the fire was still burning. "I heard the soldiers say 'Let's go. Witches could come out of the fire.' Then they left to go on what they called a 'combing operation' in the houses on the hills. I started walking and walked for three nights. In the daytime I hid because there were troops everywhere."

Amaya, as well as the two boys who said they witnessed their families being killed, emphasized that the troops appeared to be in regular radio contact with someone.

I later saw Amaya in the civilian camps down the road, where I also met the two boys. Although they were the only ones who claimed to have witnessed the killing, nearly everyone in the camp said they had come there because of "the repression in December" and claimed to have lost members of their families.

In Washington, Ambassador Rivas, in denying the accuracy of this account Tuesday, said that "serious efforts" were being made to stem armed forces abuses and that this was the "type of story that leads us to believe there is a plan" to discredit the ongoing electoral process in El Salvador, and to discredit the armed forces "or to take credit away from the certification President Reagan must make to Congress."

This week the Reagan administration must by law certify to Congress that the Salvadoran leadership "is achieving substantial control over all elements of its own armed forces, so as to bring to an end the indiscriminate torture and murder of Salvadoran citizens by these forces," or risk a cutoff of aid to El Salvador under congressional restrictions.

RURAL LIFE

39

ROBIN HYDE

WHO SAYS THE ORAKEI MAORIS MUST GO? *AND* NO MORE DANCING AT ORAKEI (1937)

from *The New Zealand Observer*

INTRODUCED BY JAMES HOLLINGS

New Zealand

Visitors arriving at Auckland by sea must approach from the east. As they enter its Waitemata Harbour, and motor up the channel toward the city's business district, they pass, on their left, a series of imposing bluffs. One of the most prominent is named Bastion Point. For centuries, it guarded the gateway to Auckland for the native Maori inhabitants, the Ngati Whatua *iwi*, or tribe.

It has been a bastion in other ways, too. For it was here, for 507 days in 1977 and 1978, that the Ngati Whatua made a final stand to stop the last of their land from being taken. Although it started as a sit-in, a protest against a government plan to sell the sacred ancestral seat to property developers, it became much more than that. It became a long, bitter, and at times violent protest against the alienation of all Maori from their land. It ended, at dawn on May 25, 1978, when eight hundred police and army personnel began pulling down tents and dragging protesters to waiting vans, in full view of television cameras from around the world. The scenes were disturbing to many New Zealanders. Many have described it as a watershed. Within a few years a process was begun of addressing Maori claims to their land, fisheries, and other property. The Bastion Point claim was the first to be heard under this process.

The seeds of this remarkable event were sown forty years earlier. In

Excerpts from Robin Hyde, "Who Says the Orakei Maoris Must Go?" and "No More Dancing at Orakei," *New Zealand Observer*, July 8, 1937, and August 19, 1937.

1937, a young woman reporter began the first serious journalistic investigation into the Maori claims to Bastion Point. Robin Hyde would not be the last reporter to set foot on the point, but she was one of the most original, effective, and determined, and one of the few who were able to see past the patronizing colonial fog that enveloped most journalism of the period. Her stories helped galvanize supporters of Ngati Whatua, and were a direct forerunner of the 1977–78 protest.

Hyde's real name was Iris Wilkinson. Born in South Africa to an English father and Australian mother, she'd grown up in Wellington, the wind-ripped, earthquake-battered capital city to the south. Her parents were committed socialists, and Robin had grown up soaked in left-wing politics. Always ready to argue a point, and with a flair for writing, a burning energy, and a passion for the underdog, she soon found her way to journalism. She started, still in her teens, at *The Dominion* newspaper, then worked her way around many others, including the *NZ Truth*, a hard-biting, scandal-ridden organ of the left. There she learned the art of investigation. Hyde was a natural journalist, her incredible energy turning out copy on political reporting, book reviews, domestic advice, and colorful undercover forays exposing charlatans such as the growing fashion for the occult ("Wicked witches weave wily spells"). By the age of twenty-four she had given birth to two sons out of wedlock, the first of which had died (she later retrieved his name, Robin Hyde, as her pen name), and the second was fostered out. By 1930 she was in Auckland, an editor at the weekly pictorial *New Zealand Observer*, working feverishly to report on the plight of the poor as the Great Depression deepened. By 1933, aged just twenty-seven, she was exhausted. She became a voluntary patient at Auckland Mental Hospital. Over the next four years she began to recover, finding time to write four novels and two outstanding collections of poetry, which cemented her reputation as one of the country's foremost poets. But she had not forgotten journalism, and it was while a patient that she heard about the plight of a small Maori village at Bastion Point, in the suburb of Orakei (pronounced OR-*RA*-KAY).

The village was nestled at the pretty beach at Okahu Bay, on the point's western edge. Hyde heard that the Auckland City Council planned to demolish a Maori settlement there. The village (in Maori: *papakainga*) was perched on a few acres, all that remained after the rest of the point had been taken by the government for a military base during the Russian invasion scare of the 1880s. The base had never been built, and the government had given the land to city hall for a park. However, city fathers, egged on by do-gooder public health officials, claimed the village, lacking proper sewerage and water, was a health hazard, and wanted to sell it to developers for prime waterfront housing. Hyde, with her well-honed ear for cant, knew something was up, and took up the cause.

Her reports were a classic example of the investigator's art. Instead of simply interviewing officials, she went and saw for herself, and interviewed the inhabitants. She backed that up with hours digging through documents, finding an unpublished report of a Native Land Court hearing, by Judge F.O.V. Acheson, that showed the government had promised Ngati Whatua the land would be returned to them when it was no longer needed for defense. Her reporting was unusual for the time; it saw past the stereotypes of the poor uneducated native put out by City Hall, and gave the inhabitants a dignity that did much to broaden their support. It galvanized supporters into petitioning the country's new socialist prime minister, Michael Joseph Savage. He eventually put a stop to the development plan.

Hyde's Orakei stories were the culmination of, and a fitting tribute to, her journalistic career in New Zealand. She left soon after for Europe, travelling via China to report on the Japanese invasion. She made her way to the front line, where despite almost losing an eye in a beating from Japanese soldiers, she sent back reports that helped spur the New Zealand government to send 10,000 pounds' worth of medical supplies. From China, she travelled to London, reaching there in late 1938. Just three weeks before the outbreak of war, she was living alone, depressed and in ill-health. Friends in the New Zealand government arranged to bring her home, but the day an embassy official arrived with her documents, she was found dead, apparently from an overdose of Benzedrine. Almost a contemporary of that other great woman New Zealand writer of the period, Katherine Mansfield, Hyde is remembered today almost entirely for her fiction.

Hyde's reporting on Orakei provided a stay of execution for the village, but only a stay. A year after she died, Savage died in office. He was buried, after a funeral procession attended by an estimated two hundred thousand people, at Bastion Point. During the Second World War, more land was taken by the government for defense, crowding Ngati Whatua onto a tiny strip of land. Even this was eyed by developers, and in 1951, taking advantage of a McCarthy-like anti-left paranoia gripping the country, the city council evicted the remaining Maori and burnt their houses. In 1977, the government decided it no longer needed the land it had taken for defense, and proposed a high-income housing development. Two days before bulldozers were due to start work, Ngati Whatua and supporters occupied the land. International supporters arrived to join the occupation, including U.S. country singer John Denver. Although the protesters were evicted, the development was stopped. Ten years later, a new Labour Government began a national conciliation process aimed at restoring rights guaranteed to Maori under the Treaty of Waitangi, signed in 1840. The first claim to be heard by the Waitangi Tribunal under this process was Bastion Point. The tribunal recognised Ngati Whatua's claim, and returned most of the point to it, along with other land and compensation. In its report, the Tribunal quoted extensively from Hyde's newspaper articles, including her phrase "Rainbow visions."

"Nobody wishes to deal harshly with these people" [was the] conclusion reached, and expressed in the dulcet tones of Sir Ernest Davis, after it was announced at the last meeting of the Auckland City Council that the Acting-Minister for Native Affairs, Mr. Langstone, had arrived at his decision—the "73 native adults and 48 children, including 13 Raratongans," now resident at the native village of Orakei, must go.

"This is my home. Here will I rest forever, for I have desired it." You mayn't recognise the quotation, but it is from the Bible, and to be seen on the grave of an old Maori at Orakei. He may, or may not, have relied upon an appropriate pakeha text. According to the New Zealand Herald, "The owners of two small areas of an acre and an acre and a half respectively declined to sell, and are still in possession. The church and cemetery site of a quarter of an acre was also not alienated. The price paid by the Crown for the 40 acres was about £10,000. As no immediate use was to be made of the property, the natives were allowed to go on living there." Now, though apparently in the interests of a garden suburb and a view, the white residents of Orakei are perfectly willing to hunt the living natives from lands which have been their ancestral right and property for so many years, surely the Maori dead will be allowed to lie in peace. Or will tombstones also clash with the rainbow visions and the town-planning schemes?

If you take a 'bus and go to Orakei (a blue clear curve before Mission Bay and St. Helier's, with hills above and the garden suburb mincing like Agag on those hills), you won't see anything very picturesque. As the reports obtained by Sir Ernest remark, "of 17 dwellings, 13 were shacks and only three really suitable for habitation." On one hand is a clay path through a paddock to the little graveyard, on the other a small, not very ornamental meeting-house, which is kept clean, and does harbour an elderly piano—Orakei's home grown fun, if the young people wish to hold concerts or dances. There is a church, small-size, and behind the paddock (where on the day of my first visit one melancholy Jersey was tethered and lowed her sorrow), the first group of dwellings. [. . .]

By risking your shins and your stockings scrambling up a steep hillside, you will come on other Maori houses, much the same, except that some of them are tents instead of shacks, poorly furnished, and with an occasional plot of kumaras or other vegetables. Most of what is said against the Maori dwelling places, as at present constituted, is true enough—except that they are the dwelling-places of very decent people, who, given a chance, would probably keep their premises as creditably as anyone could expect, and who have hung on to their long-threatened shacks at Orakei with the courage of despair.

Nia Hira, one of the Orakei leaders, expressed himself with quiet dignity in saying that one could not expect the Maori people to put much heart into their homes, until they knew that these shacks were their homes. One comes across minor anomalies. A smiling Maori offers a string of wet schnapper for sale . . . one of the biggest fish businesses in Auckland gives the Orakei Maoris sacks of fish-heads, and these, boiled up, serve as a staple article of diet.

The incidence of notifiable infectious diseases, "including tuberculosis, dysentery and enteric fever" is nearly twice as high at Orakei as anywhere else in Auckland city. On the other hand, the Maoris have said it is impossible for them (their titles to land or dwellings having been under dispute for years), to obtain facilities for proper sanitation, drainage or lighting. They also point out that the old Maori system of drainage wasn't bad of its kind. But every winter, loose metal washed down from the motor-road above their flat blocks up their drainage, such as it is, with results that can be imagined. It is awkward, but the road is not their road, and the motor cars most certainly are not their motor cars. [. . .]

My knowledge of the Orakei people is very cursory, but nobody who visits them once or twice can come away with the impression that they are so much human driftwood. In the lightless and ill-sanitated shacks are young Maori men and women of excellent education, whose knowledge of English would probably put our knowledge of Maori to shame. Many are probably in very poor circumstances but others have fought to qualify themselves for a civilised way of living. One Maori resident is a qualified nurse, for instance: another, as quiet and pretty an eighteen year old girl as you could wish to meet, fully qualified herself at an Auckland college for work as a shorthand typist. Given a little security, and a chance to exercise the racial pride and self-respect which is never dead in the Maori, there is no reason to suppose that the rest of Orakei's young people and children can't do as well. [. . .]

This proposal of bulk transportation of a community of people, numbering over a hundred, without regard to their will, is the most dictatorial suggestion, and would be the most dangerous precedent, any Government could adopt. The people responsible for the bright idea (it is hard to think that the Hon. F. Langstone thought of it lone-handed) should come out into the open, and say where the Maori must go, why they must go, and at whose bidding they must go. [. . .] This is only the moral aspect of the case—a moral aspect which gives the Orakei Maoris the right to remain, under improved conditions, at Orakei. The legal aspect is an extremely complicated one. The facts can only be given piecemeal. [. . .]

In the Observer, a few weeks back, you may have read the salient points of the Acheson Court Report, 1930, which had never been published before. Still more documents important to the Orakei case are allegedly in the files of the Government departments. Will the last ever be produced? The fate of Orakei may perhaps rest on this.

What the Orakei Maoris themselves say, according to people, pakeha and Maori, who have worked among them and known them for many years, is simple enough. No other forty acres would be the same as the papakainga at Orakei. Orakei is not only a village, but is dignified as a marae. Their heart is with their land, and they believe that if the Prime Minister and his Government know all the facts, it will be proved the 40 acres was reserved for them.

At least one of these promised reservations is recorded, in deed form, and should be in Government possession, according to Judge Acheson's Court report. Judge Acheson stated that he could himself remember having seen the deed, years ago, but at such a distance of time could not recall its exact terms. The Maori concerned was a notable man of Orakei, Wiremu Watene: two early settlers who remember Wiremu Watene very well say that to the end of his days, Watene protested he had never sold the six acres on the flat. The subject used to excite the old man to passionate oratory, but Watene is gone, his title never confirmed. Another person, very deeply versed in the affairs of Orakei Maoris, told me that what happened was this. Watene was given definite assurance that the six acres were his for ever, even though he argued with the Crown's purchasing officer that he might be signing away his whole land interests. Some time afterwards, he applied for concreting work to be done on the six acres, and was then informed that by a regrettable misunderstanding, he had sold his whole possessions, after all. He was given a chance to buy back this reservation, but by then he had no money to do so. Such irregularities, or suspicion of irregularities, are not very healthy matters for consideration of a tribe rendered landless against provision of the Native Lands Act. Even what Chief Judge R.N. Jones has to say in his report, given in 1932 after the fiasco of the Native Land Court enquiry presided over by Judge Acheson, is not reassuring:

"As for the promises said to have been made about the papakainga portion, the Court finds that it is unable to report adequately upon them, and it refers to other matters, including suspected irregularities in connection with the part of the officers of the Crown, in connection with such purchase, but it must be remembered that the Judge (Judge Acheson) had only one side before him." (This, after the Crown representative, Mr. Meredith, had withdrawn from Court under instructions from Wellington, taking with him both his documents and his as-sociates, and failing to produce for inspection the files the Native Land Court applied for, seems an odd comment.) "Doubtless, if a wrong had been proved, the Crown would endeavour to rectify it, although its title could not be assailed for that reason."

Put in language less polite, if it could be proved to the satisfaction of a white Appeal Court that any of the purchasing agents for the Crown had talked the Or-akei Maoris into a belief that they could sell their other land interests and keep their papakainga, the Crown would apologise and do its best—but the Crown would still be the title-holder. It is interesting to remember that while these land-sales were going on at Orakei (the Crown purchasing officer buying on the spot, cheque-book in pocket), Maori petitions from Orakei, asking for investigation of the actual ownership of the land, were lying on the table at Parliament. [. . .] Again, the Labour Government was not in power when the land was auctioned off by the Crown; nor yet in 1930, when the Native Land Court enquiry with Judge Acheson on the Bench, produced his report. Another Government then held the reins. [. . .]

So much can be said against the argument that the Government is the chief or only villain of the Orakei place. The Government, none the less, is situated right in the middle of a quicksand of ugly rumours about Orakei. [. . .] Firstly it has been very widely suggested that at the auction of Orakei land sections, three sections at least, were never open to public purchase.

The story [. . .] is that private persons, acquiring these sections, disposed of the options to a syndicate of prominent Auckland business men, who have un-der consideration the building of a large block of residential flats, but who do not intend to exercise their options unless the Maori village, which "spoils the view," is cleared away. Secondly, it has been said as often, and from as many quarters, that a further intention is to procure a license for this building, if erected, and also to license a hotel at St. Helier's Bay. [. . .]

For the past several months, Orakei has given up holding any dances. It has its own hall, a piano and young people who loved dancing, but as soon as its lights went on, an undesirable element in the form of white visitors with the usual flasks arrived. Rather than risk any suggestion of rowdyism, Orakei dances no more.

40

PALAGUMMI SAINATH

FROM DUST UNTO DUST (2000)

from *The Hindu Sunday Magazine*

INTRODUCED BY ANANYA MUKHERJEE-REED

India

P. Sainath is the leading reporter in India on rural affairs and poverty, having written extensively on these subjects for decades. The rural affairs editor of *The Hindu* (one of the most prestigious dailies in India), Sainath is also known for his outspoken criticism of mainstream media houses that report on the concerns of the urban elites while ignoring those of the rural poor.

There are two key distinguishing features of Sainath's work. The first is the resilience of ordinary people that his work documents—their daily struggles, their challenges, and the sheer endurance of their humanity that refuses to be crippled by the injustices they face. The second is the indifference of the elite, including policy makers whose actions rob people of their rights and aspirations. Sainath's work is that mirror which reflects the unacceptable moral failures of our times, and inspires us to act. In his thirty-three-year career, Sainath has won over forty global and national awards.

Sainath's book *Everybody Loves a Good Drought* (Penguin India, 1996) remained a nonfiction bestseller for years and is now in its fortieth printing. A collection of sixty-eight stories, the book involved covering one hundred thousand kilometers across India (over five thousand kilometers of that on foot). From the toddy tapper who climbed five thousand feet a day on his hands and legs, with no protection (a height greater than that of the Empire State Building), to the women who were bonded or ill-paid

Excerpt from Palagummi Sainath, "From Dust Unto Dust," *Hindu Sunday Magazine*, December 3 and 10, 2000.

laborers in granite quarries and through their struggles transformed their community—we can meet them all in Sainath's book.

More recently, Sainath's work on the agrarian crisis has produced the largest journalistic body of work ever on India's farming communities. Sainath is clearly the most influential voice in the public discourse on agriculture, in particular with his groundbreaking work on farmer suicides. Close to three hundred thousand impoverished Indian farmers—many driven by indebtedness—have taken their own lives in less than two decades since 1995. That is the largest wave of such suicides in recorded history. Sainath was the journalist who first established the scale of the disaster, locating it within a larger—policy-driven—agrarian crisis afflicting the peasantry.

The piece in this volume is a classic example of Sainath's work. Set in the Kolar gold mines in southern India, it depicts the inhuman conditions in which the miners live and toil and how they struggle for their rights. And how in the process the miners have created a unique society, one that Sainath finds to be perhaps "the most secular and egalitarian space in the country in many ways."

Theirs is no choreographed identity postulated by disengaged elites, but a real, lived identity of genuine coexistence and collective struggle. By the close of the decade ending 2000–1, the community produced approximately $9.6 billion in value. And their reward? Destitution, disintegration, and closure. The mines were formally closed in 2001 but the workers continue their fight and have encountered both victories and defeats along the way. They are now in a last-ditch battle in the Supreme Court to prevent the privatization of the mines. The workers had all along suspected that privatization was the real government-corporate agenda, especially now that the price of gold is about seven times what it was in the year 2000 when Sainath published the story below. Their struggle continues.

KOLAR GOLD FIELDS (KARNATAKA, INDIA)—It's 2,000 feet below the surface of the earth. The air hangs stale and thick and the electric blowers don't help much. It's dimly lit in long stretches and dingy everywhere. Puddles of water punctuate the winding tunnels we traverse. And their serrated roofs stare downwards at us, glumly.

Below us, from Level 21—or 2,100 feet—the mine is flooded. Men are at work drawing out the water, but there's a break just now and even the pumps are quiet. The cranky wheezing of the blowers is the only sound piercing the sour stillness of the mine. That, and the deep hum of the "cage" as it drones through a damp, desolate trajectory, ferrying miners up and down the sullen silence of the shaft.

Yet this subterranean maze yielded wealth in profusion. This is where, for over a century, "numbers lived like men." Hundreds died in these timeless tunnels, buried in rock bursts. Many more succumbed to disease and despair. People whose labour yielded tens of billions of rupees—for others. Those who "never saw the sun," going in before dawn, emerging after dusk. Many working here right now are the grandsons and great grandsons of those who first toiled here.

"This is where we work," he said simply. General Foreman David Prasad is one of those grandsons.

Welcome to the Kolar Gold Fields. This could be India's most secular, egalitarian *and* multi-cultural community. The KGF is about a half-hour drive from Kolar town and two hours from Bangalore, India's information technology hub, in the southern state of Karnataka.

It isn't always this silent in the shaft, explains David Prasad. There's a shift change underway and we run into others in the cage at different levels in this maze of tunnels. There's over 1,300 kilometres of them in the KGF. Placed in a straight line they would reach Mumbai in western India.

Prasad, a Science graduate who's worked 15 years in the mines, earns only Rs. 3,000[1] a month from his employer, the Bharat Gold Mines Ltd. (BGML). He's showing me around the New Trail, one of just three working shafts left in the KGF.

The jagged tunnels recall yesterday's visit to M. Kanickraj's house.

Kanickraj is a skilled worker, an electrician. "I slogged 41 years," he says smiling. "I retire this month." And his last salary will be just Rs. 4,500—gross. He joined on 75 paise a day in 1959.

"I had a young son, sir." He speaks calmly, with dignity, but you can sense the tears. "These BGML people, they make money renting out our labour. That's what they did with my boy, Don Prasad. They sent him to the Eastern Collieries Ltd (ECL) in another state."

In 1990, Don Prasad died in an ECL mine rock burst. His shattered family got a meagre Rs. 80,000 in "compensation." "And from that," Kanickraj laughs, "they cut Rs. 8,000 in taxes." He had been sent to a risky mine. "It was like condemning him to death."

Another death sentence now looms over the whole community.

The union government that took over these mines in 1962 to run them properly and save jobs now says it will shut them down. It has asked the workers to go.

It's where Krishna Prasad, a Hindu, can be the "son" of David Winston Benjamin, a Christian. Or where Harry Walter is recorded as the offspring of Anbazhagan.

Where a Tamil family from Arcot will claim progeny who could be Telugu or Kannadiga. Christian names in Hindu families. Classic Tamil names in Telugu homes. A giddy mix, cutting across region, religion, language and culture.

How does that happen? These are mines where the same family has laboured for generations. That does happen in public sector units (PSUs) across the country. Often, the son or daughter of a retiring employee is offered a job at the same factory.

Here, though, the community goes further in looking after its own. What if the retiring worker has no children? Or has a son with a job in Bangalore who doesn't to want to toil underground for a living? Well, there are others who could do with a job. And so what if their fathers were not miners? Each of them is still "one of us." Their families are in a crisis. Let's talk to the retiring miners about it.

And the retirees are very willing. They too, feel an obligation towards the larger community. So a Christian father can send in a Hindu "son" or vice versa. As the "son" of a miner, the applicant is more likely to land a job.

It's been going on for decades.

But the mainly Tamil miners of the KGF do share something in common with the few Andhras, Kannadigas and Malayalees who work here. This egalitarian culture was built around a workforce dominated by Dalits. (Those once known as the "outcastes" and who still suffer untouchability and other forms of oppression and exclusion.) The KGF workforce was built through huge struggles for survival that shaped class consciousness in this region.

The big strength working people here have is each other. A crisis in a single family worries the whole neighbourhood. There are the firm bonds and sense of community that miners everywhere seem to develop. Beyond that is a Dalit workforce built around a class rather than a caste identity, with a strong sense of its own radical and democratic traditions. For decades May 1 (International Workers' Day) was a bigger event here than any religious festival and cut across all faiths.

This unique culture now fights for its very existence.

The miners of the KGF have always laboured under exploitative systems. Earlier under the old British private owners in the former Mysore. (Which functioned as a "princely state" under the British Raj.) Subsequently under the Indian state into which Mysore merged when the country gained independence in 1947.

"My father dug tunnels after coming here in 1927—for around 36 paise a day," says A. Kasi, a miner who retired as foreman at the Edgar Shaft in 1989. "Almost all the men in my family, which came from Tamil Nadu, worked in these mines. Some earned as little as 25 paise a day. Sometimes, four families lived in each of those eight-by-eight-foot hovels that you've seen. The idea of one family to one house was accepted much later. That was after the Communist-led 1946 strike in which six miners died when the British masters resorted to firing."

Pay was wretched, conditions worse. Debt was as deep as the tunnels they dug. In the 1930s, each family, on average, owed lenders six times its monthly income.

John Taylor & Sons, the British company that exploited the mines from the 1880s to 1956, sought to ensure that miners from Tamil Nadu could not "escape." The Tamils, even if they did not always return home, believed they had a right to do so. The company felt it owned their dirt-cheap labour forever.

"The older generations were forced to wear a metal bracelet saying 'John Taylor & Sons' on the left hand," says S.M. Irchappan, a miner who worked here from 1949 till 1988. "This tight metal band had a mine name and number on it. Anyone trying to 'run away,' switch mines or the like, was traced on this basis." A kind of updated slave collar.

Miner protests saw the "bracelet" practice collapse by 1930, say Kasi and Irchappan. That year, the mine bosses tried forcibly finger-printing the workers, sparking a 24-day strike by 16,000 of them. Police fired on the workers and 44 were injured. The Dewan of Mysore (the highest official of the princely state after the Maharaja himself) had to intervene. The "Labour Registry Office" the workers hated was abolished and the strike ended.

Both Kasi and Irchappan dropped out of the fourth class. Even today, decades after freedom, schools that workers' children go to stop at middle school. They were, after all, only meant to be cheap labour. The children of officers attend English-medium institutions that go up to the secondary schooling certificate level.

"There were whole generations of miners who never saw the sun," says veteran trade unionist K. Savaridoss of the Centre of Indian Trade Unions (CITU), "The work day was 12 hours till 1946. And the workers used candles and hand drills. They went in before dawn and came out after dusk. There was no electricity for much of the mine's existence."

Odd, since Kolar was the first part of old Mysore to get electricity by 1902. "That's true," says Savaridoss. "But the power was for the establishment above. Not for the miners below. Their safety was not a priority. At best, power was used for hoisting the workers up and down. Not for their personal needs."

Abysmal conditions claimed hundreds of miners' lives. Deadly rock bursts killed many and buried several alive in the 1920s and '30s. Flooding and accidents caused still more deaths.

A little mining had taken place here in the time of Tipu Sultan (the implacable foe of British colonialism who ruled the kingdom of Mysore between 1782 and

1799). And perhaps earlier too, but always at a crude and limited level. Organised mining began with John Taylor & Sons in the 1880s. "The miners came mainly from Tamil Nadu," says T.S. Mani, a workers' leader and a former elected member of the state legislature. "A few were from Andhra and Kerala." Most of them were Dalits. Landless labourers who often stayed on as permanent settlers.

The mine workforce peaked at 35,000 in 1940, with 60 per cent of workers holding jobs beneath the ground. In 1956, the state of Mysore took over the company from John Taylor. Six years later, the government of India acquired it to form the Kolar Gold Mines Undertaking. In 1972, it launched the present Bharat Gold Mines Ltd. as a corporate entity.

In independent India, work conditions improved marginally. Pay remained pathetic.

"Till April 1972, an unskilled worker got Rs. 1.25 to Rs. 1.50 a day," says CITU's Savaridoss. "This was up from 25 paise in the '30s, and 50 paise in the '40s."

M.C. Adiseshan laboured 40 years as a miner in the KGF. "And my period was entirely in the post-independence era," he points out. He worked from 1955 to 1995. "I earned a 'coolie rate' of Rs. 1.25 a day when I began. Annual increments," he laughs, "were five paise." (For the lowest category of workers, increments were just Rs. 10 a year till the 1980s.) In 1995, he was 2,600 feet below when struck by a rock burst. "Some 60 tons of ore collapsed on us in the Nandydroog mine."

Adiseshan lived but still can't move his neck properly. He got no compensation. And like many here, gets no pension. What about medical treatment for the injury? He laughs: "It was free but meaningless. Our hospital here has nothing to offer."

In his 40th working year, Adiseshan took home less than Rs. 4,000. "Those workers covered by pension agreements—those joining after 1982—will get around Rs. 300 a month," he says. "If they and the mines last 30 years, their pensions could reach Rs. 500 at best." Most will get nothing.

In the mines, the payslips the workers show me, speak. Many record around 25 years of work and a basic pay of Rs. 1,340. "After 30 years," says Edison, a General Foreman officer at the Golconda mine, "you could make Rs. 4,250. And lose Rs. 1,720 of that in deductions." Making this the one public sector entity where you can work 40 years and take home less than Rs. 4,000 each month. Those wages have remained unchanged through a decade in which prices have shot up as almost never before.

"Isn't it hilarious?" ask the miners. "Thousands have suffered silicosis here over decades. That's a miner's disease and treatment costs money. Yet people at Bharat Earth Movers Ltd. (BEML) get a 'dust allowance.' We, who are miners, don't."

"They give us a clothing allowance of Rs. 100 or less. Not enough to pay the tailor's charge, let alone buy the dress. And this is the No.1 gold mine in the country."

Successive governments have tried to shut down the BGML for over a decade now. Oddly, this happens where the veins of gold have not run out and where large seams remain unexplored. Where worker productivity has risen but the workers are perhaps the lowest paid in any PSU in the country. Where a single region has produced a precious metal worth Rs. 450 billion over the years. And despite the Legislature of Karnataka state unanimously appealing to the Centre to try and revive the mines, not close them down.

The battles are still on, though the Union government declared that the loss-making mines would cease to exist by end of May 2001. Many insist the losses were management and government-inflicted. Some say consciously inflicted. At any rate, the losses of Rs. 3 billion are far less than those of other PSUs in the country where there has been no talk of closure.

"Oh! Government should hand over the mines to these great union leaders. They're all such experts!" That's R. Gupta, BGML Managing Director, mocking worker claims that the mines are viable. "At no time since 1956," asserts Gupta, "have these mines been profitable. It now costs Rs. 20,000 to produce 10 grams of gold. The reserves are depleted. It is not viable to continue."

Gupta scoffs at technical experts who say the government's numbers don't add up. But he does give me a pass allowing me to go down the shafts. (He has since left BGML on a promotion.)

In the New Golconda mine, General Foreman officer Edison says: "The government of India crushed us by 'buying' our gold at far below market prices." That relationship holds the key to BGML's losses. "Import of gold, starving us of investment, closing shafts. All the government's policies smashed us."

As the miners find a journalist in the shaft, a small crowd gathers around, joined by men emerging from the "cage." Edison, Shekhar, Sagainathan, Thomas, Krishnan and others, until there's nearly 30 of us. Almost all are from families that have produced three generations of miners or more. It's many voices at once.

"We got cheap electricity from the Shivasamundaram plant built exclusively for us. Then the government of Karnataka took it over, crippling us. We are paying this government's power bill."

"There's a lot of gold even now in No. 45 and No. 1 shafts. They don't want to find it."

"They'll sell off this place to some multinational corporation. Then they'll 'find' the gold at once."

"We've worked here 20–30 years. Where will we go now?"

"We've accepted diversification, innovation. We never resisted new technologies. What are we to do? Simply die?"

"We'll fight. We did in the past, too. We'll fight again."

At his union office, former Legislator T.S. Mani says: "Closure will crush the whole town, not just the mines. It's being pressed for by powerful lobbies, though several government committees have themselves suggested the mines run much longer." Former BGML Technical Director S. Natarajan believes they could run another 40 years.

K. Anbazhagan, President of the officially recognised workers union here, also points to a fudging of BGML's annual reports. "The 1990–91 report shows 7.6 million tons of ore deposits. These yielded 4.70 grams of gold per ton. The next year, they claim ore deposits are only 1.3 million tons, with roughly the same yield per ton. Where did 6.3 million tons of deposit disappear in 12 months' time? They faked these figures to submit this company to the Board for Industrial & Financial Reconstruction (BIFR)."

The idea being to prepare a case that would justify closure.

There's more. "A parliamentary sub-committee inquiry found that Rs. 300 million of gold was pilfered each year," says S. Savaridoss. This confirmed a charge often made by miners. It even implied official connivance at some levels. Yet, till just two years ago, "security checks" at the mines "were for workers only, not officers."

Money can be raised in other ways, too. There's 36 million tons of "tailings" lying outside the mines. These are giant dumps of sodium cyanide–treated waste from which the gold has been extracted. They retain a small percentage of gold dust that can be recovered by modern technical processes. Estimates of this gold vary from 22 to 26 tons. (A fortune that, at current prices, would be worth Rs. 60–75 billion.)

Worker productivity has risen these past two decades. A glance at the tons of ore handled and grams of gold extracted would show that. There were more than 13,000 workers in 1980, today only 4,036.

Employees say S. Natarajan and other experts have suggested further exploration and shallow mining. They point to the huge potential of "an untouched giant reef several kilometres long." They also assert that rich layers of gold exist even within the present complex. This strengthens the miners' belief that what is literally a gold mine, is being dressed up as a "gone case." To be flogged off cheaply to privateers with links to management and higher ups in government.

And what of the losses? "See the official reports," says V.J.K. Nair, General Secretary of CITU, Karnataka. "Especially the report of K.S.R. Chari, former Mines Secretary."

"From when BGML was registered in 1972, the gold was 'made over' to the government. Not at market rates. Compare the market value of that gold with the so-called subsidy BGML got from government. You'll find they owe BGML more than ten billion rupees.

"Even if we paid 17 per cent interest on the so-called subsidy," says Nair. "Even if this were brought up to year 2000. Even if all our dues were cleared and all government loans were paid off. The BGML would still have a surplus!

"On what basis can BIFR recommend closure? They have to show we have had five years of commercial operations and two years of losses. But we have never once been allowed to function as a commercial entity. Only as a satellite to government." The government, however, is going ahead with closure, anyway.

And so, as miners at the Golconda shaft put it: "We're going from Gold Dust to dust."

Postscript

The mines were formally closed in 2001 but the workers continued their struggle. In 2003, the Karnataka High Court ordered the government to hand over the mines to the workers for revival. In 2010, on being admonished by the High Court for reneging on the deal, the Ministry of Mines claimed the government had decided to revive the mines on its own. In November 2012, the government of India declared it would "clear all legal hurdles" in the way of resuming mining in the KGF. Instead, it repackaged its case at the level of the Supreme Court on dubious grounds to get privatisation of the mines okayed there. The workers are now pursuing a "revision petition" in the Supreme Court to overcome the setback and halt the privatization which they knew was the government's intention all along. They point out that the price of ten grams of gold was around Rs. 4,400 in 2000, but nearly seven times higher at around Rs. 30,000 in 2014. Making the gold mine, well, a gold mine.

41

ANUPAM MISHRA

NA JA SWAMI PARDESA (1993)

from *Gandhi Marg*

INTRODUCED BY ROHINI NILEKANI

India

For decades Anupam Mishra has been a storyteller and chronicler who shares his experience of local traditions and knowledge widely, through different media and in multiple languages.

His work carries forward the legacy of Mohandas Gandhi in its appeal to scientific humanism, as well as "swaraj" (self-discovery leading to independence of thought and action). For the past forty years, Anupam*ji* has been associated with the Gandhi Peace Foundation. His life of ideas has been suffused with an enthusiasm for what people can do, individually and together, empowered by their moral force.

This piece originally appeared in the newsletter of the Gandhi Peace Foundation in 1993, and has since been reprinted multiple times. Here he describes how messages about the importance of water are transmitted through time and across communities, and how one village's attempts to save its forest from destruction evolved into a broader movement to preserve and enhance water resources.

The lessons from his writing have been applied many times over with amazing results. Often, he documents how local leadership, combined with a citizenry engaged with the issues, can surmount impossible obstacles by combining old wisdom with new technology. Much of his writing is about the refined aesthetic and social structure behind traditional water supply systems. He has beautifully documented the centuries-old rainwater

Excerpt from Anupam Mishra, "Na Ja Swami Pardesa," *Gandhi Marg*, 1993.

harvesting systems of regions like Rajasthan. For him, these systems are about more than water, they are about the truth around living.

By demonstrating a positive path built on ecological intelligence, Anupam*ji* provides a narrative of action and hope amidst the tyranny of outrage and despair. Underneath, there is a powerful critique of the current socio-economic model. It does not romanticize the past, poverty, or subsistence; it is open to new thinking. But his piece asks incisive questions on sustainability and the future. Anupam*ji* observes and documents ruinous models that are expanded in the name of prosperity for all, but instead accumulate abundance for a few and over a short time. He takes the long view on human civilization, and does so with humor and humility.

His voice echoes that of poets and writers across many centuries in India. He recounts a world that seems untouched by colonialism. In many parts of the country, the presence of the Empire was almost invisible. Even though the article is postcolonial, it could well have been written earlier, as its protagonists seem unaffected by the impact of the 200,000-odd British who tried to establish control over millions of local people.

Here is a tantalizing glimpse into a successful strategy for living and organizing, with old rules that have survived waves of rulers, regimes, and externalities. It is part of a five-thousand-year-old continuum of ideas and practice, and yet its essential message is timeless and might be newly relevant.

> The water in the springs of my hills is cool. Do not migrate from this land O my beloved.
>
> —Anupam Mishra

In the community ground of Daund village, a [troupe] of fifteen young girls danced and set their song to this lyric. The villagers sat in front, undeterred by the heavy showers in June, with the monsoon having just arrived. Among the gathered were many young and old women—their fathers, brothers, husbands, and sons having spent several springs far away in the plains of northern India. [. . .]

This village is small enough to not make a mark on any map of the Himalayas. About six thousand feet above sea level, it is as removed from the rest of the country as the rest of the country is removed from it. Even the stream flowing deep in the valley seems little more than a thin line that soon gets hidden behind sheets of rain and blankets of fog.

The clouds recede, the water does not. The upper reaches send it down with velocity. Every drop erodes a little bit of the soil, and carries it into the stream that will join the Ramganga river, and turn the soil into the silt of Corbett National Park.

The dance [troupe] winds up its instruments and prepares for the next stop on its road show. Today it is Daund, tomorrow Dulmot, then Jandriya or Ufrainkhal. Village after village hears the message—to slow down the water gushing downhill, to hold together the soil, to revive the forest and farming that has suffered torrents of neglect. The musical instruments attempt to bring back an ecological melody and rhythm to the cacophony of mindless development that has overrun the Himalayas.

This alignment of culture and ecology started in the village of Ufrainkhal, in Pauri Garhwal district of the state of Uttarakhand. That was about twenty-five years ago. Today, it spans 136 villages. Its aim: to create an atmosphere of environmental conservation, to help people rediscover that their lives cannot improve without an improvement in the ecology. To encourage everyone to tend to their forests, their water sources, their pastures, their fuel sources, and their dignity.

Sachhidanand Bharati is the guide of this [troupe]. He teaches in Ufrainkhal's Inter College. His own education, however, was in the neighboring district of Chamoli, best known for the Chipko (Hug the Trees) movement, which became a symbol of popular environmental conservation in the face of the State's ecological shortsightedness. From Chipko, Bharati had realized that protest and constructive efforts go hand in hand. He returned home to find that the state's Forest Department had granted fresh logging leases in the forests around Ufrainkhal.

Bharati and friends went from village to village, persuading people. Villagers could see the good sense in what the local boy was saying. But dealing with government officials—known for arrogance and corruption here—required tact. His calm approach, backed by the strength of the support he had mobilized, convinced a senior official to send up a team to enquire if the terrain was unsuitable for logging. The government faced what the villagers had encountered shortly before: a man armed with truth.

The enquiry team agreed with Bharati's claim. The logging leases were scrapped. The villagers realized that a united village could stand up to the unfavorable decisions of the government. They could join forces to reverse ecological destruction. Bharati decided to hold a two-day environment camp, inviting neighboring villagers to Ufrainkhal. [. . .]

July of 1980 saw the first environment camp in the Doodhatoli mountains. It ended with the plantation of seedlings and saplings. The Doodhatoli Lok Vikas Sansthan was formed in March of 1982 in Ufrainkhal, a small organization with no signboard, no budget, and no funding, governmental or foreign. It would take the organization another thirteen years to take up water conservation on a large scale.

In the beginning, it was primarily about forests. The Forest Department nurseries offered saplings of commercially viable trees like pine, which are of no use to the hill ecology or to the village economy. This meant Bharati's [troupe] had to create their own nurseries. This required people to collect seeds. So children and women were recruited for the job—for no payment and no benefits.

Nurseries required water, which was becoming scarce, especially in the summer months when the seeds germinate. The answer lay closer than they imagined, in the village's name. While Ufrain is the name of a goddess, the suffix *khal* refers a type of water body characteristic of this region. It is smaller than a *taal* (which means a lake, as in Nainital), but bigger than a *chaal*, which is a series of very small water bodies along a slope. Several places here carry such suffixes to their names. It tells us that habitations often developed around water bodies.

Bharati learned the relevance of these names in a book he read.[1] With no examples to follow, he decided to experiment, beginning by constructing the smallest form of water body: *chaal*. It was suitable for the steep slopes of Ufrainkhal, as its small size allowed water retention without the danger of landslips. The Doodhatoli group experimented with varying shapes and sizes of water retention structures in the early 1990s. Soon, they settled on a calibrated size and shape for what they had in mind.

From 1993 to 1998, the water bodies in their mind materialized on the hill slopes. [. . .] The first dramatic impact was on a dry rivulet called Sukharaula. In 1994, some water flowed in it for a few months after the rains. Each subsequent year, water stayed for progressively longer durations in the river. By 2001, it was a full-fledged seasonal river. [. . .]

Bharati's [troupes] have built twelve thousand *chaal*s in 136 villages till date. There are several patches of thick forests, varying in size from thirty hectares to three hundred hectares. In several portions, the forests regenerated are healthier than the government's reserved forests. There is a greater diversity of vegetation in them, with several broad-leaved trees like oak, alder, rhododendron and fir. [. . .]

Bharati has three associates who have led this transformation. [. . .] There is Devi Dayal, a postman who has to walk through villages to deliver the post, for there are no automobiles or motorable roads here. On his beat, he observes the forests, gathers information, and delivers ecological messages without charging any stamp duty!

There is Dinesh, a medical practitioner trained in the Ayurvedic system of traditional medicine. Like Devi Dayal, his line of work involves meeting many people and talking to them. He wraps the little medical remedies in social and ecological messages. And there is Vikram Singh, who runs a small grocery in a neighboring village. His shop is the hub of conversation and social exchange.

This quartet maintains regular communication with about two dozen volunteers in each village. Invariably, these are women, for the menfolk have migrated to the plains for employment. The thousands of *chaals* built here and the hundreds of hectares of regenerated forests is their only hope. [. . .] They number in the hundreds and their names are not on any roster. They have devised an ingenious system for handing over forest protection duties to the next volunteers— typical of how the women here combine music and rhythm in daily chores.

The woman in charge of the vigil carries a baton with a string of mini-bells tied on top. The sound of the bells works like Morse code across the hill forests. When a woman is done with her shift, she returns to the village and leaves the baton at the doorstep of a neighbor. Whoever finds the baton in front of her house takes up the guard duties the following day. [. . .]

This is the routine. It's broken only by periodic environmental camps which all the women turn up for. There is much singing and dancing to an ecological melody . . .

"The water in the springs of my hills is cool. Do not migrate from this land O my beloved."

42

HENRY NXUMALO

THE STORY OF BETHAL (1952)

from *Drum*

INTRODUCED BY ANTON HARBER

South Africa

Founded in 1951, *Drum* magazine captured the emerging spirit of defiance in postwar South Africa, giving a voice to a new urban culture that was radicalizing black opposition politics and expressing itself in a burst of creativity in writing, music, and dance. As the apartheid government, which had come to power in 1948, tightened its grip, the African National Congress turned to protest and defiance under the youthful influence of Nelson Mandela and Walter Sisulu. The few racially mixed areas around the big cities were cauldrons of political and cultural activity through the 1950s and Sophiatown, on the outskirts of Johannesburg, was one such area.

Under the patronage of Jim Bailey, heir to a mining fortune, and the editorship of Anthony Sampson, later to become Mandela's biographer, *Drum* captured this Sophiatown spirit. It was a commercial venture, which came out monthly, but was driven by the maverick Bailey's passion for black journalism, Sampson's knack for finding talent, and a brilliant team of writers and photographers, such as Can Themba, Nat Nakasa, Casey Motsitsi, Lewis Nkosi, and Bob Gosani.

The magazine's pages carried a heady mix of American-style gangsters, radical politicians, illegal taverns, jazz singers, sex across the color line, and tough exposés in print and picture. It was a pioneer expression of an exuberant and confident African perspective, celebrating African leadership, achievement, and creativity.

Excerpt from Henry Nxumalo, "The Story of Bethal," *Drum*, March 1952.

East and West African editions turned it into an early pan-African venture, distributed in eight countries, with considerable success.

One man in particular, Henry Nxumalo, who often wrote under the name Mr. Drum, pioneered firsthand investigative reporting, immersing himself in stories to give vivid descriptions of life under white minority rule. He tackled the toughest stories, such as prison, labor conditions, and church segregation, with extraordinary courage.

In 1954, to experience and write about harsh conditions in a Johannesburg prison, Nxumalo set out to have himself arrested for not carrying the notorious "pass book" which all black men were obliged to have with them at all times. After a few days of frustration, he broke a shop window to get the attention of the police.

Since authorities had denied previous reports of the conditions in the jail, "we believed that only by sending a member of our own staff to jail could we be certain of an accurate report," the editor wrote.

Nxumalo told his story of racism, violence, and degradation in deadpan language: "I was kicked and thrashed every day. I saw many other prisoners being thrashed daily. I was never told what was expected of me. Sometimes I guessed wrong and got into trouble . . . all prisoners were called Kaffirs at all times."

He described the "tausa," a strange dance that naked prisoners returning from work had to go through to show they were not hiding anything on their bodies. *Drum* photographer Bob Gosani, a German who was himself to become a legend at the magazine, pretended to be doing a fashion shoot with an office secretary on top of a nearby building to get a picture that remains one of the most unforgettable images of the indignities of apartheid. There was an outcry, and shortly afterward a new law was passed with severe penalties for publishing "false information" about prisons.

Nxumalo's most politically significant work, however, was in exposing brutal labor conditions on farms. In 1952 he focused on Bethal, a major farming area east of Johannesburg known for its use of prison labor and for a series of convictions of farmers for assault and brutality. He interviewed workers who told of being tricked into signing contracts to work in slave-like conditions, and to confirm the details he signed up himself. Pictures showed prisoners being transported in wire cages on the back of trucks to work on the farm.

Others wrote about farm conditions, but Nxumalo was the only one to go in and experience it himself. In 1955, he wrote a piece headlined I WORKED ON SNYMAN'S FARM. Snyman was a notorious farmer in Rustenberg, west of Johannesburg, who had been repeatedly convicted for assaulting his workers. Nxumalo wrote of back-breaking corn picking with bare hands, numerous assaults by the farmer, and how workers were kept against their will. When he felt he could work no longer, he was told: "On this farm you don't just quit when you want to." He was asked for his pass. "He tore it up into little pieces and threw them away on the lawn. 'Now you can't leave without my permission: I can have you arrested and imprisoned . . .'" Mr. Drum fled in the dead of night.

Again, this was accompanied by an extraordinary set of photographs, taken covertly, including a silhouette of a guard on a horse wielding a whip.

Nxumalo was stabbed to death in 1957 while on his way to meet a source while investigating an illegal abortion racket by a well-known doctor. His murderer was never identified, but it was widely presumed to be related to the story.

Repeated coverage of these labor conditions by Drum and others led to an organized potato boycott in 1959, a critical moment in the mobilization of the ANC. But the severe security clampdown after the Sharpeville massacre of 1960 and the arrest of most political leaders drove many of the *Drum* writers into exile, and the magazine never recovered. The residents of Sophiatown were forcibly removed in 1964. Bailey soldiered on until he was forced to sell the magazine in the 1980s. It is still published, though the current version bears little resemblance to the magazine of the 1950s.

In 2005, Nxumalo was given the Order of Ikhamanga in Silver by the ANC government and a Johannesburg street was named after him. *Drum* is remembered as a high moment in the history of black journalism, and a symbol of what might have been if apartheid had not crushed its spirit.

Full copies of the magazine can be found at Bailey's African History Archives: www.baha.co.za. The story was captured in the 2004 film *Drum*, and the stage production *Sophiatown*. For further reading, see Sampson's memoir, *Drum: The Making of a Magazine* (Jonathan Ball, 1983), and Mike Nicol's *A Good-Looking Corpse: The World of Drum—Jazz and Gangsters, Hope and Defiance* (Secker & Warburg, 1991).

Evil Record

For many years Bethal has been notorious for the ill-treatment of the African labourers on the farms. As far back as April 12, 1929, there was a case (Rex v. Nafte, at the Circuit Court at Bethal) of a farmer who was found guilty of tying a labourer by his feet from a tree and flogging him to death, pouring scalding water into his mouth when he cried for water. [. . .] On June 3, 1947 (see De Echo

Bethal of 6.6.47) there was a case of a farmer assaulting two labourers, setting his dog on them, flogging them and chaining them together for the night; and only a week later, on June 11 (De Echo, 13.6.47), a farm foreman was found guilty of striking a labourer with a sjambok and setting his dog on him. [. . .] These cases all came up in court and were strongly condemned by the magistrates; Mr. B.H. Wooler, described the incident as being sordid, despicable and reminiscent of slavery, and the local European paper, De Echo, described the conditions disclosed as being "tantamount to slave-driving." And it seems clear that for every case that came before a magistrate there were many more that were never found out. [. . .]

Conditions Still Bad

Since 1947 there have been many statements made to the effect that conditions at Bethal have improved, and in 1949 an act was passed to safeguard the interests of labourers under contract. More inspectors were appointed by the Director of Native Labour, were supposed to supervise and witness the signing of contracts, and to satisfy themselves that they were fully understood by the recruits.

But, in spite of everything said to the contrary, there is still plenty of evidence that conditions at Bethal and the system which causes them are a disgrace to the country. [. . .]

Mr. Drum Finds Out

In order to discover the truth about the way contracts are signed, Mr. DRUM himself decided to become a farm recruit. He was soon picked up outside the Pass Office by one of the touts or "runners" who look out for unemployed Africans, and are paid for each man they collect for the agencies. [. . .] He said he had no pass, and, with many others, was told that he would be given a pass if he signed a contract to go and work out of Johannesburg: this is the normal way of dealing with people without passes. He chose to work on a farm in Springs, and was sent to _____'s compound, where he waited nearly a day before he could sign the contract.

Running Past the Contract

When the contract came to be signed the interpreter read out a small part of the contract to a number of recruits together, while the attesting officer held a pencil over the contract. [. . .]

N.A.D. African Clerk (calling roll of everyone on the contract sheet): You're going to work on a farm in the Middelburg district; you are on a six months' contract. You will be paid £3 a month, plus food and quarters. When you leave here you will be given an advance of 5s. for pocket money, 10s. 4d. for food, and 14s. 5d. for train fare. The total amount will be deducted from your first months' wages. How you got that?

Mr. DRUM and other recruits: Yes.

Clerk: You will now proceed to touch the pencil.

Mr. DRUM: But I was told before that I was going to be sent to a farm in Springs. Why am I now going to Middelburg?

Clerk: I'm telling you where you are going, according to your contract sheet, and nothing else.

So Mr. DRUM refused to touch the pencil when he reached the attesting officer, and was told to wait outside for his pass.

The other recruits then ran past the attesting officer, each hold the pencil for a moment, which was not even touching the paper. [. . .] As a result of holding a pencil for a second (50 recruits were attested in a few minutes), the recruits were considered to be bound to a contract. But in fact the contract had not been fully understood. So it seems that none of the contracts "signed" in this way are valid at all. (Native Labour Regulation Act of 1911, as amended 1949). [. . .]

Touts' Trick

A man from Nyasaland described how the touts employed by a certain labour agency in his country worked. There was a certain boundary which many people crossed in order to get to the Union. The touts wait there to intercept, and when they saw one trying to cross the area they immediately pounced on him and threatened him with arrest for trespass if he did not accept the offer of a contract for work for South Africa as a waiter. The victim only realized on arriving in the Union that he had been tricked and contracted to work on a farm. [. . .]

Compulsion, Not Persuasion

We wish to emphasize that while the Industrial Revolution is causing as much chaos in South Africa as it caused in the 19th Century Europe no lessons have been learnt from the industrial past whatever. The same abuse of labour is repeated in the same style.

Farm prisons and contracted labour bypass the normal need to attract men by improved working conditions and higher wages. They depend upon compulsion not persuasion.

Most men who touch a pencil for a farm contract are hungry, ignorant, and urgently in need of work. Once they have touched a pencil they have handed themselves to an unknown employer in an unknown area under largely unknown conditions.

It is obvious that care has been taken by the authorities to protect these people.

We asked, when farm life is so often satisfactory, what are the conditions which have given Bethal so fearful and exceptional [a] history—and we reply, it is the system; the farm contract system that has had so vile a result. [. . .]

43

CARLOS SALINAS MALDONADO

A DECIMATED CHICHIGALPA BURIES ITS DEAD (2013)

From *Confidencial*

INTRODUCED BY SILVIO WAISBORD

Nicaragua

Watchdog reporting in Latin America has long focused on the plight of the downtrodden, the vast majority of the population living amid unbelievable hardships. Salinas Maldonado, a frequent contributor to Nicaragua's leading newsweekly *Confidencial*, best represents this tradition. His reporting regularly documents social problems particularly affecting rural populations that are rarely covered by the urban-based media. His hope is the same that underlies watchdog reporting: to bring the attention of the public and authorities to urgent issues. His story focuses on how the municipality of Chichigalpa copes with the unusual number of deaths among men from chronic kidney disease, presumably related to contamination caused by sugar-cane agriculture. The story deftly blends personal testimonies from various affected parties with data. The resulting picture is all too common in the region: communities try to find answers, are skeptical of official explanations, and feel that authorities lack interest in their situation. The mix of human tragedy and official obliviousness produces a grim reality of hopelessness.

A group of women sing their hearts out in the municipal cemetery of Chichigalpa. It's a hymn of farewell, as three young men lower the coffin containing the

Excerpt from Carlos Salinas Maldonado, "A Decimated Chichigalpa Buries Its Dead," *Confidencial*, May 13, 2013. Translated by Nicolo Gnecchi-Ruscone.

remains of Víctor Ramiro Baldelomar, seventy-six years old, dead, say his family, of chronic kidney disease (CKD). It is a strange sickness that plagues this little town of Chichigalpa, one which the government ignores and whose infection rate the Ministry of Health keeps in total darkness.

The song rises with force, drowning the sobs of the family. [. . .] "All the men are dying of this," says Telma Francisca Medrano, fifty-three years old, watching the coffin disappear under the fine, coffee-red earth stinging the eyes of onlookers. [. . .]

The town has a population of fifty thousand inhabitants; an area of sugar cane producers in which both the government and Ministry of Health show no interest in developing a strategy to combat the scourge.

[. . .] Telma lost her husband, David Gutiérrez Téllez, four years ago. He was fifty-six years old. He worked for a long time at the San Antonio sugar plant, the largest employer in the area, whose lands the widows blame for the evil that killed their husbands.

Two of Telma's sons worked for the same plant because, she says, they had no alternative. They are also suffering from the sickness. The first, Francisco, twenty-two years old, just emerged "stuck" but he continues working, assures the woman. "As for the second, Alexander, I have him at home and they haven't given him anything, not even his insurance," she added.

Telma readjusts the cross that is falling off her husband's grave. [. . .]

We don't know the cause of this severe epidemic that is affecting most of the west part of Nicaragua. But it is punishing the communities of Chichigalpa with all its fury. Experts say that long exposure to high temperatures—between 32 and 36 centigrade—in the fields, exacerbated by dehydration and tough work, damages the kidneys, which begin to progressively lose nephrons, the cells that compose the organs, until they stop functioning. The sickness is diagnosed by measuring the levels of creatine in the body, a waste excreted by our kidneys. In a grown man, the normal levels of creatine are 0.9 to 1.4. In their final stages, those affected by CKD can measure above 20. [. . .]

It has not been possible to determine if there is a direct relation between the chemicals used by the cane plantations, or the water of the plant, with the CKD epidemic. Recently the School of Public Health of the University of Boston conducted research to determine the causes of the epidemic. Researchers and experts even travelled to Chichigalpa. For three years, between 2009 and 2012, the scientific team interviewed and analyzed cane farm workers and examined thirty-six agrochemicals used by the plant, as well as the water sources of the San Antonio (ISA) plantations. However, the researchers did not gather enough evidence to blame the epidemic on the agrochemicals or the water used by the plant.

"We found limited proof that the practices at work or the exposure to the chemical products used by ISA, presently or in the past, have any direct relation with CKD. It's a plausible association, but it has not been established," confirmed the researchers in their report. [. . .] In one of their recommendations, the researchers said that it was necessary to conduct further studies to determine the causes of CKD.

[. . .] Apart from the accusations towards the plant, the ex–cane workers resent the fact that the public authorities have not shown the slightest attention to their plight. Miguel Ángel, fifty-nine years old, says that four of his brothers have died, and he names them: Félix Paredes, Reynaldo Paredes, Santiago Paredes, and Rubén Paredes. "And I am about to die too," he says. Next to him, José Antonio Díaz, fifty-two, complains of the lack of medicines. "The attention from the interns and the doctor is good, but sometimes they don't have medicine, I don't know why," said Díaz, who is insured and receives a monthly pension of 1,800 córdobas. "With this I can pay for my electricity and water, some of us are lucky in that our partners also work or we have some other skill. I also work in construction, so if a job pops up, I go despite my sickness. If not I will die of hunger," says the man. [. . .]

According to an analysis of WHO and PHO data conducted by the International Consortium of Investigative Journalism (ICIJ), in the last two decades, the number of men who have died due to CKD has risen five-fold.

"Now more men are dying from the ailment than from HIV/AIDS, diabetes and leukemia combined," an ICIJ report said.[1]

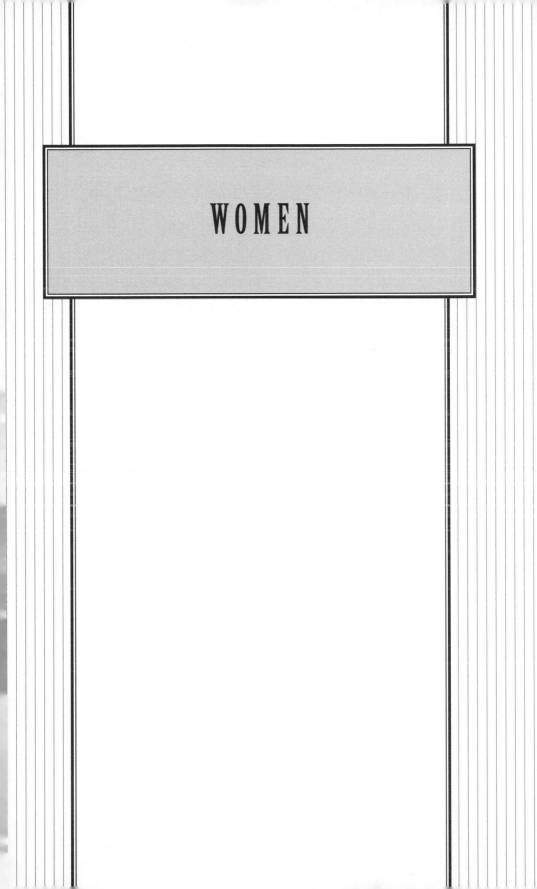

WOMEN

44

ALICIA LITTLE

FOOTBINDING: TWO SIDES OF THE QUESTION (1895)

from *Chinese Recorder and Missionary Journal*

INTRODUCED BY YEN-WEI MIAO

China

The general consensus among historians is that Chinese footbinding originated in the court and upper classes in the tenth century, and became a well-practiced custom by the end of the Qing dynasty (1644–1912). According to a census conducted by the colonial government in Japan-ruled Taiwan in 1905, the number of women with bound feet at that time was 800,616, or about 57 percent of the total female population. For centuries, the feet of Chinese girls of about five years old would be tightly bound with strips of cloth. Gradually, the pressure of the binding broke the bones of their feet, and though the feet became deformed, they also remained very small. In spite of its obvious pain and cruelty, the practice of footbinding in traditional China embodied various positive cultural values, such as beauty, femininity, sexuality, morality, higher social status, as well as Han ethnicity.

In the eighteenth and early nineteenth centuries, some intellectuals recorded their opposition in writing. By the mid-nineteenth century, the Taiping rebel regime severely prohibited footbinding. However, the impact of these efforts was limited. The basic cultural-social framework that supported the custom of footbinding remained unchallenged until certain "grievances" were constructed by Westerners in the late nineteenth century. In this vein, Alicia Little (1845–1926; a.k.a. Mrs. Archibald Little), the author of the article introduced here, played a significant role in

Excerpt from Alicia Little, "Footbinding: Two Sides of the Question," *Chinese Recorder and Missionary Journal* 26, no. 12 (December 1895).

mobilizing Westerners to participate in changing such a custom far from their homeland.

The wife of a British merchant who arrived in China in 1887 and stayed for decades, Little traveled extensively throughout China and wrote many books about her experiences in the Middle Kingdom. But perhaps her greatest contribution was her anti-footbinding activism, which gave the expatriate crusader a degree of notoriety before her husband's illness required her to return to England in 1907. While she admired many aspects of Chinese culture, she was deeply upset by a custom that crippled Chinese girls and women. She devoted herself to uprooting this "evil practice," gathering over twenty women from various Western countries—wives of diplomats, merchants, missionary-scholars, and other foreign power elites in the Shanghai settlement—to join her in her crusade. In April 1895, she founded the Natural Feet Society (tianzu hui), condemning footbinding as a cruel and injurious practice, and calling for funds and friends to aid in creating public sentiment against the practice.

The establishment of the Natural Feet Society owed much to the help of missionaries such as Rev. John Macgowan of the London Mission Society, who founded the first organized anti-footbinding group in China in 1874 in Amoy (Xiamen), Fujian province. The missionary even gave a speech at the opening meeting of Little's new organization, sharing his anti-footbinding experience with this group of secular women. The network of missionaries also functioned as the organizational base of this new society. Indeed, missionaries were automatically absorbed as members of the Natural Feet Society, while the society wives who wanted to become members were required to donate money. Because none of these women could speak or read Chinese, they had to rely heavily on the missionaries' ability to translate between Chinese and English. In fact, the article shown here was translated by Rev. Timothy Richard and his Chinese assistants, and published in an influential missionary magazine.

However, Little came to realize that, if mission influence was too prominent, natural-footed women might become the focus of antiforeign and anti-Christian violence. Also, missions were mainly associated with the poor and the humble, while the practice of footbinding was more popular among families of higher classes. Therefore, to disassociate the Natural Feet Society from the mission-oriented anti-footbinding societies, Little not only avoided speaking of such notions as "God," "Church," and "Christianity," but also frequently appealed to native authority, including the edicts of early Qing emperors and the teachings of Confucius and Mencius. Instead of trying to impose her own cultural convictions, she tried to explain the terrible consequences of footbinding from a Chinese cultural perspective, beginning with refuting the many commonly held assumptions about the practice.

Little's crusade was so remarkable that, by the turn of the twentieth century, her Natural Feet Society (1895–1906) became the only active anti-footbinding group in China. Indigenous efforts were suppressed as a consequence of the failure of the Reform Movement, and church-based activities diminished due to the Boxer Rebellion and a growing anti-Christian movement.

Full of energy and resolve, between 1899 and 1900 Little went on tour to promote the movement, traveling to major cities in the Yangtze river valley and along the southeast coast. In each city she was introduced to both Chinese and British officials and community leaders. With tireless leadership, Little organized Society gatherings in over thirty cities, and was the principal contributor to a total of 162 recorded meetings. At the end of each event, a number of leaflets, tracts, placards, and pledges were distributed. By the end of 1906, over one million copies of anti-footbinding campaign material had been printed and circulated out of Shanghai, without counting leaflets printed elsewhere.

Although almost no evidence shows that the Natural Feet Society directly persuaded a noteworthy number of Chinese women to unbind their feet, it's reasonable to conclude that Little's writings and activism played an important role in enlightening indigenous intellectuals, thus engendering reform.

After footbinding was redefined as an evil practice, various abolishing efforts developed within different regional and historical contexts. For example, there were anti-footbinding campaigns organized by Westerners who lived mostly in treaty-port communities. There were also campaigns in colonial Taiwan initiated by native elites who agreed with the colonial authorities' condemnation of footbinding. Late-Qing and early-Republican intellectuals, nationalists, and revolutionaries also led crusades against footbinding, along with state regimes with relative stability, such as the warlord regime in Shanxi Province, the Nationalists' Nanjing regime, and the Communists' Yanan regime. These were localized campaigns with the broader goals of promoting greater economic productivity and mobilization in preparation for war.

Many indigenous social reformers and nationalists regarded footbinding as lewd, wasteful, and nationally humiliating. Moreover, they recognized that, in an era of rebellion, riots, civil war, and foreign invasions, footbinding made it next to impossible for women to flee the violence and save themselves. Eventually, under the unanimity of condemnation, the practice declined. By the first half of the twentieth century, it was no longer a social stigma for Chinese women to have natural feet on the long march to modern-day China.

Part I. Refutation of the Reasons Brought Forward in Support of Foot-Binding.

1. "It is an old custom."—No! In Chinese history the time before the introduction of foot-binding is longer than the time after its introduction. [. . .]
2. "It looks nice."—No! The natural form of the foot is far more beautiful, especially where, as in China, the women have especially pretty feet by nature. Besides, think of the ugliness and even the bad odour of the bound feet if not covered!
3. "All the high class ladies bind their feet."—There was a time when no high class ladies did so. Even now the Empress of China and all the ladies of the court have feet of the natural size, nor is any woman with deformed feet allowed within the court. It is for all you ladies in the eighteen provinces to follow this good example and return to the good customs of your ancestors.
4. "It preserves the chastity and modesty of the women."—No! Or are all women with bound feet chaste and modest? Certainly not. Chastity and modesty are not preserved by outward forms but by moral principles in the heart.
5. "Should I in my family begin to give it up everyone would laugh at me."—They might do so for a little time. But already in many parts of China women are beginning to unbind their feet; sometimes to please their husbands, sometimes because they are themselves convinced of the hurtfulness of the practice. Besides it is the truest honour to endure the mockery of foolish people for right principles. [. . .]

Part II. Why Foot-Binding Is a Bad Custom.

1. Because it is contrary to nature.—Nature makes no mistakes. If the feet ought to be so small they would have been made so by nature. You must not try to correct nature. [. . .]
2. Because the wives of all the sages and the old ancestors did not bind their feet.—Think of the innumerable women in China who lived before this custom arose. Think of the mother of Mencius! Is it not good to return to and conform to their example?

3.   Because it hinders the free movements of the body.—Thus it spoils the growth and development of the body, often causes sterility, and is the principal cause of many of the diseases of women. [. . .]

4.   It sometimes causes death, for instance, by fire or in floods. [. . .]

5.   It is in the way of women earning money. Foreigners in Shanghai object to employing small-footed Chinese women, because they cannot trust them to carry their children or their crockery. Whilst in the factories managers try always to employ women with natural sized feet, as for the others it is necessary to provide seats, and they often remain seated when they ought to be attending to their machines.

6.   Because it has very bad consequences in the social relations.—Women with bound feet are always dependent on the help of others. Girls cannot run quickly to carry out the orders of their father and mother. Wives cannot fulfil their household duties as they would be able to do with unbound feet. Mothers cannot watch and look after their children properly when they are playing in the open air. Women cannot clean their houses, thus the houses remain dirty and become unhealthy. [. . .].

7.   It is a cruel custom, making the hearts of mothers hard even to their own children.—It inflicts a great deal of pain and suffering among young girls. Parents have no right thus to cripple their little girls for life, and doing so must harden and brutalise the whole family, making mothers cruel to their children, and fathers and the other children indifferent to suffering. [. . .]

The mother of Confucius and the mother of Mencius had unbound feet. The wives and daughters of all the other nations in the world have unbound feet, and are happy. Therefore ye Chinese fathers and mothers, ye ought not to bind the feet of your daughters, but follow the example of the mothers and wives of the Chinese sages and ancient Emperors.

45

MAE AZANGO

GROWING PAINS: SANDE TRADITION OF GENITAL CUTTING THREATENS LIBERIAN WOMEN'S HEALTH (2012)

from *Front Page Africa*

INTRODUCED BY PRUE CLARKE

Liberia

When Mae Azango wrote her cover story on the health effects of female genital cutting (FGC) for Liberia's major newspaper on International Women's Day in March 2012, she had little idea of the firestorm she would ignite. Within days Mae and her nine-year-old daughter were in hiding—the targets of death threats from leaders of the "Sande"—a female society thought to be at least centuries old and followed by tribes in Liberia, Sierre Leone, and Guinea. The Sande holds FGC as a sacred rite of passage for Liberian girls as young as three months old. In a series of stories for the *Front Page Africa* newspaper and website, Mae pointed out that there was more than tradition motivating the elders of the Sande. Many were making their livelihoods from the practice and they used membership in the society to wield power over others in the community.

Liberia's women were paying a heavy price. One in every ten pregnancies ended in the death of the mother. Maternal and infant mortality rates were among the highest in the world. Many of those deaths were caused simply because the mother's vagina had been so scarred by FGC that it could no longer stretch enough to allow a baby to pass. For others cutting meant terrible trauma, infections, bleeding, and lifelong complications. An unknown number had died.

Many Liberians were completely unaware of this before Mae's reporting.

Excerpt from Mae Azango, "Growing Pains: Sande Tradition of Genital Cutting Threatens Liberian Women's Health," *Front Page Africa*, March 8, 2012.

Sande rules dictated that anyone who spoke about the secret ceremonies be killed. Politicians, including President Ellen Johnson Sirleaf, needed Sande support to be elected. No media houses or political leaders had been brave enough to publicly discuss the impact the practice was having on Liberia's women.

At first the Liberian government and police dismissed the threats to Mae and *Front Page Africa*. But after an international campaign led by New Narratives, the U.S. media NGO that I run and that worked with Mae to produce the series, was joined by the Committee to Protect Journalists, Nicholas Kristof of the *New York Times*, the Columbia Journalism School, and Amnesty International, the Liberian government made its first public statements condemning FGC. Several Liberian leaders came forward to denounce FGC. The government even signed a number of international agreements and treaties that forbid the practice, and the Supreme Court upheld the first conviction of perpetrators in a cutting case. The Liberian government also announced it would shut down the Sande and prosecute anyone practicing Sande activities, including cutting. This did not end the practice. Indeed, rights groups found 750 girls were cut in a ceremony in the country's remote north months after the ban. The difference is the subject is now talked about openly. The local media keep a steady vigil exposing violations of the ban and the topic is discussed on the opinion pages. Most significantly for us, many young girls in Liberia—who once would have had no idea about FGC until it happened to them—started telling their parents they did not want to be cut.

Ma Sabah was only 13 when she was taken from her rural home to the "Sande Bush." The Sande is where women and girls are sent to be circumcised and groomed into women ready for marriage, as culture and tradition demand.

"It can hurt much more than delivery pain when they be cutting your clitorises with a knife," says Ma Sabah, now 47, as she recalls how five women held her down while another woman cut off her clitoris.

The removal of the clitoris is a central element of the Sande initiation ritual. Ten out of Liberia's 16 tribes practice cutting (commonly known as FGC). No one has reliable numbers on how many women have been cut. The Association of Female Lawyers of Liberia (AFELL) says as many as 85 percent of our population practices it.

Many girls and women who experience complications from the procedure do not seek treatment until they are in dire condition, because they have taken an oath to keep secret what happens in the Sande. The promised punishment for speaking out, according to women FPA asked to interview on the subject, is death.

Ma Sabah, who requested that her real name not be used, has only agreed to speak hidden in a small, dark room. Even then she is still scared that she will be spotted and hunted down. She whispers as she recalls what happened to her. The cutting is especially vivid in her mind because it was done without anesthesia.

Bleeding is the initial major risk from FGC says Dr. Torsou Y. Jallabah, medical director of the James N. Davis Jr. Memorial Hospital on the outskirts of Monrovia.

"If a fresh tissue is cut and not sewed, the person bleeds, the patient could go into shock and die," says Jallabah. "Recently some children who underwent genital cutting were bleeding and rushed to our hospital by the police . . . and some stitching was done to stop the bleeding."

Cutting is often carried out in an unsanitary environment using unsterilized instruments such as razor blades or knives and natural herbs for healing.

"We was plenty girls who join the Sande," says Ma Sabah. "And the time they was ready to cut us, they use only three knives on all of us and just mashed the leaf and put it on our sore."

Contamination could lead to urinary tract infections, tetanus or worse, says Jallabah.

"If one knife is used . . . without being sterilized, it is a possibility that a person could be infected with the HIV virus and it can be transmitted to the next person," says Jallabah.

Cutting also carries long-term risks, especially when giving birth says Mary Toe, a hospital midwife who also did not want her real name used. Liberia ranks among the world's worst countries for death among pregnant women and infants. Toe says cutting is a major factor.

"The baby would be endangered if it stays long to come down because the [scarred vagina will no longer] extend for the baby's head to come out, and brain damage or death could come about," says Toe.

The removal of the clitoris is a sacred cultural practice that people in the Sande say will prevent promiscuity. Others view cutting as a harmful tradition that needs to be abolished outright.

"I always advise my patients not to send their daughters to where they went and got cut, because their children would face the same difficulties in delivery as they are," says Toe.

But others caution that coming down hard on cutting would not stop the practice because it is so deeply rooted in culture. Legally banning FGC would only cause it to be done in even more secrecy and unsafe conditions, warns Dr. Jallabah.

"The most important thing is to teach ways to minimize or control the complications," says Jallabah. "Then let people know that while there are some positives [to the Sande culture], the negative effects of this particular practice are greater than the positive. Make them see reason to do away with it. But if you just come down hard people will hide and still do it, and more women will suffer."

Twenty-one African countries including Senegal and Somalia have banned or partially banned cutting. Only Liberia and five other countries are still holding onto this cultural heritage that has been passed down from generation to generation.

For Ma Sabah, there is no question about the future for her two daughters.

"I won't send my children to the Sande because it will cripple them in the future," she says. "All our eyes are open now."

46

NAFISA SHAH

KARO KARI: RITUAL KILLINGS IN THE NAME OF HONOUR (1993)

From *Newsline*

INTRODUCED BY NICOLE POPE

Pakistan

Violence against women is a global phenomenon that takes different forms around the world. In the past couple of decades, awareness of honor killings, and more broadly of a wide variety of crimes committed in the name of "honor," has increased worldwide largely thanks to the work of journalists and activists who shone a light on the dynamics of these gruesome crimes in their own communities.

I chose this article on karo kari (the name given to men and women allegedly involved in illicit relationships, which means *black*) by journalist and activist Nafisa Shah, published in 1993 in Pakistan's *Newsline* magazine, because it explains the powerful hold of an ancient code of honor that continues to kill in the tribal and feudal belt of Pakistan. Her matter-of-fact style makes the cruelty and injustice of the system all the more striking.

The practice was known but rarely discussed publicly until journalists and activists, in Pakistan and other countries where such traditional practices still prevail, revealed the full extent of its impact. Key to their battle to bring honor killings to the fore was the revelation that law enforcement agencies and judicial institutions were willing to turn a blind eye and were complicit in accepting that the perpetrator, whose "honor" had allegedly been besmirched, was the real victim.

Nafisa Shah's groundbreaking articles showed how the custom was

Excerpt from Nafisa Shah, "Karo Kari: Ritual Killings in the Name of Honour," *Newsline*, January 1993.

perpetuated in her native Sindh. Her award-winning essay "Of Female Bondage," published in the same issue of *Newsline*, focused on the commodification of women that underpins the honor system.

Shah, who has now become a member of the national assembly, was not alone in combating the practice. Other activists, lawyers, and writers in Pakistan have also played a prominent role in combating karo kari killings. In Jordan, journalist Rana Husseini was among the first to turn the spotlight on a code of "honor" that killed many women and forced others into protective custody, as if they, rather than the people who targeted them, needed to be locked up.

Their work found fertile ground because momentum was slowly building up worldwide toward acknowledging violence against women, in all its forms, as one of the most pervasive, yet least recognized, human rights violations.

In 1979, the Convention on the Elimination of All Forms of Discrimination Against Women (CEDAW), now adopted by most countries, set binding standards for the empowerment of women. In its Declaration on the Elimination of Violence Against Women, issued in 1993, the United Nations stated that "violence against women is a manifestation of historically unequal power relations between men and women" and "is one of the crucial social mechanisms by which women are forced into a subordinate position compared with men."

Pioneering journalists, brave enough to break taboos and tackle issues that society keeps under wraps, can be a trigger for social change. Karo kari killings haven't ended in Pakistan, nor have crimes committed in the name of honor been eradicated around the world. But media attention and growing public outrage have challenged the immunity too often afforded to the perpetrators, forcing governments in a number of countries, including Pakistan, to confront the issue and change legislation. Against a strong patriarchal background, implementation of the new laws is often weak, but activists continue to campaign for justice, in spite of strong criticism and threats.

Awareness of crimes committed in the name of honor, which fit within a broad spectrum of violence against women, also reached Western countries with large migrant communities affected by such murders. Interestingly, for many years courts in European countries were willing to accept "culture" as a mitigating factor. This stemmed partly from the fact that all too often, relations between the authorities of the host country and their migrant communities were limited to contacts with male community leaders. But groups representing women from an ethnic background started speaking out in the media, calling for their own rights to be respected and rejecting these brutal traditional practices as part of their culture.

Thanks to their efforts, honor-based crimes, which also include forced marriages, intimidation, and widespread domestic violence, have now been brought out into the open. But while courts are less likely to be lenient toward perpetrators and the victims' perspective is more often taken into consideration, in the aftermath of the 9/11 attacks, crimes committed in the name of honor have often been seen in Western countries as Islamic in origin and used to fuel anti-Muslim sentiment.

Honor killings are sometimes given a religious cover, and local journalists and activists combating discriminatory customs are often labelled traitors to their faith and culture or accused of promoting immorality. But the concept of honor pre-dates Islam and isn't directly linked to religion, even if many religious fundamentalists, just as intent on restricting women's freedoms as patriarchal tribal leaders, turn a blind eye or even condone it. In this article, for instance, Nafisa Shah refers extensively to a tribal and feudal code of honor, but she doesn't mention religion as a source.

———————

The village of Khairpur Juso near Larkana still talks about that gory night a year ago when a young Baloch woman nine months pregnant was hacked to death. A young man of the Channa tribe had gone to visit a friend in a neighbouring Baloch village. The friend welcomed him, told his young wife to cook a festive dinner for the two of them, and asked Channa to stay overnight. The next thing Channa knew was that the woman's uncles suspected him of having a liaison with his friend's wife.

Channa ran back to his village. The woman had nowhere to run. [. . .] As though driven by intuition, she hid in a graveyard. Her uncles brought her back the next day, collected all the village women, gave the young woman a glass of water and just as she was about to drink, chopped off her head with a kulhari. The poor husband helplessly watched his wife being butchered to pieces. The uncles forced the husband to swear that he was the killer and had him sent to jail for murder. The Channa tribesman had to pay two lakh rupees in protection money to save his life.

The man was a karo (literally, black), the woman a kari and the murder was a tribal ritual which demands that a man and a woman involved in an illicit relationship should be killed. The ritual has survived all the legal, political and ethical developments of our times and is now convenient cover for all kinds of murders.

The Baloch woman's murder was not an unusual occurrence: hundreds of women in the tribal belts of Sindh, Balochistan and lower Punjab are killed every year on charges of being karis. Young girls who have not yet reached puberty, married women with children, even grandmothers are killed on charges of having illicit relations with men whom they have often never seen.

Karo kari is a Baloch tribal tradition that is now also practised by Sindhis and Punjabis living in the tribal belt. [. . .] And although the tradition is supposed to apply equally to both men and women, the dice is heavily loaded against women since the accusations are always made by men who are the custodians of power in the feudal set-up. [. . .]

About six months ago a 14-year-old boy and a 10-year-old girl from the Chandio tribe were branded karo kari and killed in the village of Akil Khuhro in Larkana district. The boy, who had taken his younger siblings to visit neighbours from the same tribe on a hot summer afternoon, was spotted drying his sweat-drenched shirt while the ten-year-old girl slept on a charpoi nearby. The girl's elder brother saw him and jumped to the wrong conclusion. A few days later, the boy was killed on his way to school and subsequently the girl was also murdered. A few cases come to light, but the vast majority of karo kari murders go unreported. [. . .] And it is not just illiterate tribals who engage in this practice: there have been several cases in which the wives of well-to-do men have been killed and the murders hushed up. In one such case, the nephew of a member of the Sindh government killed his mother and her alleged paramour in Sanghar. No case was registered.

The law seems to be deliberately blind to these incidents. It is the sardar or feudal chief who takes the decisions that are literally a matter of life or death; no one even bothers to investigate the truth or falsehood of the charges made. No record is kept of such cases since the police either charge a fee to keep them off the record or are intimidated into silence by the economic and political clout of the feudal. "The police in Kashmore charges 7,000 rupees to keep silent about karo kari murders," says one villager who has seen it happen again and again. "They never record cases and so we have a zero crime rate."

Police stations in Jacobabad are considered gold mines in police circles because of the high incidence of karo kari murders there. A conservative estimate puts the number of karo kari murders in Jacobabad at between 55–60 a month. [. . .]

Karo kari are an integral part of the feudal and tribal systems. They serve more than one purpose. In some cases, they are motivated purely by tribal concepts of honour. But frequently they are just another element in the conflict between two warring tribes, and the women who die are no more than pawns in the game of vendetta played by feudal warlords. Men get back at their enemies by killing their own women, and then accusing their opponents of doing so. The accused is often forced to pay a price to avoid a heavy sentence. If money alone is not considered sufficient, a woman is added to it. Bartered and traded, she has no more value than a piece of property, like a cow or a piece of land that the man may dispose of at his pleasure. [. . .]

Asked why women are equated with money, Ghulam Hussein Mazari, a local sardar and muqaddam (manager) of Sindh food minister Salim Jan Mazar says, "We prefer to give a woman in exchange for a murder: relations with a woman cool the man to whom injustice has been done." [. . .]

Sometimes the karo kari pretext helps a man escape a life sentence. Says Zuheida Mathelo, a lecturer in Jamshoro University: "In a village in Larkana, a man in my servant's family committed a murder. His father told him to immediately murder his sister-in-law if he wanted to escape a death sentence. He took a kulhari and hit his bhabi on the head while she was cooking food for the family, declaring her kari with the man he had murdered." [. . .]

Killing a woman and crying karo kari is also a good way to make a fortune overnight. In the village of Gujrani, 12 miles from Kandkot, a man murdered his 85-year-old mother last year declaring her a kari. He needed 25,000 rupees and got it—from the man he called karo.

The kot or house of the sardar is the only sanctuary for a woman accused of being a kari. Here she is given refuge till the tribal court pronounces its verdict. But in most cases they do not dare go back to their families, and therefore become the property of the sardar. [. . .] A few lucky ones manage to build a new life for themselves. [. . .]

Not all murders are committed to settle tribal feuds or to make money. Women do frequently elope with men of their choice. But in the value system of the feudal and tribal set-up, pride and honour are important components and the woman is a measure of both. She is in fact the prime instrument these systems use to sustain themselves. Woman is the price or property that negotiates all kinds of faislas ranging from marriage to murder. [. . .]

Karo kari enforces the strength of the sardar. It makes him richer and mightier. The sardar leads the jirga that decides the fate of a karo—who in most cases escapes before the jirga can be held. Compensation can take the form of either money or women. Different tribes apply different rates of blood money to exempt a karo from punishment. Women, however, are often preferred to even a hefty sum of money. The standard rate is one girl above seven years of age or two girls under seven. "There have been cases in which parents have broken the milk teeth of a girl far below seven years of age so that they only have to pay one girl as the price for murder," says a Sindhi doctor. [. . .]

Using karo kari as a means to amass wealth [. . .] is also common. In Jacobabad it has turned into a full-fledged industry. Women are ruthlessly killed to exact a fine from the enemy tribe, one of whose tribesmen is branded the karo. Jacobabad is full of gory stories of women being killed while cooking food, fetching water or even sleeping. [. . .]

Shaikh Ayaz, the doyen of Sindhi poetry, has come across numerous cases of karo kari in his practice as a criminal lawyer, and states than 90 per cent of these are based on false charges. He sees no hope of change unless the system that fosters the custom is dismantled. "This will go on and on until we get rid of the male-dominated system that subjugates women," he says. "The Sindhi woman will never be liberated until society is rid of the curse of feudalism."

47

ELISABETH WYNHAUSEN

DEATH EXPOSES AGONY OF SEX SLAVES (2003)

from *The Australian*

INTRODUCED BY KATHLEEN MALTZAHN

Australia

In late 2002, I received a phone call from Charandev Singh, a human rights advocate at the Brimbank Community Legal Centre in Melbourne's outer west. We had never met, but Singh had heard that Project Respect, where I worked, had been following the case of a young woman who had died in late September 2001 in the Villawood Immigration Detention Centre in Sydney.

Questions had been raised in parliament about the death of Puong-tong Simaplee and we were concerned. In 2001, we had received funding from the Myer Foundation to research trafficking, and we had uncovered a pattern of the detention and deportation of trafficked women. Victims of crime, it seemed, were being treated like criminals—held in immigration detention and deported without recourse to justice. Simaplee had been apparently picked up during an operation in Sydney against people smuggling within the sex industry. We did not know anything about the young woman who had died, but her death raised significant questions. [. . .]

In the year leading up to Singh's call, Project Respect had had more and more contact with trafficked women. A clear pattern had emerged. Women—at that time often Thai women—were coming to Australia on the promise of decent conditions and good pay. Many knew they might

Introduction from Kathleen Maltzahn, *Trafficked* (Sydney: UNSW Press, 2008). Excerpt from Elisabeth Wynhausen, "Death Exposes Agony of Sex Slaves," *The Australian*, March 15, 2003.

be doing prostitution, or at least would be connected to the sex industry through karaoke bars or strip clubs. Some, a small minority, had no inkling that they would have anything to do with prostitution. Either way, their experience was similar. Women told us of being lied to, raped, beaten and locked up, of having no control over how or if they had sex with customers, having to have sex when they were sick or menstruating, being deprived of their passports and threatened with violence and deportation. Some women were sold on from one trafficker to the next. All were paying off "debts" of at least $35,000. Some escaped and, if found, were beaten and fined. They saw all the same things happening to other women. [. . .]

At that time, despite the many crimes committed against the women, if they were found by the Department of Immigration to be in breach of their visa conditions they were put in detention and deported. No charges were laid: even leaving aside the federal sexual slavery legislation, crimes under state law—rape, battery and imprisonment—were going undetected by the authorities. Compounding the women's fear of deportation, traffickers themselves threatened to and in fact at times did report women to immigration authorities.

It was difficult to know how many women were being trafficked. The authorities weren't counting—they didn't believe trafficking existed—and it was hard for a small organisation like ours to come up with national estimates. [. . .]

The coronial inquiry launched in 2003 into the death of Puongtong Simaplee got people asking what sort of crimes foreign women in Australia were experiencing, how were traffickers able to exploit women in this way, why were authorities missing the problem, and what were trafficked women doing to survive in the absence of a humane government response?

Arriving at the point where trafficking was being discussed at all was testament to Charandev Singh's skill and inordinate hard work. Months before the case, when we had little reason to expect that we would get legal standing, let alone anything more than that, he was clear. We needed a legal strategy, he said, and a media strategy, and he proceeded to pull them together. [. . .]

The first step in the legal strategy was to gain legal standing. As experts on trafficking, our expertise could help the court and our organization had a stake in the outcome of the inquiry, which could impact public rights in our field. Much to my surprise, the coroner gave us standing. But my sense that the coroner was not entirely open to our participation was soon confirmed. "This is not an enquiry into the sex industry," he told the court. "This is not an enquiry into immigration detention." When we asked questions relating to the sex industry or trafficking, our lawyer was told she was out of line. Having been given legal standing solely on the basis of our expertise on trafficking, we were told we could not ask questions on that issue.

So we didn't. At least not immediately. Having read through the brief again and again, it was devastatingly clear that Puongtong Simaplee had died without reason. There was no doubt she was vulnerable. Court documents show that before her detention she had a heroin addiction, was homeless and, in the words of an older friend, was "not in a positive state of mind." [. . .]

For the two days of witnesses, we asked questions about Simaplee's medical treatment, welfare measures and the processes in place at Villawood to protect vulnerable detainees. The coroner made it clear, however, that his court was not the place for further conversations about what role trafficking had played in getting this woman into Australia and ultimately immigration detention. "This is not a human rights court," he said succinctly.

It was here that Charandev Singh's second strategy kicked in. We took the questions we weren't allowed to ask within the coronial inquiry and asked them outside. It's a well-worn approach of course, but in this case the strategy of using the legal process as much as we could and then working with the media to raise questions that weren't allowed in the hearing was crucial.

Crucial, but not without risk. It didn't take a lot of imagination to work out what some members of the media could do with the story of a heroin-addicted Asian prostitute. The Department of Immigration had already set the tone in its 2001 media release on Simaplee's death. A Thai drug addict, the release said, had died from an overdose in Villawood in a pool of her own vomit. The text seems since to have been removed from the department's website.

We were fortunate though. Singh had previously dealt with *Australian* journalist Elisabeth Wynhausen on stories about immigration detention, and he knew we could trust her to tell the story fairly. I know now that Wynhausen is an award-winning journalist and book author who worked for twelve years in New York as correspondent for the *Age* and the *National Times* and had also worked for the *Bulletin*, but at that time all I really knew was that Singh trusted her.

I first met her in November 2002 when I walked, dazed, out of a long night in a brothel, having heard story after story from women who had been trafficked to Australia. A train ride later, unwashed and sleep-deprived, in a cafe over the road from the *Australian*'s shiny headquarters, I blurted out what I had spent the last months listening to. Wynhausen listened for a bit, cut me off, fired questions at me, interrupted a bit more, and told the waiter off for wishing her Merry Christmas. For a community worker schooled in letting people speak, it was a surprise, but I was sold. I could tell she understood the issues.

By the time the coronial inquiry began in early 2003, Wynhausen was ready to go, and the *Australian* soon teamed her up with its new investigative editor, Natalie O'Brien. The *Australian*'s stories began with Puongtong Simaplee's death and the fact that despite her claims that she had been trafficked into Australia as a child, and despite her vulnerability, neither the Villawood Immigration Detention Centre nor the Department of Immigration took the steps needed to address these issues and keep the young woman alive. Many news agencies jumped on the story that Puongtong Simaplee had been trafficked to Australia as a child—a statement that was not investigated in the coronial inquiry and was later shown to be untrue—but Wynhausen and O'Brien saw the broader story.

The child-trafficking claim pulled in media outlets that might not ordinarily have bothered with a death-in-custody story and some of these lost interest once it was established that Puongtong Simaplee had not been trafficked into Australia as a child. In contrast, Wynhausen and O'Brien had just begun. In the months that followed the coronial inquiry, they ran story after story about trafficking: about bungled immigration raids, about women's shock and despair at the violence they'd faced in Australia, about the authorities' deafness to allegations of crime. After years of steadfast inaction, the official response, when it finally came, was surprisingly swift. By the second day of the *Australian*'s stories, the federal government had set up a high-level interdepartmental committee. At last, the Department of Immigration, the Attorney-General's Department, the (then) Office for the Status of Women and other government departments were talking to each other about trafficking. The *Australian*'s stories made sure that those initial discussions didn't stop there—the government knew that this was not a one-off media flurry. The *Australian* promised—and delivered—ongoing scrutiny on the previously invisible subject of trafficking. It was the beginning of a genuine shift by the federal government on trafficking.

When Puangthong Simaplee, affectionately known to friends as Popo, was picked up in a raid on a brothel in Sydney's Surry Hills, the tiny, emaciated 27-year-old had endured years of abuse and indignity. Sold as a child and trafficked to

Australia on a fake Malaysian passport at the age of 12, she was enslaved as a prostitute.

The girl from a hill tribe in Thailand's Chiang Mai province was addicted to heroin by the time Immigration Department officers raided the brothel at 359 Riley Street. Simaplee was taken to the Villawood Detention Centre. Three days later she was dead. The sordid tale unfolded at the Westmead Coroners Court this week at the inquest into her death.

"It is not an inquiry into Australian immigration policy; it is not an inquiry into the sex industry," said Michael O'Brien, counsel assisting deputy coroner Carl Milovanovich. Project Respect, which works on behalf of trafficked women, nonetheless raised concerns about the fate of trafficked women in detention, many of them virtual slaves.

"They don't expect the brutality—they may be forced to have sex without condoms; they can't refuse customers; they are made to keep working when they're sick," Project Respect co-ordinator Kathleen Maltzahn told The Weekend Australian. "The women who don't know they've been brought here for prostitution are brutalised and raped to force them to do what the traffickers want."

Simaplee was one of hundreds of trafficked women held against their will and forced to work as prostitutes to fulfil so-called contracts. That means having sex with hundreds of men to pay the traffickers as much as $50,000, the "fee" for getting them to Australia.

Industry sources say the women are held captive, have their passports confiscated and are escorted between the brothels and the dormitories where they sleep.

They have no life of their own and they are beaten and starved if they try to run away.

Some traffickers threaten the women, telling them "we know where your children are."

Women like Simaplee, who have been trafficked as children, simply may not know their real name or date of birth.

But catching sex traffickers remains a low priority, according to Ms Maltzahn. Despite the introduction of federal anti-sex trafficking laws in 1999, there has not been a single prosecution under the act.

"The legislation was supposed to go after Mr Big and not punish the women and what we have is the opposite," Ms Maltzahn said.

"The DIMIA (Department of Immigration and Multicultural and Indigenous Affairs) compliance branch is funded according to the number of deportations. That means if they have a choice between investigating and deporting, they deport."

DIMIA disputes this, claiming compliance is funded on the number of illegals who have been picked up.

Opposition justice spokesman Daryl Melham said the Government and DIMIA appeared to be more interested in rapidly deporting the sex-trade victims than encouraging them to act as witnesses to target the criminals.

Ten illegal immigrants were picked up late last year in a joint raid on a brothel in Sydney's Woolloomooloo by immigration officers and police. Nine have been deported. DIMIA does not know if they were trafficked or not.

Insiders claim there are no serious attempts to combat crime syndicates organising the trafficking that "milks" the system for all it's worth.

If they want to get rid of the women who have been around a while, "old stock," the traffickers may tip off DIMIA.

To speed up the deportation and ensure the girls are not talking to investigators or giving evidence, the traffickers may actually drop their passports off at Villawood.

Industry sources say women would be happy to reveal details in exchange for concessions from DIMIA if given a chance.

"DIMIA unwittingly assists the traffickers," private investigator Chris Payne, a former federal police officer, said. "In their haste to get the women out of the country, they are in a way exporting the evidence."

A DIMIA spokesman said illegal sex workers were questioned about whether they had been trafficked and, if they had, the matter was referred to the federal police for investigation.

The Australian Federal Police has investigated six matters in the past two years. Four had been referred by DIMIA. Three are still under investigation. There was insufficient evidence to proceed with the others.

Five other women were picked up with Simaplee in September 2001. All were deported that month. DIMIA does not know if the women had been trafficked or not.

ACKNOWLEDGMENTS

Above all, I owe a tremendous debt to Jane Folpe. It was her research that led me to Adam Hochschild, Roger Casement, and E.D. Morel and her thoughts on how journalism in developing countries is often overlooked that led me to think of editing a book on the subject. Jane was involved throughout in reading and thinking and talking through the material and her research skills and passion for accuracy were essential. However, we found our way to the old newspaper collections because the historian Richard John invited me to teach with him at Columbia University's Graduate School of Journalism. Under his guidance I began looking at the history of newspapers around the world, and he kept me on track through the different paths that my reading took. Vanessa Pope has spent years in the British Library working with me and is now an expert on nineteenth-century reporting from India and Africa. She sees connections and patterns that cut across time and place and has an instinct for what matters. Vanessa is also a crack editor with an eye for detail and good writing. I am grateful for the many months she spent working on this book and for her efficiency, kindness, and smarts.

Marc Favreau, from The New Press, decided that this book should include samples of the journalism, and Rebecca Hopkins, Laura Quintela, Branwen Millar, and Nicolo Gnecchi-Ruscone tracked down many contributions. As my summer researcher, Zach Hendrickson kept this project on track, reading, organizing, and clarifying the connection between journalism and human rights. Chandrika Kaul also generously shared ideas and sources. Many friends, acquaintances, and colleagues came up with good ideas early on: Liza Featherstone, Sean Jacobs, Mila Rosenthal, Jonathan Birchall, Nicole Pope, Peter Rosenblum, Michael Staunton. Many enthusiastic people got the idea of the project right away and spent time pointing out interesting pieces they had seen. These include Kevin Cassidy, Mei Fong, Manoah Espisu, Yuli Ismartono, Musikilu Mojeed, Mirta Ojito,

Sheridan Prasso, Aline Sara, Ashwini Sukthankar, and Jo Weir. Michael Schudson, Sheila Coronel, Catherine Higgs, and Algirdas Lipstas made helpful comments on my introduction as did my beloved husband, Joseph E. Stiglitz. My father, André Schiffrin, lived just long enough to know that I had turned in the manuscript. I thank him for his enthusiasm about the book and for the suggestions he made about what should be included. I miss so many things about my father, including his wonderful editing.

For their constant support and friendship, deepest thanks to Hannah Assadi, Julia Cunico, Eamon Kircher Allen, Eliza Bates, Scott Sherman, Dean Starkman, and my assistant, Estelle Drent. Samantha Marshall edited parts of the book and, as always, brought her narrative flair and news judgment to this task. I also enjoyed reading other collections of journalism, particularly *Muckraking!: The Journalism That Changed America*, edited by Bill and Judith Serrin; *Shaking the Foundations: 200 Years of Investigative Journalism in America*, edited by Bruce Shapiro; *Troublemakers: The Best of South Africa's Investigaitve Journalism*, edited by Anton Harber and Margaret Renn; *Tell Me No Lies: Investigative Journalsm That Changed the World*, edited by John Pilger; *Investigative Journalism in China: Eight Cases in Chinese Watchdog Journalism*, edited by David Bandurski and Martin Hala; and Mark Lee Hunter's *Global Investigative Journalism Casebook: An Anthology for Teachers and Students of Investigative Journalism*. Helping judge some of the entries submitted for awards given by the Overseas Press Club in New York also inspired me as I read so many remarkable pieces of reporting.

Finally, the contributors: thank you for your patience with my edits, your generosity, and for sharing your work.

Why?" by Carlos Cardoso, December 1, 1999, *Metical*, No. 617. Available at www .cip.org.mz/metical/pdata/M-0617.pdf.

Excerpt from "The Tale of a Brave Woman," by Rafael Marques de Morais, July 25, 2005, *A Capital*. Used by permission of the author.

Excerpt from "Oil Boom Enriches African Ruler," by Ken Silverstein, January 20, 2003. Reprinted by permission of *Los Angeles Times*.

Excerpt from "Pipeline to Justice?" by Lisa Girion, June 15, 2003. Reprinted by permission of *Los Angeles Times*.

Excerpt from "Villages Swallowed by Coal," by Tatiana Escárraga, *El Tiempo*. Reprinted by permission of the author.

Excerpt from "Tiger Leaping Gorge Under Threat," *Southern Weekend*, Liu Jianqiang and Cheng Gong. Reprinted by permission of *Southern Weekend*.

Excerpt from "Milking the Poor," by Mike Muller, *The Guardian*, February 7, 1974. Reprinted by permission of Guardian News & Media Ltd © 1974.

Excerpt from *Rebellion in the Backlands* by Euclides da Cunha. Reprinted by permission of University of Chicago Press © 1944.

Excerpt from "Bloody Trail of the South African Police," by Jacques Pauw, November 19, 1989, *Vrye Weekblad*. Reprinted by permission of Max du Preez.

Excerpt from *Chile, Pinochet, and the Caravan of Death* by Patricia Verdugo. Permission granted by the Center for Hemispheric Policy, University of Miami.

Excerpt from "First He Pulled the Pin, Then He Handed Over the Grenade," by Mehmet Baransu, August 28, 2009, *Taraf*. Permission granted by *Taraf*.

Excerpt from "Salvadoran Peasants Describe Mass Killing," by Alma Guillermoprieto, January 27, 1982, *Washington Post*. Used with permission of Watkins/ Loomis Agency.

Excerpt from "From Dust Unto Dust," by Palagummi Sainath, December 2000, *The Hindu Sunday Magazine*. Reprinted by permission of *The Hindu*.

Excerpt from "Na Ja Swami Pardesa," by Anupam Mishra, 1993. Reprinted by permission of Gandhi Peace Foundation.

Excerpt from "The Story of Bethal," by Henry Nxumalo, March 1952, *Drum*. © Baileys African History Archive Henry Nxumalo.

Excerpt from "Growing Pains: Sande Tradition of Genital Cutting Threatens Liberian Women's Health," by Mae Azango, March 8, 2012. Reprinted by permission of *New Narratives*.

Excerpt from "Death Exposes Agony of Sex Slaves," by Elisabeth Wynhausen, March 15, 2003. Permission granted by *The Australian*.

Excerpt from *Trafficked* by Kathleen Maltzahn, University of New South Wales Press, 2008. Permission granted by author, University of South Wales Press, and Swinburne University.

NOTES

Anya Schiffrin, Introduction

1. Also known as investigative reporting.

2. Given to him by the gathering of European countries at the Berlin conference of 1884 and 1885.

3. For more information, please see Mike Kaye, "1807–2007: Over 200 Years of Campaigning Against Slavery," Anti-Slavery International, 2005, www.antislavery .org/includes/documents/cm_docs/2009/1/18072007.pdf.

4. See Catherine Higgs, *Chocolate Islands: Cocoa Slavery and Colonial Africa* (Athens: Ohio University Press, 2012). On page 75 she notes that although slavery officially ended in Portuguese Africa in 1875, labor laws were introduced in 1889 that required colonized people to work. The result was that many "found them selves locked into renewable five-year contracts that usually became life sentences."

5. Ibid., p. 75.

6. Ibid., p. 130.

7. Lowell Satre, *Chocolate on Trial: Slavery, Politics, and the Ethics of Business* (Athens: Ohio University Press, 2005), 141.

8. Reported on by Dr. Cicely Williams, "The Slaughter of Innocents," *Straits Times*, April 3, 1941, 3.

9. Alexander Dyck and Luigi Zingales, "The Corporate Governance Role of the Media," in *The Right to Tell: The Role of Mass Media in Economic Development*, ed. Roumeen Islam (Washington, DC: World Bank, 2002).

10. Sendhil Mullainathan and Andrei Shleifer, "The Market for News," *American Economic Review* 95, no. 4 (2005): 1031–53.

11. For example, the support given by Google Ideas to the Organized Crime and Corruption Reporting Project for Investigative Dashboard, which was funded originally with seed money from Open Society Foundations' media program.

12. See Richard J. Tofel, "Non-profit Journalism—Issues Around Impact: A White Paper from ProPublica," February 2013, s3.amazonaws.com/propublica/ assets/about/LFA_ProPublica-white-paper_2.1.pdf or "Mapping Donor Decision Making on Media Development," School of International and Public Affairs,

Columbia University, May 2011, sipa.columbia.edu/academics/workshops/docu
ments/InternewsMediaDevelopment.pdf.

13. Josh Greenberg and Graham Knight, "Framing Sweatshops: Nike, Global
Production, and the American News Media," *Communication and Critical/Cultural
Studies* 1, no. 2 (2004): 151–75.

2. Benjamin Saldaña Rocca, "The Wave of Blood"

1. Hardenburg translated Muriedas's letter for inclusion in his book manuscript about the Putumayo atrocities. I have left Hardenburg's translation unaltered
apart from three minor changes: (1) when his sentence construction is awkward, I
have returned to the original Spanish and translated the sentence again; (2) when
his punctuation is jarring for today's readers, I have simplified it; and (3) when people or places are mentioned with which today's reader will not be familiar, I have
added a short explanation in parentheses.

3. Dwarkanath Ganguli, "Slavery in the British Dominion"

1. The rest are immigrants from other parts of India and Assam, with 44.7 percent coming from Santhal Parganas.

4. Henry Woodd Nevinson, "Part VI—The Islands of Doom"

1. For more on Nevinson's career, see Angela V. John, *War, Journalism and the
Shaping of the Twentieth Century: The Life and Times of Henry W. Nevinson* (London:
I.B. Tauris, 2006); and Lowell Satre, *Chocolate on Trial: Slavery, Politics, and the Ethics
of Business* (Athens: Ohio University Press, 2005).

8. Liu Zhiyi, "Youth and Destiny Spent with Machines— 28 Days Undercover at Foxconn"

1. See mnc.people.com.cn/GB/126636/8132476.html. *People's Daily* quoted
Samsung Economic Research Institute on the 20 percent of Shenzhen's exports and
tax of RMB 5 billion in 2007.

2. Two more suicides followed the publication of this report.

3. Per the request from the source, Wang Kezhu is a pseudonym.

9. E. Benjamin Skinner, "The Fishing Industry's Cruelest Catch"

1. Michael Field, "Slavery at Sea Exposed," *Sunday Star-Times*, April 3, 2011.

2. Christina Stringer, Glenn Simmons, and Daren Coulston, "Not in New
Zealand's Waters, Surely? Labour and Human Rights Abuses Aboard Foreign
Fishing Vessels," New Zealand Asia Institute Working Paper Series, No. 11–01,
September 2011, docs.business.auckland.ac.nz/Doc/11–01-Not-in-New-Zealand
-waters-surely-NZAI-Working-Paper-Sept-2011.pdf. It was subsequently pub-

lished in the *Journal of Economic Geography* (2013), joeg.oxfordjournals.org/content/
early/2013/09/23/jeg.lbt027.full.

11. Albert Londres, "The Court of Miracles"

1. See the chapter on Prisons and the Colonial Press in Peter Zinoman, *The Colonial Bastille: A History of Imprisonment in Vietnam, 1862–1940* (Berkeley: University of California Press, 2001).

2. Erwin James, "Among the Ghosts," *The Guardian*, December 3, 2006, www.theguardian.com/world/2006/dec/04/france.prisonsandprobation.

12. Nguyễn An Ninh, "Is a Revolution Possible?"

1. Jürgen Habermas, *The Structural Transformation of the Public Sphere* (Cambridge: MIT Press, 1989).

2. Nguyễn An Ninh, "La France en Indochine," serialized essay published in *La Cloche Fêlée*, November 1925.

3. Despite Ninh's contemporary fame, the one-party regime of Vietnam never fully recognized his legacy. His name is attached to a minor street in Saigon's Bến Thành district.

4. Philippe Peycam, *The Birth of Vietnamese Political Journalism* (New York: Columbia University Press, 2012), 127–28.

5. Nguyễn An Ninh traveled to the Mekong Delta with the French writer Léon Werth to collect unpaid subscriptions to the newspaper. Most of the journey was done by bus and boat. Mỹ Tho and Trà Vinh were at the time medium market towns, respectively located at sixty and two hundred kilometers from Saigon.

6. The name *Annam* designated both the whole of Vietnam and its central region (*Trung Kỳ*), which, like the northern part of the country Tonkin (*Bắc Kỳ*), was under the regime of a "protectorate" since their conquest by the French in 1884. The southern part of Vietnam, by contrast, called Cochinchina (*Nam Kỳ*), was a "colony" since 1863. It was directly administered by the French Republic. Cochinchina, Annam, and Tonkin, together with Cambodia and Laos, formed the federation of French Indochina. The name *Annamite* referred to inhabitants of Vietnam and the Protectorate of Annam. In spite of its sino-centric undertone, *Annam* (from the Chinese "Peaceful South") was kept by the French authorities. We will keep the terms of *Annam* and *Annamite* throughout the whole article.

7. Cần Tho' is the second largest city in the Mekong Delta, situated 120 kilometers south of Saigon.

8. *Tiên* or spirit consultations were widespread practices among middle-class Vietnamese. Originating from Taoist practices, they were also influenced by *spiritisme*, in fashion in Europe during that time. The prediction mentioned by Ninh may, as it turned out, have been right: from 1926 onward, a new religion, Caodaism,

which borrowed much from *spiritisme*, gained hundreds of thousands of adepts in the rural areas of southern Vietnam, a process that revolutionized the local socio-political landscape. The year 1926 was also a turning point in the Saigon political scene dominated by the Vietnamese "newspapers' village," when sixty thousand people crossed the city on April 4 on a silent march for the funeral of Phan Châu Trinh, one of Vietnam's nationalist figures depicted elsewhere in Ninh's article. Ninh's involvement in the movement led to his first imprisonment. See Peycam, *Birth of Vietnamese Political Journalism*, 136–41.

9. Nguyễn An Ninh refers to a number of "anticolonial" events that kept being reported from the northern and central parts of Vietnam. In southern Vietnam, the last spectacular event took place in 1916, with the attack on the Central Prison by a politico-millenarianist group led by the charismatic Phan Xích Long.

10. Ninh lists the grievances shared by many Vietnamese intellectuals at that time: regular cases of mistreatment of Vietnamese by French *colons*; censorship of the Vietnamese-language press; lack of educational facilities for "natives"; huge social inequalities; corruption; and the cost of maintaining princely families in Huế, Luang Prabang, and Phnom Penh.

11. Ninh refers to the succession of seditious movements and actions springing up across Vietnam against which the French authorities used brutal force: the *Cần Vương* (Aid the King) insurgency between 1885 and 1889, the 1907 peasant tax revolts, the 1908 attempt to poison the French garrison in Hanoi, the Đề Thám's thirty-year guerrilla campaigns (1883–1913), the Phan Xích Long–led attacks in Saigon in 1913 and 1916, or in 1917, the Thái Nguyên uprising in the northern part of the country. One month after the article was published, on June 19, the young Phạm Hồng Thái threw a bomb at the governor general of Indochina, in Guangzhou, China. The attempt failed and Thái committed suicide.

12. The term *race* was used to signify *nation*.

13. Ninh uses the French spellings *Hindous* or *Indous* to refer to the Indian people. No religious connotation was implied.

14. The way French attitudes toward Vietnamese changed on ships from/to Vietnam was described by many Vietnamese and French writers, including Nhất Linh, Clara Malraux, and Léon Werth. Léon Werth (1878–1955) was a French intellectual and a bohemian writer of anarchist and pacifist leanings. Both men probably befriended each other in Paris. An unclassifiable author, Werth wrote with an acid prose against colonialism. His essay "Cochinchine," which appeared in 1928, was the result of his visit to southern Vietnam and his trip with Ninh to the Mekong Delta. Werth later wrote against Stalinism and criticized the mounting Nazi movement in Germany. He later joined the French Resistance.

15. Bạc Liêu is a town situated in the extreme south of the Mekong Delta, 350 kilometers from Saigon. Ninh refers here to the election to the *Député* of Cochinchina, at that time underway, and in particular of the shady governor of Cochinchina Maurice Cognacq (1921–26), who was notorious for his corrupt practices and his brutal handling of Vietnamese—and even French—opponents. For Ninh

and many of his contemporaries, Governor Cognacq personified all of what was wrong with colonialism. He had a direct altercation with Ninh following a presentation the young man gave at the Mutual Education Society in October 1923, in which he openly stated that Vietnam "does not need intellectuals." This event earned Ninh instant popularity among the Vietnamese.

20. Carlos Cardoso, "The Tip of the Iceberg: Who Wants to Kill Albano Silva and Why?"

1. Frente de Libertação de Moçambique, or Mozambique Liberation Front, overthrew the Portuguese colonial rulers of Mozambique and has remained the ruling party to date (2013).

2. Paul Fauvet and Marcelo Mosse, *Carlos Cardoso: Telling the Truth in Mozambique* (Cape Town: Juta and Company Ltd, 2003), 29.

3. This was one of Cardoso's most successful causes, since the public scandal led to the strengthening of environmental policy, avoiding an environmental disaster, and the sacking of the two ministers involved.

4. *Carlos Cardoso: An Independent Spirit*, documentary directed by Rehad Desai (2001), 33 min.

5. On February 21, 2014, Vicente Ramaya, who had been on probation for almost a year, lost his life, gunned down in a vehicle in Maputo thirteen years after Cardoso's death. The motive and murderers haven't yet been confirmed.

6. Nyimpine Chissano died of heart failure at age thirty-seven, seven years after Cardoso's murder.

7. A new free weekly newspaper that circulates throughout most of the country.

8. A weekly paper, also a product of the Mediacoop cooperative.

9. Dr. Albano Silva was the BCM's lawyer and he was investigating the BCM $14 million fraud case in collaboration with Carlos Cardoso. Although Albano Silva was lucky to survive the attempted murder in 1999, a year later Carlos Cardoso was not so fortunate.

10. Mao Tse Tung, Julius Nyerere, and Amilcar Cabral are all names of streets in Maputo, named after important figures of communist history after the country reached independence.

29. Ian Stephens, editorial, *Indian Statesman*

1. Ian Stephens, *Monsoon Morning* (London: Benn, 1966), 173.

2. For more information as to why the famine happened—and the role of the British—please see Madhusree Mukerjee, *Churchill's Secret War* (New York: Basic Books, 2010).

3. Stephens, *Monsoon Morning*, 192.

4. Amartya Sen, "Food Battles: Conflict in the Access to Food," Coromandel Lecture, December 13, 1982, reprinted in *Mainstream*, January 8, 1983.

5. Timothy Besley and Robin Burgess, "Political Agency, Government Responsiveness and the Role of the Media," *European Economic Review* 45, no. 4 (May 2001).

35. Patricia Verdugo, *Chile, Pinochet, and the Caravan of Death*

1. David Sugarman, "Obituary: Patricia Verdugo," *The Guardian*, February 28, 2008, www.theguardian.com/world/2008/feb/29/pinochet.chile.
2. Ibid.
3. From research conducted in Copiapó by the journalist Maria Eugenia Camus for *Analisis*, November 19, 1985.
4. Ibid.

36. Ogen Kevin Aliro, "Uganda: Heroes Turning in Their Graves?"

1. According to a Human Rights Watch report, *kandoya* means "tying hands and feet behind the victim." Jemera Rone, *State of Pain: Torture in Uganda* (New York: Human Rights Watch, 2004), available at www.refworld.org/docid/412f03434.html.

38. Alma Guillermoprieto, "Salvadoran Peasants Describe Mass Killing"

1. Alma Guillermoprieto, *Dancing with Cuba* (New York: Pantheon, 2004).
2. Alma Guillermoprieto, "Shedding Light on Humanity's Dark Side," *Washington Post*, March 14, 2007.
3. Stanley Meisler, "The Massacre in El Mozote," in *Thinking Clearly: Cases in Journalistic Decision-Making*, ed. Thomas Rosenstiel and Amy S. Mitchell (New York: Columbia University Press, 2003).
4. Mark Danner, *The Massacre at El Mozote: A Parable of the Cold War* (New York: Vintage Books, 1994).
5. Guillermoprieto, "Shedding Light on Humanity's Dark Side."
6. Alma Guillermoprieto, "Telling the Story, Telling the Truth," in *Telling True Stories: A Nonfiction Writers' Guide from the Nieman Foundation at Harvard University*, ed. Mark Kramer and Wendy Call (New York: Plume, 2007).

40. Palagummi Sainath, "From Dust Unto Dust"

1. At the time of writing, the exchange rate was roughly Rs. 46.8 to the dollar. Subsequent figures in the story remain in rupees and paisa as they are from very different eras (from the 1930s till year 2000). And a few of the payment figures till the 1980s work out to just one U.S. cent or less. In January 2014, the dollar was worth around Rs. 62.

41. Anupam Mishra, "Na Ja Swami Pardesa"

1. Editor's note: Anupam is too modest to say that Bharati was influenced by his own book.

43. Carlos Salinas Maldonado, "A Decimated Chichigalpa Buries Its Dead"

1. Sasha Chavkin, "Thousands of Sugar Cane Workers Die as Wealthy Nations Stall on Solutions," Center for Public Integrity, December 12, 2011, www.public integrity.org/2011/12/12/7578/thousands-sugar-cane-workers-die-wealthy-nations -stall-solutions.

ABOUT THE CONTRIBUTORS

Guilherme Alpendre is the executive director at the Brazilian Association for Investigative Journalism (Abraji). He holds a BA degree in Journalism from São Paulo University (USP) and has studied the history of Spanish journalism at the Carlos III University in Madrid.

Ira Arlook is the chief of advocacy campaigns at Fenton, a communications agency specializing in social change.

Jeff Ballinger started trade union work in his teens, registering voters in minority and working-class neighborhoods of Gary, Indiana. After getting a law degree in New York City, he has lived half of the last thirty years in Asia doing organizing, writing, and research about sweatshops and global trade.

Robert Barnett founded and directs the Modern Tibetan Studies Program at Columbia University in New York. His books include *Tibetan Modernities: Notes from the Field* (with Ronald Schwartz); *Lhasa: Streets with Memories*; *Leaders in Tibet*; and *A Poisoned Arrow: The Secret Petition of the 10th Panchen Lama*. A former journalist, he is a frequent commentator on Tibet-related issues for the BBC, NPR, the *New York Times*, and other media outlets.

Beibei Bao is a Chinese economic analyst and writer based in New York. She graduated from the Columbia Journalism School in 2013 and writes about China's economic, labor, and health care.

Leopoldo M. Bernucci holds a chair in Latin American studies at UC Davis and has written extensively on nineteenth- and twentieth-century Brazilian and Spanish-American literature, including the great Brazilian book *Os Sertões*.

Clifford Bob is Raymond J. Kelley Chair in International Relations and professor of political science at Duquesne University. His books include *The Marketing of Rebellion: Insurgents, Media and International Activism*; *The Global Right Wing and the Clash of World Politics*; and *The International Struggle for New Human Rights*.

Ying Chan is journalism professor and founding director of the Journalism and Media Studies Centre at the University of Hong Kong. She directs the China Media Project at the JMSC with Qian Gang.

Aviva Chomsky is a professor of history and coordinator of Latin American studies at Salem State University in Massachusetts. Her books include *Linked Labor Histories: New England, Colombia, and the Making of a Global Working Class* (Duke, 2008); *A History of the Cuban Revolution* (Wiley-Blackwell, 2011); and *They Take Our Jobs! And 20 Other Myths about Immigration* (Beacon, 2007).

Reg Chua is the executive editor, editorial operations, Data & Innovation, at Thomson Reuters, which he joined in early 2011. Previously he was editor in chief of the *South China Morning Post* and spent sixteen years at the *Wall Street Journal*, including eight years as the editor of its Hong Kong–based Asian edition.

Prue Clarke is co-founder of New Narratives, a project helping build the financial independence of media businesses in Africa. She is an Africa projects manager at BBC Media Action and a former reporter with the *Financial Times* and the Australian Broadcasting Corporation and has reported from Africa since 2004 for the *Times, The Guardian, Newsweek,* CBC, NPR, and others.

Sheila Coronel is the current director of the Toni Stabile Center for Investigative Journalism at Columbia University. In 1989, Sheila and her colleagues founded the Philippine Center for Investigative Journalism to promote investigative reporting, which has since become the premier investigative reporting institution in the Philippines and Asia.

Andrew Finkel has reported from Istanbul for over twenty years and is a founder of P24, an NGO that supports independent journalism in Turkey. He is the author of the book *Turkey: What Everyone Needs to Know.*

Robert Friedman is editor at large for Bloomberg News, where he manages long-term features and projects for the global finance team. Prior to joining Bloomberg in April 2008, he was the international editor of *Fortune.* Robert was also an assistant managing editor of *Life* magazine from 1995 to 2000.

Ray Gamache taught journalism for more than thirty years. His book *Gareth Jones: Eyewitness to the Holodomor* was published in 2013 by the Welsh Academic Press.

Jordan Goodman is an honorary research associate in the Department of Science and Technology Studies at University College London. He has published widely in the fields of cultural history, the history of science and medicine, and in the history of human rights. His most recent publications, highlighting the history of human rights abuses, are: *The Devil and Mr. Casement* (2009) and *Paul Robeson: A Watched Man* (2013).

Anton Harber is the Caxton Professor of Journalism at the University of the Witwatersrand, Johannesburg, and a columnist for the newspaper *Business Day.* He was the founder-editor of the *Weekly Mail* (now the *Mail & Guardian*) and is the chair of the Freedom of Expression Institute. His books include *Diepsloot* (Jonathan Ball, 2011) and *Gorilla in the Room* (Mampoer Shorts, 2013).

Catherine Higgs is the author of *Chocolate Islands: Cocoa, Slavery, and Colonial Africa* (Athens: Ohio University Press, 2012), which chronicles the response—in the early 1900s—of the chocolate manufacturer Cadbury Brothers to accusations that it was buying slave-harvested cocoa from the Portuguese colony of São Tomé and Príncipe. She is a professor of history at the University of Tennessee, Knoxville.

Adam Hochschild is the author of *King Leopold's Ghost, Bury the Chains, Half the Way Home,* and other books.

Dr. James Hollings is a senior lecturer in journalism at Massey University, Wellington, New Zealand. He practices, researches, and teaches investigative journalism and is a founding member of the New Zealand Centre for Investigative Journalism.

Mark Lee Hunter is an adjunct professor and senior research fellow at the INSEAD Social Innovation Center in Paris and an expert in investigative journalism. He is the editor of *The Global Casebook* published by UNESCO, a handbook for teachers and students of investigative journalism.

Perry Link is Chancellorial Chair for Teaching Across Disciplines at the University of California, Riverside, and emeritus professor of East Asian studies at Princeton University. His books include *The Uses of Literature: Life in the Socialist Chinese Literary System* and *Two Kinds of Truth: Stories and Reportage from China.*

George W. Lugalambi, PhD, is a media trainer and public affairs analyst based in Kampala, Uganda. A former journalist and newspaper editor, he also spent fifteen years in academia and was active in advocacy for media development and freedom of expression in Africa.

Yen-Wei Miao is associate professor, Department of Sociology, National Chengchi University, Taiwan.

Lisa Misol is a senior researcher in the Business and Human Rights Program at Human Rights Watch, based in New York. She covers human rights issues related to corruption and poor governance in resource-rich countries, including Angola, Azerbaijan, and Equatorial Guinea.

Madhusree Mukerjee is the author of *Churchill's Secret War: The British Empire and the Ravaging of India During World War II* (2010) and *The Land of Naked People: Encounters with Stone Age Islanders* (2003).

Ananya Mukherjee-Reed is a professor of political science and development studies at York University, Toronto. She is the founding director of the International Secretariat of Human Development (ISHD) at York University. Her recent publications include *Human Development and Social Power: Perspectives from South Asia* (Routledge); *Business Regulation and Non-State Actors: Whose Standards? Whose Development?* (co-edited, Routledge Series in Development Economics); and *The Paradox of Profits: Perspectives on the Indian Corporate Economy* (Palgrave).

Kathleen Maltzahn is an Australian human rights activist. In 1998 she founded Project Respect, an organization dedicated to ending violence against women in the sex industry. Her book *Trafficked* (UNSW Press) was published in July 2008 and was shortlisted for the Human Rights and Equal Opportunity Commission's Human Rights Literature Non-Fiction Award.

Mike Muller is a member of South Africa's National Planning Commission and was director general of the national Department of Water Affairs. In another life, he also wrote *Tobacco and the Third World: Tomorrow's Epidemic* and "The Health of Nations," an investigation of drug companies in poor countries.

Vincent Weifeng Ni is a correspondent for Caixin. An Oxford graduate, he joined Caixin initially as its Europe correspondent, then as its U.S. correspondent. In 2011, he won a runner-up prize from London's Foreign Press Association (FPA).

Rohini Nilekani is a former journalist, has authored two books, and is now an active philanthropist. She is founding chairperson of Arghyam, a foundation working on issues of water and sanitation, and founding chairperson of Pratham Books, a not-for-profit children's publisher.

Philippe M.F. Peycam is a historian who specializes in the modern history of Vietnam. He is the director of the International Institute for Asian Studies, Leiden University, the Netherlands. His most recent book is *The Birth of Vietnamese Political Journalism: Saigon 1916–1930.*

Angela Pimenta holds a BA in journalism from São Paulo University (USP) and an MA in journalism from Columbia University. Since March 2012, she has been based in São Paulo as a partner at PATRI, the leading Brazilian public affairs consultancy.

Nicole Pope is a Swiss journalist and writer based in Istanbul. She was the Turkey correspondent for the daily newspaper *Le Monde* for fifteen years and currently works as a columnist and independent researcher. She is the author of *Honor Killings in the Twenty-First Century* (Palgrave Macmillan) and a co-author of *Turkey Unveiled: A History of Modern Turkey* (Overlook Press).

Katie Redford, an international human rights lawyer, is the co-founder and director of EarthRights International, an NGO that combines the power of law and the power of people in defense of human rights and the environment.

Erica Rodrigues is an anthropologist who has researched the extractive sector for years and has master's degrees from the University of Capetown and Columbia University.

Mica Rosenberg is a reporter for Reuters in New York and previously was a correspondent for the agency in Mexico City and Guatemala, covering news from ten Latin American countries including the earthquakes in Haiti and Chile. In 2012, she was a Knight Bagehot Fellow in business journalism at Columbia University.

Ernesto Semán is a historian and a writer. His most recent book is *Soy un bravo piloto de la nueva China*, a novel. He is an assistant professor at the University of Richmond's Jepson School of Leadership Studies.

Jayeeta Sharma is an assistant professor at the University of Toronto Scarborough. Her most recent book, *Empire's Garden: Assam and the Making of India*, discusses the connections between "coolie" labor and the politics of race, gender, language, and ethnicity.

Dr. Glenn Simmons is a research fellow at the New Zealand Asia Institute at the University of Auckland. His research focuses on fisheries' global value chains and how seafood businesses can sustainably create, deliver, and capture more socio-economic value from their activities.

Francisca Skoknic is a Chilean journalist. She serves as the deputy director of CIPER, the country's premier investigative reporting center. She has a master's degree in public administration at Columbia University and is a member of the International Consortium of Investigative Journalists.

Dr. Christina Stringer is a senior lecturer in international business at the University of Auckland. She has a long-standing research interest in the fishing industry with a focus on the globalization of fisheries value chains.

Silvio Waisbord is a professor in the School of Media and Public Affairs at George Washington University. Waisbord is the author of, among other books, *Reinventing Professionalism: News and Journalism in Global Perspective* and

Watchdog Journalism in South America. He is the editor of the *International Journal of Press/Politics.*

Hugh Whittaker is a professor of management and director of the New Zealand Asia Institute at the University of Auckland. His research includes East Asian economic development and globalization, from the perspective of "compressed development," as well as growth and change issues facing businesses in New Zealand.

PUBLISHING IN THE PUBLIC INTEREST

Thank you for reading this book published by The New Press. The New Press is a nonprofit, public interest publisher. New Press books and authors play a crucial role in sparking conversations about the key political and social issues of our day.

We hope you enjoyed this book and that you will stay in touch with The New Press. Here are a few ways to stay up to date with our books, events, and the issues we cover:

- Sign up at www.thenewpress.com/subscribe to receive updates on New Press authors and issues and to be notified about local events
- Like us on Facebook: www.facebook.com/newpressbooks
- Follow us on Twitter: www.twitter.com/thenewpress

Please consider buying New Press books for yourself; for friends and family; or to donate to schools, libraries, community centers, prison libraries, and other organizations involved with the issues our authors write about.

The New Press is a 501(c)(3) nonprofit organization. You can also support our work with a tax-deductible gift by visiting www.thenewpress.com/donate.